Quiet Water

MASSACHUSETTS, CONNECTICUT, AND RHODE ISLAND

AMC's Canoe and Kayak Guide to 100 of the
Best Ponds, Lakes, and Easy Rivers

3RD EDITION

ALEX WILSON & JOHN H

Appalachian Mountain Club Books
Boston, Massachusetts

AMC is a nonprofit organization, and sales of AMC Books fund our mission of protecting the Northeast outdoors. If you appreciate our efforts and would like to become a member or make a donation to AMC, visit outdoors.org, call 800-372-1758, or contact us at Appalachian Mountain Club, 5 Joy Street, Boston, MA 02108.

outdoors.org/publications/books

Front cover photograph © Jerry and Marcy Monkman, EcoPhotography.com
Back cover photograph © Caleb Kenna
All interior photographs © Alex Wilson and John Hayes, except where noted
Maps design by Nadav Malin and Vanessa Gray, © Alex Wilson and John Hayes
Book design by Eric Edstam

Library of Congress Cataloging-in-Publication Data

Wilson, Alex, 1955-
  Quiet water Massachusetts, Connecticut, and Rhode Island : AMC's canoe and kayak guide to 100 of the best ponds, lakes, and easy rivers / Alex Wilson & John Hayes. -- 3rd edition.
     pages cm
  Previous edition had subtitle: canoe & kayak guide.
  Includes bibliographical references and index.
  ISBN 978-1-62842-000-5 (pbk. : alk. paper) 1. Canoes and canoeing--Massachusetts--Guidebooks. 2. Canoes and canoeing--Rhode Island--Guidebooks. 3. Canoes and canoeing--Connecticut--Guidebooks. 4. Massachusetts--Guidebooks. 5. Rhode Island--Guidebooks. 6. Connecticut--Guidebooks. I. Hayes, John, 1944- II. Appalachian Mountain Club. III. Title.
  GV776.M4W55 2014
  797.1220974--dc23
                    2013050025

The paper used in this publication meets the minimum requirements of the American National Standard for Information Sciences-Permanence of Paper for Printed Library Materials, ANSI Z39.48-1984. ∞

Outdoor recreation activities by their very nature are potentially hazardous. This book is not a substitute for good personal judgment and training in outdoor skills. Due to changes in conditions, use of the information in this book is at the sole risk of the user. The authors and the Appalachian Mountain Club assume no liability for accidents happening to, or injuries sustained by, readers who engage in the activities described in this book.

Interior pages contain 30% post-consumer recycled fiber.
Cover contains 10% post-consumer recycled fiber.
Printed in the United States of America,
using vegetable-based inks.

10 9 8 7 6 5 4 3 2 1   14 15 16 17 18 19 20

MIX
Paper from
responsible sources
FSC® C005010

Tent site

Lean-to

Picnic area

Campground

Boat access

Parking area

Marsh

Peak

Dam

Interstate highway

State highway

Paved road

Less-traveled road

Rough dirt road

Foot path

River

} arrow indicates
direction of flow

Stream

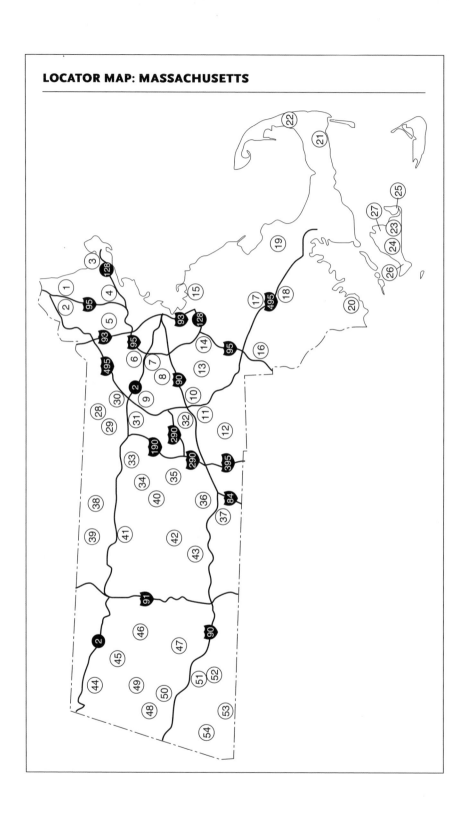

LOCATOR MAP: MASSACHUSETTS

LOCATOR MAP: RHODE ISLAND / CONNECTICUT

Contents

SECTION 1: EASTERN MASSACHUSETTS

SECTION 2: SOUTHEASTERN MASSACHUSETTS AND CAPE COD

SECTION 3: MARTHA'S VINEYARD

SECTION 4: CENTRAL MASSACHUSETTS

SECTION 5: WESTERN MASSACHUSETTS

SECTION 6: RHODE ISLAND

SECTION 7: EASTERN CONNECTICUT

SECTION 8: SOUTHERN CONNECTICUT

SECTION 9: WESTERN CONNECTICUT

NATURE ESSAYS

At-a-Glance Trip Planner

#	Trip	Page	Access Location	Area/ One-Way Length	Estimated Time
	EASTERN MASSACHUSETTS				
1	Parker River	2	Newbury	8 miles	5 hours
2	Crane Pond and Parker River	6	Georgetown; Newbury	3 miles	6 hours
3	Essex Marsh and Choate (Hog) Island	9	Essex	3,000 acres	8 hours
4	Ipswich River and Wenham Swamp	13	Topsfield	8 miles	1 to 2 days
5	Stearns Pond and Field Pond	16	Andover; North Andover	41 acres; 59 acres	3 hours
6	Concord River and Great Meadows National Wildlife Refuge	19	Bedford; Concord	6.5 miles	6 hours
7	Walden Pond	21	Concord	61 acres	2 hours
8	Sudbury River	24	Wayland; Lincoln	10.6 miles	8 hours
9	Assabet River	28	Maynard; Stow	5.5 miles	6 hours
10	Ashland Reservoir	30	Ashland	157 acres	2 hours
11	Whitehall Reservoir	33	Hopkinton	592 acres	4–6 hours
12	Blackstone River	36	Uxbridge	4 miles	5 hours
13	Charles River	40	Millis; Medfield; Dover; Natick	13.4 miles	8 hours

NOTES
[1]MPH or HP limit imposed
[2]few motorboats
[3]no personal watercraft

Hiking Trails (Y/N)	Swimming (Y/N)	Motor-boats (Y/N)	Permit required (Y/N)	Type of Trip
N	N	Y	N	salt marsh estuary
N	N	N	N	shallow, marshy stream and out-of-the-way pond
Y	N	Y	N	salt marsh estuary with winds, tides; island wildlife refuge
Y	N	N	Y	shallow, marshy stream, wildlife refuge; permit needed for camping
Y	N	N	N	shallow, marshy ponds within state forest
Y	N	Y	N	slow-flowing, historic river; wildlife refuge with rare plants and turtles
Y	Y	N	N	small, deep, protected, historic pond
Y	N	Y	N	slow-flowing, historic river; wildlife refuge
Y	N	Y[2]	N	slow-flowing, historic river; wildlife refuge; rail trail
Y	Y	Y[1,3]	N	wooded reservoir within state park
Y	N	Y[1,3]	N	large, former water-supply reservoir with protected coves and islands
Y	N	N	N	historic canal and slow-flowing river
N	N	N	N	shallow, wooded, historic, mostly protected river

Hiking Trails (Y/N)	Swimming (Y/N)	Motor-boats (Y/N)	Permit required (Y/N)	Type of Trip
Y	N	N	N	shallow, wooded, historic, mostly protected river
N	N	Y[3]	N	salt marsh estuary
N	N	N	N	shallow, meandering, marshy, wooded stream
N	Y	Y	N	lake provides access to huge, wild Hockomock Swamp; separate Town River section
Y	Y	N	N	shallow lake, pond, within state park
Y	Y	N	N	small, shallow lake; rare species; within huge forest with rare habitat
Y	Y	Y[2]	N	shallow, marshy estuary; hiking, swimming at state park
Y	N	Y	N	shallow, marshy estuary; hiking on Cape Cod Rail Trail nearby
Y	N	Y[2]	N	huge salt marsh; shallow at low tide
Y	Y	Y	N	large, saltwater to brackish pond
Y	Y	Y	N	large, saltwater to brackish pond
Y	Y	Y	N	small, saltwater pond that connects to Cape Poge Bay; wildlife refuge
Y	N	Y	N	large, saltwater pond open to sea
Y	N	Y	N	large, saltwater pond open to sea; wildlife refuge
Y	N	Y[1]	N	dammed up river section with protected bays, inlets, and islands
N	N	N	N	shallow, marshy, meandering river; within wildlife management area
N	N	N	N	shallow, meandering, marshy stream

Hiking Trails (Y/N)	Swimming (Y/N)	Motor-boats (Y/N)	Permit required (Y/N)	Type of Trip
Y	N	Y[2]	N	marshy river through national wildlife refuge
Y	N	Y	N	shallow, marshy, stump-filled reservoir
N	N	N	N	small, shallow, wooded pond
N	N	Y[2]	N	small, shallow, marshy northern fen
Y	N	N	N	small, shallow, marshy pond
N	N	Y[2]	N	shallow, meandering, marshy rivers
Y	N	Y	N	lakes connected by canoe trail through swamp
Y	Y	N	N	shallow, marshy, meandering river; within wildlife management area, state park, and state forest
Y	Y	Y[1] on lake: no motors on river	N	reservoir with protected islands and bays; marshy, slow-flowing river
Y	N	N	N	mostly marshy, protected, slow-flowing rivers
N	N	Y	N	shallow, marshy, elongated lake
N	N	Y[3]	N	small, marshy pond and brook
Y	N	Y[2,3]	N	slow-flowing wooded river
Y	N	N	N	small, marshy northern fens within state forest
Y	N	N	N	small, marshy, protected pond
Y	Y	N	N	wooded pond within state forest
N	N	Y[1]	N	elongated, wooded reservoir

Hiking Trails (Y/N)	Swimming (Y/N)	Motorboats (Y/N)	Permit required (Y/N)	Type of Trip
N	N	Y	N	slow-flowing river
N	N	N	N	marshy, beaver-dammed stream
Y	N	N	N	medium pond within state forest
N	N	N	N	shallow, marshy, meandering, beaver-dammed stream
Y	N	Y[2]	N	small, shallow, marshy pond
N	N	Y; shallow water, aquatic plants limit motors	N	small, shallow, marshy pond within wildlife management aea
Y	N	Y[2]	N	shallow, marshy ponds within state park
Y	Y	Y[1]	N	shallow, marshy pond
Y	Y	N	N	small pond within state park
Y	N	Y[2]	N	shallow, marshy, wooded pond
N	N	Y	N	clear-flowing outlet of water-supply reservoir
Y	N	Y	N	narrow, meandering river in urban area; hiking/biking path
N	N	Y[2]	N	slow-flowing river through broad marsh
Y	N	Y[2]	N	shallow, marshy pond
N	N	Y; no motors on rivers	N	large, shallow pond; small, shallow, meandering streams
N	N	Y[1]	N	small, natural kettle pond
Y	N	Y	N	large estuary with winds and tides
Y	Y	Y	N	large pond within state park; nearby wildlife refuge

Hiking Trails (Y/N)	Swimming (Y/N)	Motor-boats (Y/N)	Permit required (Y/N)	Type of Trip
N	N	Y[2]	N	wide, undeveloped river
N	N	N	N	marshy, meandering river
N	Y	Y	N	shallow, marshy pond; parts lie within state forest and state park
Y	N	Y	N	flood-control reservoir and protected river stretch
Y	Y	Y[1]; no motors on Bigelow	N	deep, clear lake with islands; shallow, marshy pond; partially within state park
N	N	Y[1]	N	shallow, marshy, meandering stream
N	N	N	N	small, shallow, marshy pond
N	N	Y[2]	N	small, wooded, meandering stream
Y	Y	Y[1]	N	wooded reservoir, deep coves, islands, and inlet rivers
N	N	Y[1]	N	shallow, marshy pond and river
N	N	Y[1]	N	shallow, marshy pond
N	N	N	N	small, shallow, marshy pond
Y	Y	Y[1]	N	dammed up meandering river
Y	N	Y[1]	N	dammed up meandering river
Y	N	N	N	small, wooded, mountain pond
N	N	Y[1]	N	small, wooded, protected pond
Y	N	N	N	small, elongated, wooded pond, partially within a state forest
Y	N	Y[1]	N	shallow, marshy pond within wildlife management area

Hiking Trails (Y/N)	Swimming (Y/N)	Motor-boats (Y/N)	Permit required (Y/N)	Type of Trip
N	N	Y[1]	N	large reservoir
Y	N	Y	N	shallow, marshy, tidal estuary
N	N	Y	Y	tidal estuary channel of Connecticut River; small, marshy, inlet stream; permit needed for camping
N	N	Y	N	tidal estuary, brackish marshland, protected islands and coves
N	N	Y; no motors in wildlife refuge	N	salt marsh estuary, partially within wildlife refuge
Y	Y	N	N	shallow, marshy pond; state forest
N	N	N	N	shallow, marshy pond within wildlife management area
N	N	Y	N	salt marsh estuary and tidal river
Y	N	Y[2]; no motors before Sept. 1	N	salt marsh estuary, partially within wildlife refuge
N	N	Y[2]	N	large, slow-flowing river
Y	N	Y[2]	N	shallow, marshy pond
Y	N	Y[1]	N	deep, elongated, wooded reservoir
N	N	Y[2]	N	wooded lake with protected bays
Y	Y	Y[2]	Y	wooded lake with clear water
Y	N	Y[2]	N	large, slow-flowing river and small, meandering stream
N	N	Y[2]	N	rivers through extensive marshlands with bays and side channels
Y	Y	Y[2]	N	large, natural lake; small, marshy stream

Preface

The first edition of the *Quiet Water Canoe Guide: Massachusetts, Connecticut, and Rhode Island*, written by Alex Wilson and published in 1993, was the second in a series that now includes guides to New Hampshire/Vermont, Maine, New York, and New Jersey/Eastern Pennsylvania. John Hayes, co-author with Alex Wilson of the New Hampshire/Vermont, Maine, and New York guides, has co-authored the second and third editions.

We took the opportunity in the second and third editions to add new material, nearly doubling the amount of water covered. The first edition contained 64 entries covering 93 bodies of water. For the second edition, we dropped seven of those entries: Aaron River Reservoir, Long Cove, and Squibnocket Pond because of limited access; Otis Reservoir, Benedict Pond, and Lake Waramaug because of overuse; and Holbrook Pond because its most interesting feature, bryozoan colonies, had been crowded out by invasive exotic weeds. We also added 43 new entries covering 59 bodies of water, including new sections to the Quaboag River, Pachaug River, and Wood River entries.

For this third edition, we dropped twelve entries. Lake of the Isles, Stillwater Reservoir, Glasgo Pond, and Squantz Pond are now developed. North River is difficult to paddle and has little biological diversity. New Bedford Reservoir and Pine Acres Lake were choked with weeds. The owner of Knowlton Pond posted no trespassing signs at the access. Burr Pond; Mauserts Pond; and Cliff, Flax, and Little Cliff ponds are all small, though the latter group is nice for families. Because of efforts to limit invasive species at Pottapoag Pond and Quabbin Reservoir, you may not use your own canoe or kayak in either body of water.

We did, however, add twelve new entries covering fifteen bodies of water, including Crane Pond, a new section of Parker River, Assabet River, Blackstone River, Neponset River, Bungay River, Hockomock Swamp, Town River, Lake Nippenicket, Beaver Brook, Oneco Pond, Moosup River, West Branch Reservoir, and North and South Branches of the Pawtuxet River. The second and third editions increased entries from 64 to 100 and increased bodies of water from 93 to 140, a gain of more than 50 percent.

Because descriptions inevitably go out of date, we also rechecked all bodies of water to ensure that new development had not crowded the shores, revised directions to reflect new road names, and added GPS coordinates to access points. When possible, we avoided places with substantial development, but we worried more about the effect of personal (motorized) watercraft and high-speed boating on safety, the quietwater experience, and the environment.

We thank blogger Erik Eckilson and Kevin Klyberg of the National Park Service for their help in identifying great places to paddle on the Blackstone River, and we thank David Hodgdon of Blue Hill Adventure for pointing out the great paddling available on the Neponset River.

Introduction

Quiet waters—lakes, ponds, estuaries, and slow-flowing streams—receive much less attention than whitewater rivers. If you seek the adrenaline rush of paddling cascading rivers, there are plenty of excellent resources—but this is not one of them. The peaceful solitude of out-of-the-way lakes and ponds lures us to quietwater paddling. This guide will lead you to wood ducks swimming through early morning mists; to playful antics of river otters as you round a bend in a winding inlet channel; to the thrill of an osprey diving, retrieving a silvery fish grasped in its talons; and to old-growth white pine towering above crystal-clear ponds that help us imagine what our forests looked like centuries ago.

With quietwater paddling, you can focus on *being* there instead of *getting* there. You do not need a lot of fancy high-tech gear—although a light canoe or kayak makes portaging over beaver dams a lot easier. Binoculars and field guides to fauna and flora make up our most important gear—after boats, paddles, and personal flotation devices (PFDs).

This guide will lead you to a body of water and describe why you might want to paddle it. Generally, we tried to include places that have abundant wildlife or extensive marshlands or beautiful scenery; most entries have all three. We hope that our research will allow you to spend your valuable time paddling instead of driving around for hours trying to find elusive accesses. We designed the AMC Quiet Water guides for paddlers of all experience levels, to help you better enjoy our wonderful water resources.

THE SELECTION PROCESS

This guide includes only a small percentage of the lakes, ponds, estuaries, and slow-flowing rivers in Massachusetts, Connecticut, and Rhode Island. In our selection process, we looked for great scenery; limited development; few motorboats and personal watercraft; a varied shoreline with lots of coves and inlets; and interesting plants, animals, and geological formations.

We include a variety of water types: big lakes and rivers for longer excursions and small, protected ponds and marshes for when you have limited time or when weather conditions preclude paddling larger bodies of water. We wrote this book not only for vacationers planning a weeklong trip hundreds of miles from home but also for local residents wanting to do some paddling on their afternoon off.

The book contains a wide geographic spread of small and large bodies of water from the tri-state region. We asked people about the best places to paddle; we consulted DeLorme's *Massachusetts Atlas & Gazetteer* and *Connecticut and Rhode Island Atlas & Gazetteer*; we bought other books about paddling; and we systematically searched the United States Geological Survey (USGS) 7.5-minute topographic maps of the states.

Although we tried to include the very best places to paddle, we doubtless missed some really good locations. If you have suggestions of other lakes, ponds, and streams to include, please write to Alex Wilson at alex@atwilson. com or John Hayes at jhayes@pacificu.edu.

SAFETY, EQUIPMENT, AND TECHNIQUE

We all long for the idyllic paddle on mist-filled, mirror-smooth surfaces of quiet ponds at daybreak. But if you spend any time paddling lakes and tidal rivers, you will also encounter far less tranquil conditions. Estuaries can have swift tides that, coupled with wind, can be very dangerous. On larger bodies of water, strong winds can arise quickly, whipping up 2- to 4-foot waves in no time—waves big enough to swamp an open boat. If you capsize in cold water even a moderate distance from shore, hypothermia—a cooling of the body's core that can lead to mental and physical collapse—can set in quickly. If you have just driven a long way to reach a particular lake and find it dangerously windy, choose a more protected body of water, or go hiking instead.

Safety First

All Northeast states require each boater to carry a U.S. Coast Guard–approved (Type I, II, or III) personal flotation device (PFD). A good PFD keeps a person's face above water, even if that person has lost consciousness. A foam-or kapok-filled PFD will also help keep you warm in cold water. Children 12 and under must wear their PFDs, which must be the right size so that they will not slip off; adult PFDs are not acceptable for children. Although the law does not usually require adults to wear PFDs, we strongly recommend that you do so, especially when paddling with children. If you do not normally wear your PFD while paddling, at least don it in windy conditions, when crossing large lakes, or when you may encounter substantial motorboat wakes. It could save your life. **Take Note:** Connecticut now requires all persons in manually propelled craft to wear PFDs from October 1 through May 31. Massachusetts requires all canoeists and kayakers wear PFDs from September 15 through May 15.

You should also bring along a waterproof first-aid kit. The best kit is one that you assemble yourself; make sure that it has bandages or moleskin for blisters, an antihistamine for allergic reactions, sunscreen, an extra hat, a pain reliever, and any special medications that you might require.

As for clothing, plan for the unexpected. Even with a sunny-day forecast, a shower can appear by afternoon. On trips of more than a few hours, we bring along rain gear and dry clothes in a waterproof stuff sack as a matter of course. Along with rain coming up unexpectedly, temperatures can drop quickly, especially in spring or fall, making conditions ripe for hypothermia. Lightweight nylon or polypropylene clothing dries more quickly than cotton, and wool still retards heat loss when wet. Remember that heads lose heat faster than torsos—bring a hat.

Also bring a whistle, which you may need to use if you need help, since the sound of a whistle travels farther than the sound of a human voice, especially if it's windy. Bring enough food to maintain your energy level, and carry one liter of water for short trips and two or more liters for long trips. Avoid shallow, marshy waters during waterfowl hunting season. For hunting season dates, check the states' fish and wildlife websites: mass.gov/eea, ct.gov/deep, and dem.ri.gov

Other safety issues include:
- Getting off the water during lightning storms—lightning almost always strikes the highest object in the vicinity, which would be you in a boat out on a lake
- Knowing what to do if you capsize and having experience doing it
- Avoiding dehydration by drinking plenty of liquids
- Avoiding areas with a lot of high-speed boating
- Checking the weather forecast before going out

Equipment

For quietwater paddling, avoid high-performance racing or tippy whitewater models. Borrow a boat before buying; selection will be easier with a little experience. Whether you prefer a canoe or kayak, look for a model with good initial and secondary stability. A boat with good initial stability and poor secondary stability will tip slowly, but once it starts it may keep going. The best canoes for lakes and ponds have a keel or shallow V hull and fairly flat keel line to help track in a straight line, even in a breeze. Kayaks perform extremely well in rough water, particularly if equipped with a foot-operated rudder and a sprayskirt to keep from taking on water.

If you like out-of-the-way paddling requiring portages, get a Kevlar boat if you can afford it. Kevlar is a strong, lightweight carbon fiber. We paddle a rugged, high-capacity 18-foot, 4-inch Mad River Lamoille canoe that weighs just 60 pounds, a 15-foot, 9-inch Mad River Independence solo canoe that weighs less than 40 pounds, a 14-foot Wenonah Wigeon kayak that weighs 38 pounds, and a 14-foot Wilderness Systems Chaika kayak that weighs 32 pounds. If you plan to go by yourself, consider a sea kayak or a solo canoe in which you sit (or kneel) close to the boat's center. You will find paddling a well-designed solo canoe far easier than a two-seater used solo. The touring or sea kayak with its long, narrow design, low profile to the wind, and two-bladed paddling style is faster and more efficient to paddle than a canoe.

A padded portage yoke in place of the center thwart on a canoe is essential if you plan on much carrying. With unpadded yokes, wear a life vest with padded shoulders. Attach a rope—called a "painter"—to the bow so that you can secure the boat when you stop for lunch, line it up or down a stream, and—if the need ever arises—grab on to it in an emergency. We both have embarrassing stories about not using a painter to secure the boat. Wind can cause Kevlar boats to disappear very quickly, and it's not fun to watch your boat bobbing away in a stiff wind!

Choose light, comfortable paddles. For canoeing, we use a relatively short (48- or 50-inch), bent shaft paddle. Laminated from various woods, the paddle has a special synthetic tip to protect the blade. Bent shaft paddles allow more efficient paddling, because the downward force converts more directly into forward thrust. However, straight shaft paddles also work well. Always carry at least one spare paddle per group, particularly on longer trips, in case you break a paddle or a porcupine gets hold of one.

Paddling Technique

On a quiet pond, does it matter if you use the proper J-stroke, the sweep stroke, or the draw? No. Learning some of these strokes, however, can make paddling more relaxing and enjoyable. We watch lots of novices zigzagging along, frantically switching sides while shouting orders fore and aft. People have told us about marriage counseling sessions devoted to paddling technique!

If you are new to the sport and want to learn canoeing or kayaking techniques, buy a book or participate in a paddling workshop, such as those offered by the Appalachian Mountain Club, equipment retailers, and boat manufacturers. We include recommended books on canoeing and kayaking in Appendix B.

Start out on small ponds. Practice paddling into, with, and across the wind. On a warm day close to shore, with your PFD on and others to help you out of difficulties, practice capsizing. Intentionally tipping your boat will give you an idea of how easily it can tip over. Try to get back into the boat when you are away from shore. Getting the water out of a kayak while treading water is impossible without a hand pump; you can have one mounted permanently on your boat, or you can carry a portable one. You should be able to right a canoe with two people, getting most of the water out (keep a bailer fastened to a thwart). Getting back in the boat is another story. Good luck!

PADDLING WITH KIDS

When canoeing with kids, try to make it fun, and keep calm. Even though you may be plenty warm from paddling, children can get cold while sitting in the bottom of the boat. Remember that everyone should have PFDs on at all times, and PFDs will help keep children warm. They also need protection from sun and biting insects. Watch for signs of discomfort. Set up a cozy place where young children can sleep. After the initial excitement of paddling fades, a gently rolling canoe often puts young children to sleep, especially near the end of a long day. Also, for longer excursions, make sure to bring dry clothes for everyone in a waterproof sack.

How to Use This Book

For each trip in the book, we provide a list of basic information, a map, directions, and a short description of what you'll see.

TRIP INFORMATION

At the start of each trip description, we include location, DeLorme and USGS map information, area covered by the trip, an estimate of time required for a leisurely paddle, habitat type (i.e., type of environment you will encounter), types of game fish, predominant animals and type of vegetation you should expect to see, contact information, camping information, and special notes about development or hazards to avoid.

Choose larger bodies of water and longer rivers when you have more time and a good weather forecast. Under windy conditions, paddle smaller bodies of water or rivers. Most entries include substantial shallow-water marshlands.

Campgrounds listed here are public camping areas. For information on private campgrounds, see the extensive lists in the DeLorme atlases.

Note that, although we list fish species for each destination, specific or general advisories against eating or reducing consumption of caught fish from all bodies of water exist, particularly for pregnant and nursing women and children. Advisories do not apply to stocked hatchery fish. We include specific and general advisories in Appendix A.

MAPS

We recommend that you use the DeLorme Mapping Company's *Massachusetts Atlas & Gazetteer* and *Connecticut/Rhode Island Atlas & Gazetteer*, available at bookstores, outdoor retailers, and delorme.com. We key each entry to the respective DeLorme atlas, which divides Massachusetts into 54 detailed 10" x 15" maps at a scale of 1:80,000, and Connecticut into 40 and Rhode Island into 12 maps at a scale of 1:65,000. The maps include most—but not all—access locations, campsites, road names, campgrounds, and parks, as well as other pertinent information. For more detail and information on topography, marsh areas, and so on, refer to the 7.5-minute, 1:24,000-scale USGS topographic maps listed in each section.

GETTING THERE

We give directions from the nearest city or major highway to the access. We provide distances between points, with the cumulative distance given in parentheses. We assume that you will use a detailed highway map, such as DeLorme's atlases. We also include GPS coordinates, taken on-site with a dashboard-mounted GPS unit; we report latitude and longitude values in degrees and minutes. If it's more convenient to use degrees as one number with decimals, instead of degrees and minutes, then take just the minutes, and divide by 60 to get a decimal. For example, to convert 42° 45.602′, divide 45.602 minutes by 60 minutes per degree to get 0.760031°. Then add this decimal to 42° to get 42.760031°.

WHAT YOU'LL SEE

The trip descriptions, each a few paragraphs long, give details about the area's natural features. Those details include birds, animals, and plants that you should expect to see on each trip, and in some cases we describe prominent geological features. Bringing field guides to birds, plants, and animals—along with waterproof binoculars—would be a great help in identifying and enjoying what you see.

Happy paddling!

Stewardship and Conservation

Diverse wetlands—among the richest, most readily accessible ecosystems—provide wonderful opportunities for paddlers to learn about nature. You can visit deep, crystal-clear mountain ponds, slow-flowing rivers, and unique bog habitats. You can observe hundreds of species of birds; dozens of mammal, insect, turtle, and snake species; and hundreds of plant species. Some quite rare species—such as a delicate bog orchid or a family of otters—provide a real treat when you observe them. But even ordinary plants and animals lead to exciting discoveries and can provide hours of enjoyable observation.

In the essays, we describe a few interesting plants and animals that you might encounter. We interspersed these descriptions—and accompanying pen-and-ink illustrations by Cathy Johnson—throughout. We hope that the information in these short essays will enhance your own observations.

DO WE REALLY WANT TO TELL PEOPLE ABOUT THE BEST PLACES?

People have asked us how we could, in good conscience, tell others about the more remote, pristine, unspoiled places—after all, increased visitation would make these places less idyllic. We spent many an hour grappling with this difficult issue as we paddled along. We believe that people who experience wild, remote areas firsthand will come to value them and build support for their protection.

For many lakes and ponds, protection will mean purchase of fragile surrounding areas by state or local governments, or private organizations such as The Nature Conservancy. On other bodies of water, restricting high-speed boating offers the best form of protection.

Wetlands perform extremely important functions, such as recharging groundwater, helping control floods, supporting fishing and waterfowl hunting, and providing habitat for many rare and endangered species, as well as for hundreds of other species. Even low-impact uses such as canoeing or kayaking can substantially affect fragile marsh habitat. Paddling can disturb nesting loons, eagles, and snowy plovers; rare turtles; and fragile bog orchids. And even a canoe or kayak can carry invasive plants and other harmful organisms from one body of water to another; be sure to clean off your boat before you visit other water bodies.

You can go even further than the adage, "Take only photographs, leave only footprints." Carry along a trash bag and pick up the leavings of less thoughtful individuals. If each of us did the same, we would all enjoy more attractive places to paddle. While motorboaters tend to have a bad reputation when it comes to leaving trash, paddlers should have the opposite reputation—which could come in handy when seeking restrictions on high-impact resource use.

For information on low-impact camping and other uses of fragile habitats, see Rich Brame and David Cole's book, *Soft Paths: How to Enjoy the Wilderness Without Harming It*, 4th ed. (Stackpole Books, 2011). Also, visit the website of Leave No Trace (lnt.org), an organization dedicated to teaching people how to have minimal outdoor impact.

Besides reducing our impact on the environment, we can actively work to protect fragile bald eagle, osprey, otter, and other wildlife populations. If we want to preserve these species and their habitats for future generations, we will demand that elected and appointed officials make wildlife preservation and ecosystem protection a higher priority. We can also join conservation organizations—such as AMC, Sierra Club, The Nature Conservancy, Audubon Society, and many others—so that when those organizations speak about preserving the environment, their voices carry the weight of tens of thousands of like-minded members.

Some of the waters featured in this book have more protection now than when the first edition was published in 1993. Many bodies of water in the three states now impose a 10 HP limit on motors, or prohibit internal combustion motors, or prohibit personal watercraft, or impose speed limits. The land around a number of our most treasured water resources has received protection from development forever. While The Nature Conservancy and land trusts continue to protect more of the shoreline along a few key ponds and lakes, most other bodies of water suffer from continued development and more high-speed boating. When we update this guide in a few years, we hope to report a lot more progress in protecting these lakes and ponds.

We heartily applaud Massachusetts for banning lead sinkers and jigs weighing less than one ounce, although it seems unlikely that Connecticut and Rhode Island would follow suit in the near future. Now we need to work on banning lead shot for waterfowl hunting; accumulation of lead shot in shallow marshes poisons waterfowl and is a truly substantial environmental concern.

AMC'S CONSERVATION EFFORTS

Because the lakes and ponds of New England are beautiful, their real estate value is high, which can lead to excess development and harm to the environment. In response, the Appalachian Mountain Club has worked hard to protect the undeveloped shorelines of the Northeast. AMC, with other environmental organizations and land trusts, has successfully secured millions of dollars in funding from federal and state budgets and bonds to protect critical lands with high aesthetic, recreational, and ecological waterfront values. AMC has been a leader in protecting riparian lands during the licensing of hydropower projects, knowing that in return for using the public waters, the hydroelectric dam owners have an obligation to create shoreline management plans and mitigate their operational effects on the watershed.

PUBLIC ACCESS

Private land abuts many waterways. To ensure continued access, paddlers must respect private property. Never camp or picnic on private land without permission. In many places, adjacent landowners also own the riverbed or lakebed, which means that even if you have the right to paddle there, you may not have the right to fish there.

The southern New England states have done a good job of providing public access to waterways, either by establishing conservation easements or by purchasing land and water outright. We have listed only public access locations, but private property bounds most bodies of water. Never launch your boat from private land without getting permission first, and do not get out along the shore on land posted as private. Cooperation will help keep bodies of water open to paddlers.

LEAVE NO TRACE

The Appalachian Mountain Club is a national educational partner of the Leave No Trace Center for Outdoor Ethics. The center is an international nonprofit organization dedicated to responsible

leave no trace
CENTER FOR OUTDOOR ETHICS

enjoyment and active stewardship of the outdoors by all people, worldwide. The organization teaches children and adults vital skills to minimize their impacts when they are outdoors. Leave No Trace is the most widely accepted outdoor ethics program used today on public lands across the nation by all types of outdoor recreationists. Leave No Trace unites five federal land management agencies—United States Forest Service, National Park Service, Bureau of Land Management, Army Corps of Engineers, and United States Fish and Wildlife Service—with manufacturers, outdoor retailers, user groups, educators, organizations such as AMC, and individuals.

These seven principles guide the Leave No Trace ethic:

Plan ahead and prepare. Know the terrain and any regulations applicable to the area you're planning to visit, and be prepared for extreme weather or other emergencies. This will enhance your enjoyment and ensure that you've chosen an appropriate destination. Small groups have less impact on resources and the experience of other backcountry visitors.

Travel and camp on durable surfaces. Travel and camp on established trails and campsites, rock, gravel, dry grasses, or snow. Good campsites are found, not made. Camp at least 200 feet from lakes and streams, and focus activities on areas where vegetation is absent. In pristine areas, disperse use to prevent the creation of campsites and trails.

Dispose of waste properly. Pack it in, pack it out. Inspect your camp for trash or food scraps. Deposit solid human waste in catholes dug 6 to 8 inches deep, at least 200 feet from water, camp, and trails. Pack out toilet paper and hygiene products. To wash yourself or your dishes, carry water 200 feet away from streams or lakes and use small amounts of biodegradable soap. Scatter strained dishwater.

Leave what you find. Cultural or historic artifacts, as well as natural objects such as plants or rocks, should be left as found.

Minimize campfire impacts. Cook on a stove. Use established fire rings, fire pans, or mound fires. If a campfire is built, keep it small and use dead sticks found on the ground.

Respect wildlife. Observe wildlife from a distance. Feeding wildlife alters their natural behavior. Protect wildlife from your food by storing rations and trash securely.

Be considerate of other visitors. Be courteous, respect the quality of other visitors' backcountry experience, and let nature's sounds prevail.

AMC is a national provider of the Leave No Trace Master Educator course. AMC offers this five-day course, designed especially for outdoor professionals and land managers, as well as the shorter two-day Leave No Trace Trainer course, at locations throughout the Northeast. For more information, see outdoors.org/education/lnt. For Leave No Trace information and materials, contact the Leave No Trace Center for Outdoor Ethics at 800-332-4100, or visit lnt.org.

1 | EASTERN MASSACHUSETTS

The Eastern Massachusetts bodies of water included here range from the New Hampshire border to just south of Boston, and westward to I-495. This section includes truly historic areas—such as Walden Pond and the Charles, Concord, and Sudbury rivers—along with rivers and ponds that drain into Massachusetts Bay and the North Shore.

Although this book focuses primarily on ponds and lakes, in this section the major portions of ten entries include rivers. Much of early United States history unfolded on these rivers. The Charles, Concord, Sudbury, Assabet, Neponset, and Blackstone rivers provided opportunities for navigation, mill sites, shipbuilding, and more. The Blackstone included a canal with locks and powered the Stanley Woolen Mill. Today, you can paddle sections of the Blackstone River and the Blackstone Canal, as well as walk or bike the old towpath. Perhaps surprisingly, much of these river corridors remains free from development. The lengthy upper Charles River section undulates through forests rich with birds, deer, and other wildlife, and myriad tress and shrubs; every time we visit the Charles, we revel in its wildness.

Along the North Shore, we include coastal river estuaries, as well as more inland locations. Essex Marsh provides a great opportunity to paddle an extensive estuary and to hike on an island loaded with wildlife. The marsh presents a challenge because of strong tides and winds that often blow unimpeded across the low terrain. That's when we head to the Parker River, which allows paddling in a more protected estuary.

Inland from there, you can paddle an upper Parker River section that flows on a barely perceptible current through the Crane Pond Wildlife Management Area, a swamp that stands in marked contrast to the coastal rivers. Although not quite as swampy, the Ipswich River and Wenham Swamp provide another great wilderness paddling experience; because of slightly stronger currents and an 8-mile length, many people use two vehicles, making this a one-way trip.

We also include Ashland and Whitehall reservoirs, dammed up originally to provide water for a burgeoning population. No longer used as water supplies, they now provide great recreation opportunities.

At some point, all Northeast paddlers should make a pilgrimage to Walden Pond to stand where Thoreau stood and to breathe in the air hovering over the pond that inspired so much transcendentalist literature.

1 | Parker River

Parker River offers a great opportunity to study salt marsh species close up and out of the wind and tides found in most estuaries. Look for herons, egrets, and swamp sparrows.

Location: Newbury and Rowley, MA
Maps: *Massachusetts Atlas & Gazetteer*, Map 19: O20, 21, 22; USGS Newburyport East, Newburyport West
Length: 8 miles one way; upper river, 5 miles one way; shorter trips possible
Time: 5 hours upper river round-trip
Habitat Type: tidal estuary, broad marshland, few trees
Fish: striped bass, saltwater species (see fish advisory, Appendix A)
Information: tide charts, maineharbors.com; Parker River National Wildlife Refuge, fws.gov/northeast/parkerriver
Camping: Salisbury Beach State Reservation
Take Note: little development; motors allowed

PARKER RIVER

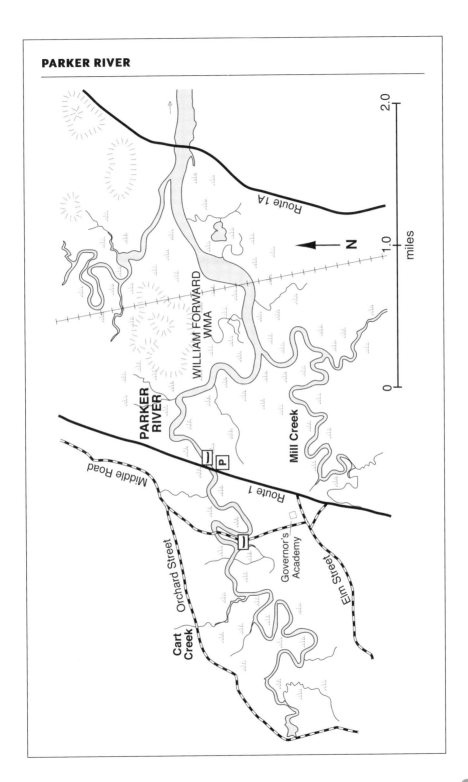

Marsh wren nests, like this one, are often woven from narrow-leaved cattails.

GETTING THERE

Route 1 (42° 45.602' N, 70° 53.974' W). From the junction of Routes 1 and 1A in Newburyport, go about 3.0 miles south on Route 1 to the access by the bridge. We prefer the quieter Middle Road access.

Middle Road (42° 45.333' N, 70° 54.081' W). From the Parker River bridge on Route 1, go 0.9 mile (0.9 mile) south, and turn right on Elm Street. Go 0.2

mile (1.1 miles), and turn right on Middle Road. Go 0.5 mile (1.6 miles) to the access on the right.

WHAT YOU'LL SEE

The Parker River, tidal in this entire stretch, flows through broad, mostly treeless marshland. The 2,000-acre William Forward Wildlife Management Area (WMA) protects much of the drainage. Upstream of the WMA, near the end of this section, a few houses and a high school loom over the marsh. Though salt marshes have very high biological productivity, they harbor fewer species than many other habitats. We felt fortunate to see red-tailed hawks soar overhead, while great blue and green herons and snowy egrets stalked the shallows. Occasional gulls flew over, tail-bobbing spotted sandpipers fled before us, swamp sparrows occasionally flitted into view, and male red-winged blackbirds serenaded us from streamside perches.

Singing marsh wrens, *Cistothorus palustris*, provided a real treat for us. They prefer nesting in narrow-leaved cattails, which abound upstream of the Middle Road bridge. Males weave several elliptical nests to attract females and use false nests for roosting. Densities of territorial males can reach one per acre. The denser the vegetation, the more successful the rearing of young. Males destroy eggs and nests of other marsh wrens and, indeed, of other bird species. Listen for metallic trilling; with patience and binoculars, you should be able to spot singing males.

We saw large stands of grasses and bulrush. Along with the more common salt marsh grasses (*Spartina alterniflora* and *S. patens*), we saw the less common *S. pectinata* and *S. cynosuroides*—the latter a quite dramatic species in fall. We also saw saltmarsh bulrush and some large stands of wild rice (*Zizania aquatica*). Beyond the sea of grasses lie stands of red and scarlet oaks, hickory, and white pine.

While in this area, visit Parker River National Wildlife Refuge on Plum Island. Because so many bird-watchers flock to this area, rare species get reported regularly. Over the years we have seen little egret, black swan, king eider, tufted duck, Ross's gull, ivory gull, and yellow-headed blackbird, along with many more common species.

2 | Crane Pond and Parker River

Narrow, marshy Parker River flows through a wildlife management area filled with birds and wetland plants. High water levels, especially in spring, make paddling through narrow meandering channels much easier. Use shorter boats here. You will see many waterfowl, a diverse array of aquatic plants, and more.

Location: Georgetown, Groveland, and Newbury, MA
Maps: *Massachusetts Atlas & Gazetteer*, Map 19: O17, 18, Map 29: A27; USGS Exeter, Georgetown
Length: 3 miles one way
Time: 6 hours round-trip
Habitat Type: shallow, marshy stream
Fish: trout, largemouth bass, pickerel (see fish advisory, Appendix A)
Information: Crane Pond Wildlife Management Area, mass.gov/eea/docs/dfg/dfw/habitat/maps-wma/northeast/cranepondwma.pdf
Camping: Salisbury Beach State Reservation

GETTING THERE

Southern Access (42° 44.704′ N, 70° 58.93′ W). From I-95, Exit 55, go west on Central Street, and turn left on Main Street at the stop sign. Go 1.8 miles (1.8 miles), and turn right on Thurlow Street. Go 1.0 mile (2.8 miles) to the access on the right. Park just before the bridge. It's easier to put in on the far side of the bridge. This is the preferred access.

Northern Access (42° 45.328′ N, 70° 56.97′ W). From I-95, Exit 55, go west on Central Street, and turn left on Main Street at the stop sign. Go 0.3 mile to the access on the right.

WHAT YOU'LL SEE

The Crane Pond Wildlife Management Area surrounding this section of the Parker River offers a superb paddling environment. The river, more like a creek here, varies from canoe width to about 20 feet as it meanders through an extensive marsh; beaver keep most of the channel open. When we paddled here in the first week of August, sunfish redds indicated that they were spawning.

With its sharp bends and 180-degree turns, the waterway will test your paddling skills. Kayakers may have a difficult time here, except maybe during

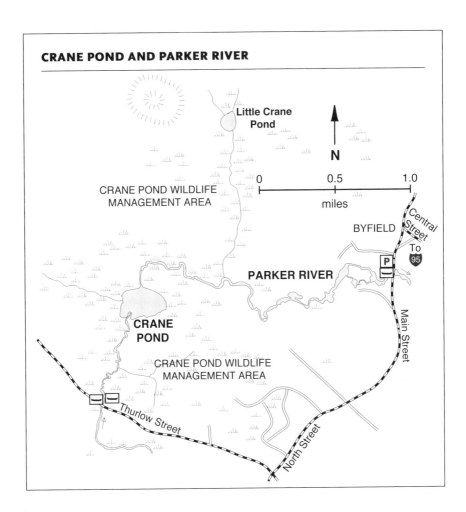

CRANE POND AND PARKER RIVER

Little Crane Pond

N

CRANE POND WILDLIFE MANAGEMENT AREA

0   0.5   1.0

miles

BYFIELD

Central Street

To 95

P

PARKER RIVER

Main Street

CRANE POND

CRANE POND WILDLIFE MANAGEMENT AREA

Thurlow Street

North Street

times of high water when the channels widen; use a short boat and short paddle here. To make any kind of reasonable progress, the bowperson in a canoe should have a perfected draw stroke; even then, a certain amount of backing and filling will be necessary to negotiate tight turns. We also prefer paddling a short canoe here. Whatever type of craft you choose, paddling here will be well worth the effort.

Aquatic plants dominate this environment. Pickerelweed lines the waterway in most areas, along with abundant swamp loosestrife, with its graceful arching bows that drape out over the waterway. The dominant underwater plant, at least in early August, seemed to be a species of yellow-flowered bladderwort. Widely dispersed dwarf red maples stand on slightly higher ground throughout the swamp. Look for clumps of arrowhead, sweetgale, narrow-leaved cattail, buttonbush, yellow pond-lily, and American white waterlily. The floating leaves of pondweed, watershield, and lesser amounts of smartweed occur sporadically throughout. In places, especially in open areas subject to wind, rafts of duckweed pile up and seriously impede paddling later in the summer. The duckweed is another reason to paddle here during spring high water.

We saw only small amounts of one invasive species, purple loosestrife. We also saw patches of an interesting parasitic plant, common dodder (*Cuscuta gronovii*), a native plant that grows throughout most of the US and Canada. Its orange, leafless, parasitic stems entwine around marshland shrubs, from which dodder absorbs its nutrients. Many other species of dodder, most of them invasives, occur throughout the US. Few species, however, inhabit wetlands, and *C. gronovii* is by far the most abundant dodder in the Northeast, especially in wetlands.

After flowing through Crane Pond, the river narrows, bumping up against some large boulders and nearby banks, whose main tree species include white pine, red oak, red maple, and hemlock. We paddled over two drowned-out beaver dams. We saw downy woodpeckers here, along with nuthatches, cardinals, robins, crows, and more. Out on the open water, look for other bird species, such as red-winged blackbird, Eastern kingbird, tree swallow, Canada goose, black duck, and wood duck.

We recommend that you start from the Thurlow Road access, paddling out and back. That way, depending on water levels, amount of surface-clogging vegetation, and your paddling skill level, you can decide to turn around at the appropriate time.

Axillary flowers and three-leaved whorls make swamp loosestrife easy to identify.

3 | Essex Marsh and Choate (Hog) Island

Essex Marsh is a large saltwater estuary that harbors a large island wildlife refuge with hiking trails. This is a wonderful place to explore and to study saltwater species. At times, tides and wind can cause difficult paddling conditions; novice paddlers should steer clear of Essex Marsh.

Location: Essex and Ipswich, MA
Maps: *Massachusetts Atlas & Gazetteer*, Map 30: E9, F9, 10, G9, 10; USGS Ipswich, Rockport
Area: 3,000 acres
Time: all day
Habitat Type: salt marsh estuary; island hiking; dunes
Fish: striped bass, saltwater species (see fish advisory, Appendix A)
Information: Crane Wildlife Refuge, The Trustees of Reservations, 978-356-4351, thetrustees.org; excellent description in *Nature Walks along the Seacoast* (see Appendix B); Great Marsh Coalition, greatmarsh.org; tide charts, maineharbors.com
Camping: Salisbury Beach State Reservation
Take Note: some development; lots of main-channel boat traffic in summer; watch out for wind, waves, and tides, especially near Route 133 bridge and in Castle Neck River; always wear your PFD; not recommended for novice paddlers

GETTING THERE
From Route 128, Exit 14, go west on Route 133 for 3.3 miles to the access in Essex (42° 37.859′ N, 70° 43.48′ W), on the right, across from Woodman's Restaurant. After unloading your boat, park at a small roadside park behind the restaurant.

WHAT YOU'LL SEE
Essex Marsh
Essex Marsh, just an hour north of Boston, offers splendid paddling and hiking. Spend a few hours or an entire day exploring this interesting area. The Essex and Castle rivers and several thousand acres of tidal creek and salt marsh comprise

ESSEX MARSH AND CHOATE (HOG) ISLAND

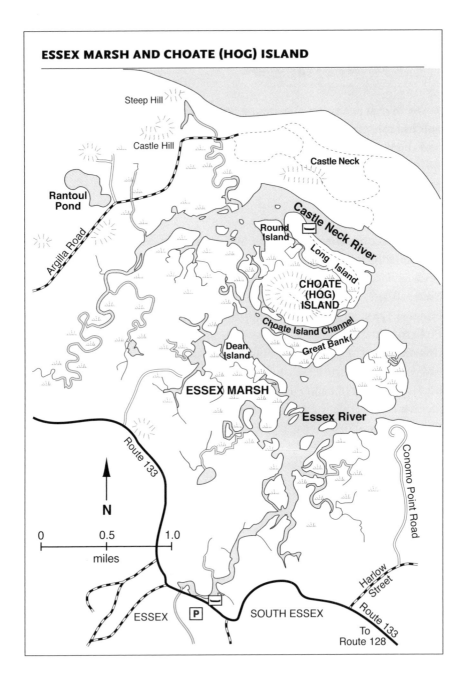

the Essex Marsh, part of the 20,000-acre Great Marsh. Castle Neck's sand dunes and beach plum and bayberry highlands protect the marsh from open ocean. In the middle of the marsh, Choate Island (also known as Hog Island), a rather dramatic drumlin—a glacial deposit formed by a receding glacier—dominates the local topography. Rising steeply on the western side to 177 feet, it then slopes gradually east. The Trustees of Reservations owns 697 acres that include Choate Island, Long Island, and three smaller islands, maintaining them as the Crane Wildlife Refuge.

We love paddling here, especially during the week when there's less boat traffic in the main channels. With an 8-foot tide differential and extensive mud flats at low tide, try to avoid paddling at low tide.

Paddling to the left on the Essex River will shortly take you to the Route 133 bridge. While the salt marsh on the inland side of the bridge offers enjoyable exploration, the tidal current under the bridge, where the channel constricts, causes very fast and tricky currents. Use caution!

We prefer paddling to the right to Choate Island, following the widening channel, rounding successive curves, and heading generally north. Look back periodically, noting landmarks that will guide your return. As water levels change, the area can look quite different. We recommend taking along a compass and a photocopy of the map in this book.

To hike on the islands and through the Crane Wildlife Refuge, head for the boat landing on the north side of Long Island. Aim initially for the steeper, western end of Choate Island. As you get near, head off into Choate Island Channel right in front of the island, following it to the right and then around the island, or—if the tide is high enough—continue around the island's west side. The more direct western route suffers from exposed tidal flats on either side of low tide. You can land your boat at Long Island between 8 A.M. and sunset year-round.

You can explore a little way into Lee's Creek between Choate Island and Round Island, but much of this area is protected as bird nesting habitat. The water around the island seems exceptionally clear, with white sand visible even 10 or 15 feet down. Paddling across to Castle Neck, you can explore the sand dunes and Crane Beach, also owned by The Trustees of Reservations. If you pull your boat up on Castle Neck, watch for rising tide, and be careful not to damage the fragile dune ecosystem.

You could also explore Castle Neck River and the inlet creeks and channels that reach into the salt marsh, an extremely interesting ecosystem dominated by smooth cordgrass (*Spartina alterniflora*) and saltmeadow cordgrass (*S. patens*). At high tide you can explore deeply into the little side creeks and look out over thousands of acres of *Spartina*. At low tide, you will see mussels clinging to the sod banks, fiddler crabs, perhaps horseshoe crabs, and clumps of seaweed clinging to rocks. On the mud flats, keep an eye out for various sandpipers and gulls. You should also see osprey and many other bird

From the south, Choate Island's distinct profile rises above the salt marsh.

species here, especially during migration.

Wind, blowing across a fairly broad expanse of water and low salt marsh, can present even more of a problem than tidal currents, generating sizable waves. Wear your PFD when paddling here; novice paddlers should avoid this area.

Choate Island

A wonderful trail extends southeast from the Long Island dock, then across to Choate Island. Maintained by The Trustees of Reservations, the trail takes you past a large barn on Long Island, a newer Cape Cod-style cottage, and the original Choate House on the main island. Thomas Choate built the house, a beautiful example of early eighteenth-century architecture, between 1725 and 1740. From Choate House, the trail extends uphill to the island's peak, passing through the oddly out-of-place 95-acre spruce forest planted in the 1930s by Richard Crane, the Chicago plumbing magnate, who purchased the island and much of the surrounding land in the early 1900s.

Until recently the Crane Wildlife Refuge hosted a large deer population, typically numbering from 50 to 75. With no hunting, and native predators long gone, the deer became quite tame. Since the mid-1980s, however, Lyme disease, borne by deer ticks, has become a major problem on isolated islands such as this. To reduce the deer population in an effort to control deer ticks, the refuge has permitted limited hunting in recent years; numbers have decreased, and deer have become much more wary of humans.

4 | Ipswich River and Wenham Swamp

The Wenham Swamp offers one of a few opportunities in Massachusetts for an on-site canoe and kayak camping trip. This pristine swamp is a favorite of bird-watchers.

Location: Hamilton, Ipswich, Topsfield, and Wenham, MA
Maps: *Massachusetts Atlas & Gazetteer*, Map 29: H30, Map 30: F1, 2, G1, H1; USGS Ipswich, Salem
Length: 8 miles one way; shorter trips possible; can be paddled both directions
Time: 1 to 2 days
Habitat Type: slow, meandering river through vast marshland; some islands; overhanging trees and vines
Fish: brook, brown, and rainbow trout; largemouth bass; white perch (see fish advisory, Appendix A)
Information: massaudubon.org/Nature_Connection/Sanctuaries/Ipswich_River
Camping: Ipswich River, Perkins Island
Take Note: no development; no motors

GETTING THERE
Route 97 (42° 37.539′ N, 70° 56.175′ W). From the junction of Routes 1 and 97 in Topsfield, go 0.7 mile south on Route 97 to the access on the right.

Asbury Street (42° 39.238′ N, 70° 54.718′ W). From the junction of Route 1 and Ipswich Road, go 1.2 miles (1.2 miles) east on Ipswich Road, and turn right on Asbury Street. Go 0.2 mile (1.4 miles) to the access by the bridge. We do not recommend this access because of limited parking and because you can't get your car completely off the road.

Ipswich Road (42° 39.539′ N, 70° 54.42′ W). From the junction of Asbury Street and Ipswich Road, go 0.3 mile east on Ipswich Road to the access on the right. This and the Asbury Street access are part of Bradley Palmer State Park.

WHAT YOU'LL SEE
We love paddling here, following the Ipswich River's narrow twists and turns as it meanders through vast, tree-filled Wenham Swamp. Silver maple dominates

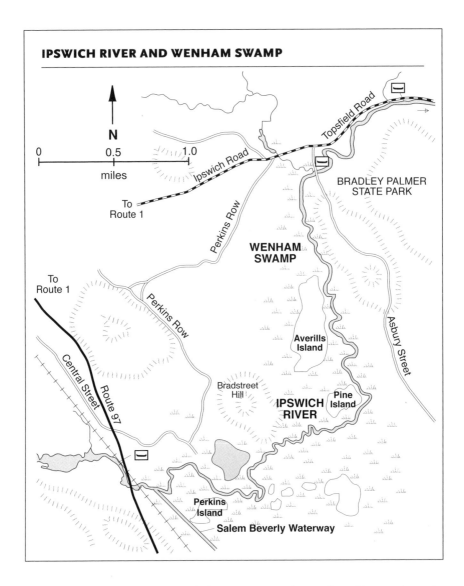

IPSWICH RIVER AND WENHAM SWAMP

the shoreline, interspersed with large swamp white oak, willow, red maple, cherry, and white pine. Trees reach out over the water, lending a closed-in, protected feeling. The section included here courses for 8 miles, which could easily require a full day to paddle, especially if you explore side channels and hidden coves and stop for a picnic lunch.

We especially enjoyed Perkins Island—where you can camp with Mass Audubon permission—with its huge straight-trunked trees. Its relatively clear understory stands in stark contrast to the brushy banks and encroaching vegetation along most of the streambed. Prominent shrubs and vines include dogwood, wild grape, arrowwood, and poison ivy. Royal and sensitive fern share the banks with cardinal flower, while patches of American eelgrass and pondweed undulate in the gentle current.

Damselflies and painted turtles sun on the many deadfalls, and the constant presence of flitting songbirds holds one's attention for much of the way. We paddled right up to a rather unconcerned great egret and found a couple of cormorants fishing in one of the more open areas. Paddling back to the Route 97 access, retracing our steps, we saw the swamp from a new perspective and continued to glimpse new things. We hated to leave this wonderful spot and vowed to return soon . . . and often.

A great egret stalks the shallows.

5 | Stearns Pond and Field Pond

Stearns and Field ponds, though relatively small, provide opportunities for extensive study of aquatic and shoreline plants. Extensive hiking trails lead to nine other ponds within the Harold Parker State Forest. Camping available on-site.

Location: Andover and North Andover, MA
Maps: *Massachusetts Atlas & Gazetteer*, Map 29: I19, 21, H21; USGS Reading
Area: Stearns Pond, 41 acres; Field Pond, 59 acres
Time: 3 hours, more if you study the plants or portage into other ponds
Habitat Type: shallow, marshy ponds; hiking trails
Fish: largemouth bass, yellow perch (see fish advisory, Appendix A)
Information: trail maps, mass.gov/dcr/parks/northeast/harp.htm
Camping: Harold Parker State Forest
Take Note: no development; no motors

GETTING THERE

From Lawrence, go south on Route 114. When Routes 114 and 125 split, go 3.8 miles (3.8 miles) on Route 114, and turn right into Harold Parker State Forest. Go 0.8 mile (4.6 miles) to the Stearns Pond access (42° 37.142′ N, 71° 4.351′ W) on the left. For Field Pond (42° 36.628′ N, 71° 6.492′ W), go another 0.3 mile (4.9 miles), and turn right on Middleton Road at the T. Go 1.1 miles (6.0 miles), and turn left on Jenkins Road. Go 0.8 mile (6.8 miles), and turn right on Harold Parker Road. Go 1.2 miles (8.0 miles) to the access on the left.

From Salem, go north on Route 114 for 3.4 miles past the intersection with Route 62, turn left into the state forest entrance, and follow directions as above.

From I-93, Exit 41, go 2.6 miles (2.6 miles) north on Route 125, and turn right on Harold Parker Road (a hard right leads to Gould Road). Go 0.6 mile (3.2 miles) to Field Pond on the right. For Stearns Pond, continue for 1.2 miles (4.4 miles), and turn left on Jenkins Road. Go 0.8 mile (5.2 miles), and turn right on Middleton Road. Go 1.1 miles (6.3 miles), and turn left on Harold Parker Road. Go 0.3 mile (6.6 miles) to the access on the right.

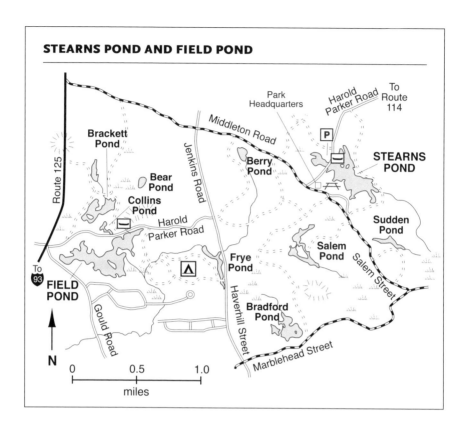

STEARNS POND AND FIELD POND

WHAT YOU'LL SEE

A collection of small ponds in Harold Parker State Forest, half an hour north of Boston, provides opportunity for very relaxing quietwater paddling. Of the eleven ponds in the forest, we include the two largest: Stearns Pond and Field Pond.

Both ponds have highly varied shorelines—full of coves, inlets, and islands—so despite their small sizes, you can do a surprising amount of exploration. White pine, red and sugar maples, red, white, and scarlet oaks, and gray birch cloak the hillsides. Sweet pepperbush, highbush blueberry, winterberry, sheep laurel, and other shrubs form a dense tangle for most of the shoreline, but intermittent patches of needle-carpeted forest floor allow you to stretch your legs or enjoy a picnic lunch.

Floating pond vegetation dominates the surface, particularly on Stearns Pond, and bur-reed, purple loosestrife, and cattail occur in the marshy spots. Bladderwort and other submerged plants provide hiding places for largemouth bass. Mossy hillocks of tree stumps remain from years ago when dams raised

The puffy, white, ball-like flowers of buttonbush, a shrub that can withstand root immersion for periods of time, bloom in summer.

water levels. Look for small, carnivorous sundews amid the sphagnum moss on these stumps. Along the shallow, sandy shores, look for freshwater mussel shells left behind by the area's industrious raccoons. The forest's vernal pools also provide habitat for rare blue-spotted salamanders (*Ambystoma laterale*).

The 3,500-acre state forest provides plenty of opportunity for exploring, especially if you don't mind a small portage. You can paddle any of the ponds as long as you park off the pavement. You can put in across the road from Field Pond into Collins Pond, for example, paddle to the north end, and then carry over to Brackett Pond. Getting to Salem Pond, the most remote, requires a considerable carry. To explore these areas, use the Harold Parker State Forest Trail Map, which shows the forest's network of trails and unpaved roads, most closed to vehicles.

6 | Concord River and Great Meadows National Wildlife Refuge

Paddling this section of the historic Concord River, although not a wilderness experience, transports us back to the time of Emerson and Thoreau. This slow-flowing river can be paddled in both directions. Look for orioles and lots of other bird species in the tall trees lining the river.

Location: Bedford, Billerica, Carlisle, and Concord, MA
Maps: *Massachusetts Atlas & Gazetteer*, Map 28: O7, Map 40: A6, B4, 5, 6; USGS Billerica, Maynard
Length: 6.5 miles one way; shorter trips possible
Time: 6 hours round-trip
Habitat Type: slow-flowing river through wildlife refuge; shrubby marshlands
Fish: largemouth, smallmouth, and calico bass; yellow perch; pickerel; northern pike (see fish advisory, Appendix A)
Information: *The Concord, Sudbury and Assabet Rivers* by Ron McAdow (Bliss Publishing, 1990); Great Meadows National Wildlife Refuge, fws.gov/northeast/greatmeadows, 978-443-4661; River Stewardship Council, sudbury-assabet-concord.org
Camping: Harold Parker State Forest
Take Note: limited development; motors allowed, 10 MPH speed limit

GETTING THERE

From Route 62 in Concord, go 0.4 mile north on Lowell Road to the access on the left before the bridge (42° 27.971' N, 71° 21.331' W). Drop your boat, and park along the street.

From the junction of Routes 4, 62, and 225, go 1.5 miles northwest on Route 225, and go off diagonally right on the access road, well before the bridge (42° 30.546' N, 71° 18.79' W).

WHAT YOU'LL SEE

The Concord River flows generally north with imperceptible current from the confluence of the Assabet and Sudbury rivers in Concord until it reaches Lowell and the Merrimack River. We include here a 6.5-mile section that flows through

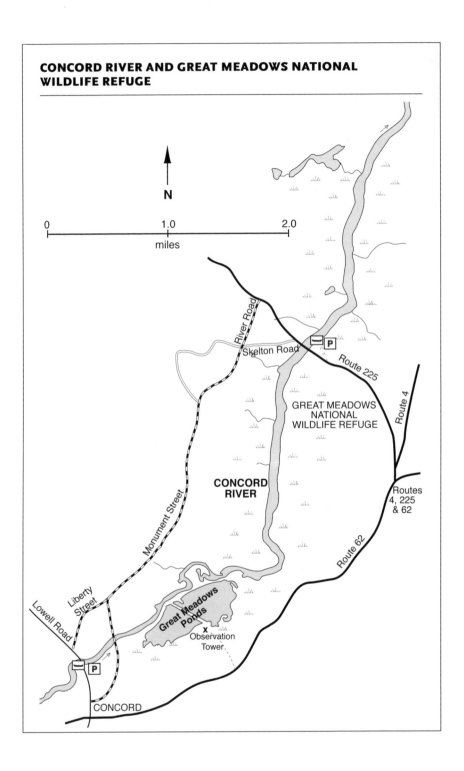

CONCORD RIVER AND GREAT MEADOWS NATIONAL WILDLIFE REFUGE

N

0   1.0   2.0

miles

River Road

Skelton Road

P

Route 225

Route 4

GREAT MEADOWS
NATIONAL
WILDLIFE REFUGE

CONCORD
RIVER

Routes
4, 225
& 62

Monument Street

Route 62

Liberty
Street

Lowell Road

Great Meadows
Ponds

X
Observation
Tower

P

CONCORD

Great Meadows National Wildlife Refuge. Thoreau wrote about his travels on the Concord in 1839 in *A Week on the Concord and Merrimack Rivers*. This historic area includes the Old North Bridge, about which Emerson penned:

> *By the rude bridge that arched the flood,*
> *Their flag to April's breeze unfurled,*
> *Here once the embattled farmers stood,*
> *And fired the shot heard round the world.*

Motorboats ply this section of the river but must comply with a 10 MPH speed limit. Paddling here on a June weekend, we saw more canoes and kayaks than motorboats. Because of the narrowness of the wildlife refuge on the river's west side, you will see a few large houses perched on large lots above the riverbank, but they do not impinge much on this mostly undeveloped section of river.

High plant diversity characterizes this area, including American lotus (*Nelumbo lutea*), with its enormous yellow flowers, found in impoundments within the wildlife refuge. This unusual plant is found only in a few New England locations. Dominant plants along the shrubby shoreline include buttonbush, smartweed, silver maple, pickerelweed, and invasive purple loosestrife. We also noticed patches of invasive watermilfoil and water chestnut. Towering oaks and white pine occur on higher ground. Common yellowthroats, white-throated sparrows, eastern kingbirds, grackles, and yellow warblers called from the underbrush, while crows, orioles, red-eyed vireos, chickadees, and robins called from the treetops. Tree swallows fed their nearly fully fledged young on a bare branch overhanging the river.

7 | Walden Pond

All paddlers in the Northeast should, at some point, make a pilgrimage to Walden Pond. Here we revere Henry David Thoreau, who penned in *Walden* the reason why many of us seek solitude in nature:

> *I went to the woods because I wished to live deliberately, to front only the essential facts of life, and see if I could not learn what it had to teach, and not, when I came to die, discover that I had not lived.*

Location: Concord, MA
Maps: *Massachusetts Atlas & Gazetteer*, Map 40: D5; USGS Maynard

Area: 61 acres

Time: 2 hours

Habitat Type: historic glacial, kettle-hole pond; hiking trails

Fish: rainbow and brown trout, largemouth and smallmouth bass (see fish advisory, Appendix A)

Information: Walden Pond State Reservation, mass.gov/eea/agencies/dcr/massparks/region-north/walden-pond-state-reservation.html, 978-369-3254; $5 launch fee; thoreausociety.org

Take Note: recreation area development only; no internal combustion motors

GETTING THERE

From the Route 2 rotary in Concord, go 3.5 miles (3.5 miles) east, and turn right on Route 126. Go 0.5 mile (4.0 miles) to the access on the right (42° 26.258′ N, 71° 20.12′ W).

From I-95, Exit 29, go about 4.5 miles (4.5 miles) west on Route 2, and turn left on Route 126. Go 0.5 mile (5.0 miles) to the access on the right.

WHAT YOU'LL SEE

Walden Pond has come a long way since the first edition of this book. In the intervening twenty years, a major revegetation effort has added tens of thousands of new native plants, restoring the shoreline and nearby trails to a condition not seen in 75 years.

The pond, a "kettle hole," formed 12,000 years ago when receding glaciers left behind a large chunk of ice buried in glacial till. Melting ice created a 100-foot-deep, sandy-bottomed pond, which provides superb swimming. The absence of any major inlet streams keeps Walden Pond relatively sterile, though; without stocking, it would provide little in the way of fishing.

We include the pond primarily for its historical significance. Simply paddling the same water that Thoreau and Emerson (two founders of the environmental movement) knew so well can give you—well, we have to say it—a transcendental experience. Henry David Thoreau lived at Walden Pond, on land owned by Ralph Waldo Emerson, from July 4, 1845, until September 1847, and he later reflected on the experience in *Walden*, published in 1854.

At the time Thoreau lived here, Walden Pond's woods were among the last in the Concord area not cleared for farming. He built a small one-room cabin near the pond's northern tip and spent his days studying natural history, gardening, reading, writing, and entertaining guests. His writing career began here, penning *A Week on the Concord and Merrimack Rivers*. About Walden

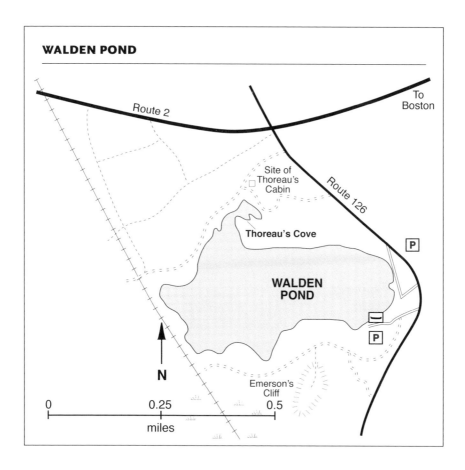

WALDEN POND

Route 2

To Boston

Site of Thoreau's Cabin

Route 126

Thoreau's Cove

P

WALDEN POND

P

N

Emerson's Cliff

0   0.25   0.5

miles

and other ponds, he wrote:

> *A lake is the landscape's most beautiful and expressive feature.*
> *It is Earth's eye; looking into which the beholder measures*
> *the depth of his own nature.*

Society's destruction of forests deeply affected Thoreau: "When I first paddled a boat on Walden it was completely surrounded by thick and lofty pine and oak woods . . . but since I left those shores, the woodcutters have still further laid them waste." To compensate, Thoreau planted 400 white pine, but the great hurricane of 1938 knocked them down; look for the few remaining stumps above the house site.

When Thoreau lived here, loons occasionally visited the pond, but they disappeared, pushed away by encroaching civilization and a lack of fish. (Today, loons nest on only four bodies of water in Massachusetts, all public water supplies and off-limits to boating.) In the twentieth century, Walden became far more crowded than Thoreau could have imagined, in part from the fame he himself brought to the pond. In the early 1900s, as many as 2,000 tourists visited the pond per day. By the summer of 1935, after an 80-acre parcel of land around the pond had been granted to the commonwealth as a public park, as many as 485,000 people visited the pond each summer, with up to 25,000 visitors on a single Sunday. Today, visitors number 600,000 annually, with folks turned away on warm summer afternoons when the park reaches capacity.

Since 1975, the Massachusetts Department of Environmental Management has managed Walden Pond and has worked to restore its eroded banks and trails. If your schedule permits, come midweek after Labor Day or before Memorial Day or perhaps on a drizzly day that will help you reflect on the pond's historic past as you paddle the deserted shores.

8 | Sudbury River

The Sudbury flows lazily through Great Meadows National Wildlife Refuge, making it easy to paddle both directions. Revel in the abundant birdlife. Interesting aquatic plants abound, as well.

Location: Concord, Lincoln, Sudbury, and Wayland, MA
Maps: *Massachusetts Atlas & Gazetteer*, Map 40: E4, F3, 4, G3, 4, H3, I3; USGS Framingham, Maynard
Length: 10.6 miles one way; shorter trips possible
Time: all day
Habitat Type: slow-flowing river through wildlife refuge; broad, shrubby marshlands
Fish: largemouth, smallmouth, and calico bass; yellow perch; pickerel; northern pike (see fish advisory, Appendix A)
Information: *The Concord, Sudbury and Assabet Rivers* by Ron McAdow (Bliss Publishing, 1990); Great Meadows National Wildlife Refuge, fws.gov/northeast/greatmeadows, 978-443-4661; River Stewardship Council, sudbury-assabet-concord.org
Take Note: some development; motors allowed, 10 MPH speed limit

GETTING THERE
Access points are given in order, starting upstream (south end).
   Pelham Island Road (42° 21.526′ N, 71° 22.153′ W). From the junction

SUDBURY RIVER

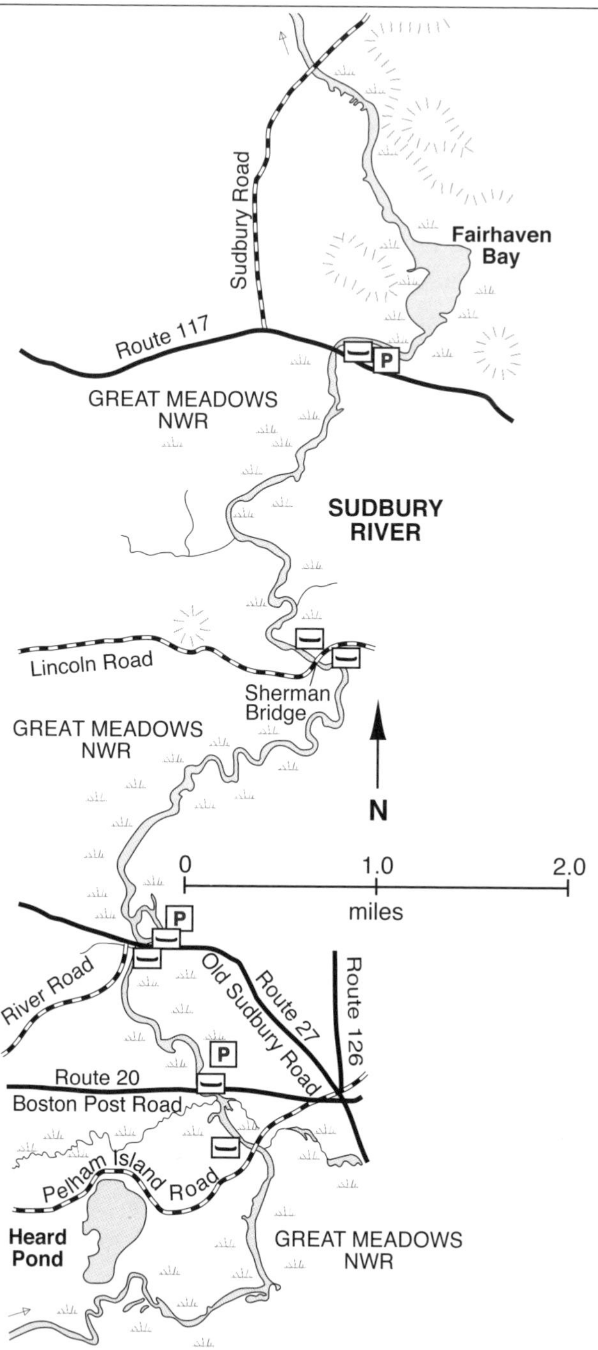

Fairhaven Bay

Sudbury Road

Route 117

GREAT MEADOWS
NWR

SUDBURY
RIVER

Lincoln Road

Sherman
Bridge

GREAT MEADOWS
NWR

N

0   1.0   2.0
                miles

River Road

Old Sudbury Road

Route 27

Route 126

Route 20
Boston Post Road

Pelham Island Road

Heard
Pond

GREAT MEADOWS
NWR

of Routes 20, 27, and 126 in Wayland, go west on Route 20. Turn immediately diagonally left on Pelham Island Road. Go 0.4 mile to the access on the right, just across the bridge.

Route 20/Boston Post Road (42° 21.806′ N, 71° 22.458′ W). From the junction of Routes 20, 27, and 126, go 0.7 mile west on Route 20 to the access on the right, just before the bridge.

River Road (42° 22.147′ N, 71° 22.917′ W). From the junction of Routes 20, 27, and 126, go 1.3 miles north on Route 27, and turn left on River Road. Access is immediately on the left.

Route 27/Old Sudbury Road (42° 22.452′ N, 71° 22.867′ W). From the junction of Routes 20, 27, and 126, go 1.3 miles north on Route 27; access is on the right, just before the bridge.

Sherman Bridge (42° 23.791′ N, 71° 21.867′ W). From the junction of Routes 117 and 126 in Lincoln, go 1.5 miles (1.5 miles) south on Route 126, and turn right on Lincoln Road. Go 0.7 mile (2.2 miles) to the access on either side.

Route 117/South Great Road (42° 25.205′ N, 71° 21.853′ W). From the junction of Routes 117 and 126, go 1.1 miles west on Route 117 to the access on the right, just before the bridge.

WHAT YOU'LL SEE

This section of the Sudbury River from Heard Pond downstream to Sudbury Road offers wonderful paddling through broad expanses of the Great Meadows National Wildlife Refuge (Great Meadows NWR). In another 2.4 miles downstream, the Sudbury joins the Assabet to form the Concord River. Like the Concord, which also flows through Great Meadows NWR, you can paddle the Sudbury both directions through the lazy current. The Sudbury lacks the breadth of the Concord but has broader surrounding meadows, filled with low-growing grasses and other marsh plants.

At times of high water, you can paddle up the Heard Pond outlet and explore the prime birding habitat of this small pond and the surrounding marshes and woods (part conservation lands, part Great Meadows NWR). At the other end of this section of the Sudbury, in Fairhaven Bay, look for osprey fishing alongside the human anglers. In between, you can spend hours paddling along, enjoying the surrounding marshlands with their abundant birdlife.

Look for buttonbush (*Cephalanthus occidentalis*), with its spherical white flowers and seedheads, growing along the banks and in the water. Purple loosestrife (*Lythrum salicaria*), an introduced species, grows on slightly higher ground. We found small patches of water-clover—aptly named *Marsilea quadrifolia*—an aquatic fern introduced into New England from Europe,

A mechanical harvester prepares to unload a few thousand pounds of water chestnuts, a very destructive invasive plant.

along with larger patches of water chestnut, *Trapa natans*, another alien and far more destructive species. When we paddled here a dozen years ago, the towns of Lincoln and Concord were harvesting truckloads of water chestnut from Fairhaven Bay, using a huge floating harvesting machine.

The birds impressed us most, however, as they called from their streamside perches. We saw or heard many species, including bobolink, white-throated and song sparrows, barn and tree swallows, wood duck, eastern kingbird, red-winged blackbird, Baltimore oriole, grackle, tufted titmouse, common yellowthroat, yellow warbler, chickadee, cedar waxwing, mourning dove, killdeer, catbird, and cardinal.

9 | Assabet River

This slow-flowing section of the Assabet River flows through an extensive marshland with inlets, islands, and multiple channels to explore. Look for typical wetland species, especially great blue heron; we saw many fishing here, along with lots of other wetland birds.

Location: Maynard and Stow, MA
Maps: *Massachusetts Atlas & Gazetteer*, Map 39: E26, 27, F24, 25, G24, 25; USGS Framingham, Hudson, Marlborough, Maynard
Length: 5.5 miles one way
Time: 6 hours round-trip
Habitat Type: slow-flowing marshy river
Fish: largemouth bass, yellow perch, pickerel (see fish advisory, Appendix A)
Information: Assabet River National Wildlife Refuge, fws.gov/northeast/assabetriver/opportunities.html; *The Concord, Sudbury and Assabet Rivers* by Ron McAdow (Bliss Publishing, 1990)
Take Note: limited development; hiking trail

GETTING THERE

Sudbury/Boon Road (42° 24.698′ N, 71° 30.487′ W). From the junction of Routes 27 and 62 in Maynard, go 1.0 mile (1.0 mile) west on Route 62, and turn right on Routes 62 and 117. Go 1.9 miles (2.9 miles), and turn left on Route 62. Go 1.1 mile (4.0 miles), and turn left on Whitman Street. Go 0.9 mile (4.9 miles), turn left on Boon Road (immediately becomes Sudbury Road), and go 0.2 mile (5.1 miles) to the access at Magazu's Landing on the right, just after the bridge.

White Pond Road (42° 25.418′ N, 71° 28.502′ W). From the junction of Routes 27 and 62 in Maynard, go 1.0 mile (1.0 mile) west on Route 62, and turn right on Routes 62 and 117. Go 0.4 mile (1.4 miles), and turn left on Hastings Street. Go 0.3 mile (1.7 miles), turn left on White Pond Road, and go 0.2 mile (1.9 miles) to the access on the left, just before the bridge.

Ice House Landing (42° 24.526′ N, 71° 28.096′ W). From the junction of Routes 27 and 62 in Maynard, go 1.0 mile (1.0 mile) west on Route 62, and turn left on Route 117. Go 0.2 mile (1.2 miles), turn right on Winter Street, and go 0.2 mile (1.4 miles) to Ice House Landing on the right.

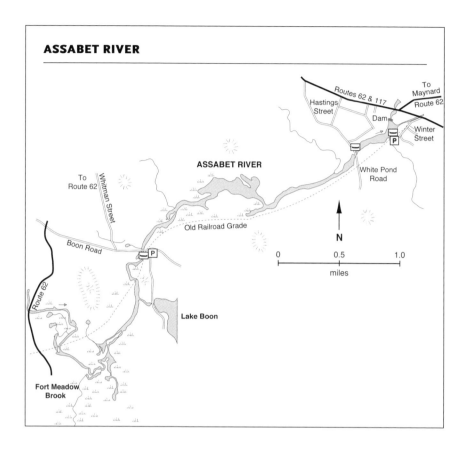

ASSABET RIVER

ASSABET RIVER

To Maynard
Routes 62 & 117
Route 62
Hastings Street
Dam
Winter Street
White Pond Road
To Route 62
Whitman Street
Old Railroad Grade
N
Boon Road
0   0.5   1.0
miles
Route 62
Lake Boon
Fort Meadow Brook

WHAT YOU'LL SEE

Marshy Assabet River, on its way to join the Sudbury at Concord, flows lazily through extensive marshlands upstream from the small Ben Smith Dam at Ice House Landing in Maynard. With limited time, we prefer putting in at Boon Road or White Pond Road and paddling upstream. You can paddle all the way upstream to the dam at Route 62. Regardless of where you start, the Assabet offers a fabulous place to paddle, with portions bordered by the Assabet National Wildlife Refuge. It's also worth reading the kiosk information at Ice House Landing, maintained by the Maynard Conservation Commission. One of the kiosks contains this quote from Nathaniel Hawthorne in *Mosses from an Old Manse*:

> *Running our boat against the current, between wide meadows, we turn aside into the Assabeth. A more lovely stream than this, for a mile above its junction with the Concord, has never flowed on earth— nowhere, indeed, except to lave the interior of a poet's imagination.*

Hawthorne's river selection, like the section covered here, flows through extensive marshlands. The most interesting paddling lies upstream of Boon Road among the islands, marshy inlets, and multiple river channels. A little less than a mile downstream from Route 62, you can paddle south under a culvert up Fort Meadow Brook into an extensive beaver marsh.

We didn't keep a great blue heron count, but we watched many of them fish the shallows and shorelines. Large groups of barn, bank, and tree swallows darted across the water, gathering in insects. We also saw or heard white-breasted nuthatches, common yellowthroats, red-winged blackbirds, brown thrashers, cardinals, song sparrows, Eastern kingbirds, spotted sandpipers, Eastern phoebes, red-tailed hawks, turkey vultures, Canada geese, and robins.

Red maple, red oak, and other trees rim the marsh, while small amounts of jewelweed, yellow pond-lily, American white waterlily, and pickerelweed appear along the grass-lined banks. Cattails sprout up here and there throughout the wetlands. Painted turtles perch on logs, plummeting into the water as you pass by, and frogs dive down through the floating aquatic vegetation.

Although we saw some clumps of invasive purple loosestrife, we were more chagrined by finding large clumps of Japanese knotweed at the Boon Road access. In the last ten years, the amount of this super invasive plant has increased dramatically, particularly along Connecticut and Rhode Island waterways. An ornamental escape, knotweed thrives in disturbed areas, spreading easily through root rhizomes and from pieces of dislodged stems carried downstream by flowing water. These plant parts easily take root and then grow in dense patches that crowd out all native vegetation.

While you're here, you can bike or hike the former Boston and Maine Railroad railway bed. The Assabet River Rail Trail association hopes to acquire the remaining sections to complete the 12-mile Acton to Marlborough trail.

10 | Ashland Reservoir

Ashland Reservoir offers a few hours of pleasant paddling along wooded shorelines over deep, clear water. The scenic shoreline harbors many tree species, with white pine and red oak in plentiful supply. Expect to see ducks and cormorant, along with other bird species.

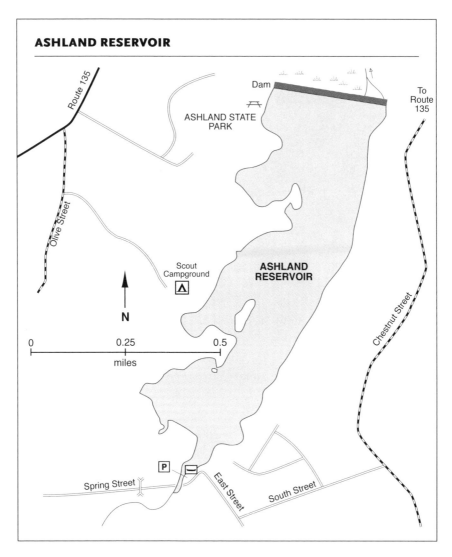

ASHLAND RESERVOIR

Location: Ashland, MA
Maps: *Massachusetts Atlas & Gazetteer,* Map 51: A27, 28; USGS Medfield
Area: 157 acres
Time: 2 hours, longer if you go for a swim
Habitat Type: deep reservoir; wooded shoreline
Fish: brook, brown, and rainbow trout; largemouth and calico bass; yellow perch (see fish advisory, Appendix A)
Information: Ashland State Park, mass.gov/eea/agencies/dcr/massparks/region-north/ashland-state-park.html, 508-435-4303

Mallards, a frequent sight on Ashland Reservoir, take a break from feeding along the shoreline.

Take Note: little development; motors allowed up to 10 HP/12 MPH; no personal watercraft

GETTING THERE
From I-495, Exit 21A, go 5.5 miles (5.5 miles) east on West Main Street and then Route 135, and turn right on Main Street. Go 0.6 mile (6.1 miles), and veer right on Chestnut Street. Go 1.3 miles (7.4 miles), and turn right on South Street (unmarked). Go 0.4 mile (7.8 miles), and turn right on East Street to the access (42° 13.938′ N, 71° 28.121′ W).

WHAT YOU'LL SEE
Ashland Reservoir, popular with canoers and kayakers, provides a great spot for a quiet morning or afternoon paddle. With a largely undeveloped shoreline, a 10 MPH limit for motors, and attractive woods surrounding the reservoir, Ashland offers some of the best lake paddling within the I-495 loop. A little more than 1 mile long and about 0.25 mile wide, the reservoir seems quite deep, with little aquatic vegetation. Ashland State Park, located at the north end off Route 135, offers picnic and swim areas, hiking trails, and a boat launch (open seasonally).

Paddling north, the reservoir quickly opens up, with some deep coves on the west shore. The west shore—with more variation—provides more interesting paddling than the east shore. Red oak and white pine dominate the heavily wooded shoreline, but you will also see red maple, American chestnut, scarlet and white oaks, gray and black birches, sassafras, blackgum, and pitch pine. Shrubs—sweet pepperbush, alder, blueberry, and winterberry—grow densely along the shore. During a mid-September paddle, we found some edible grapes overhanging the water along the east shore.

In places you will see numerous shallow depressions in the sand a foot or two in diameter. Spawning sunfish keep these locations free of debris and organic matter. During summer, adult males valiantly guard these depressions, fanning the eggs that their mates deposited to provide good aeration. Along with lots of sunfish, Ashland Reservoir harbors healthy populations of largemouth bass, yellow perch, and stocked rainbow trout.

11 | Whitehall Reservoir

Whitehall Reservoir harbors several islands and protected bays, making it seem larger than it is. It takes half a day or more to explore all the various passageways surrounded by gorgeous forests. Islands contain unusual tree species for this latitude. Avoid this popular lake on busy summer weekends.

Location: Hopkinton, MA
Maps: *Massachusetts Atlas & Gazetteer*, Map 51: A21, B21; USGS Milford
Area: 592 acres
Time: 4 hours; 6 hours for thorough exploration and a picnic
Habitat Type: reservoir; many islands and protected bays
Fish: trout, largemouth bass, white and yellow perch, pickerel, northern pike (see fish advisory, Appendix A)
Information: Whitehall State Park, mass.gov/eea/agencies/dcr/massparks/region-north/whitehall-state-park.html, 508-435-4303
Take Note: little development; motors allowed, 12 MPH limit; no personal watercraft

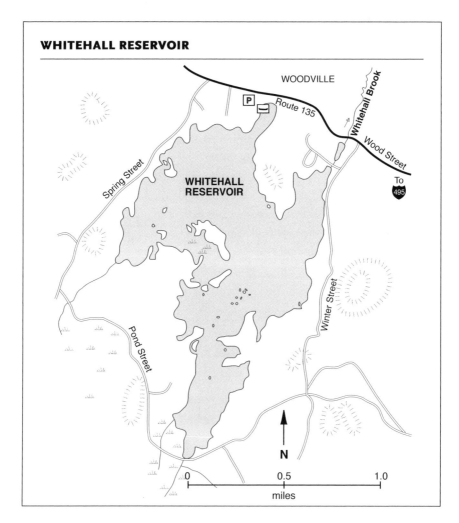

WHITEHALL RESERVOIR

WOODVILLE

Whitehall Brook

Route 135

Wood Street

To 495

WHITEHALL RESERVOIR

Spring Street

Pond Street

Winter Street

N

0   0.5   1.0
miles

GETTING THERE

From I-495, Exit 21A, go 1.2 miles (1.2 miles) east on West Main Street, and turn left on Route 135/Wood Street. Go 2.7 miles (3.9 miles) to the access on the left (42° 14.46′ N, 71° 34.338′ W).

WHAT YOU'LL SEE

Whitehall Reservoir at one time served as a water supply for areas west of Boston, but with Quabbin Reservoir's creation in 1939, drinking water from Whitehall was no longer needed, and the area eventually got turned into a state park. Its years of restricted access mean great boating today. The park encompasses the reservoir's entire shoreline but allows homeowners to erect small docks. From the water, the reservoir feels undeveloped and wild.

Mountain laurel graces Whitehall Reservoir shores, blooming in mid-June.

The highly varied shoreline includes numerous deep coves and dozens of wonderful islands to explore. A few marshy areas occur along the mainly heavily wooded shoreline. The open woods invite picnicking. Mixed deciduous trees and conifers, typical of southern Massachusetts, along with mountain laurel and highbush blueberry, grow along the shore. Near the center of the reservoir on the west side, a fantastic grouping of islands sports far different vegetation, however, including Atlantic white cedar, tamarack, and black spruce—trees you would expect to see much farther north. On a quiet weekday morning, weaving in and out of these almost magical islands on the channels that cut through them, the rest of the world can seem pretty far away.

While the wetness of the islands near the reservoir's center preclude exploration on foot, the higher islands on the reservoir's north end present a perfect place for a picnic or blueberry-picking excursion. Also, near the dam at the northeastern tip, some gorgeous open woodlands—tall white pine with a thick carpet of pine needles underfoot—invite exploration.

While Whitehall Reservoir's 592 acres offer some great paddling for a half-day or more, we would avoid it on busy summer weekends. Motorboats that routinely ignore the 12 MPH speed limit can make paddling unpleasant at times; water-skiing and personal watercraft are prohibited.

12 | Blackstone River

This is a rare trip where you can paddle in a loop: downstream on a river and then upstream on a canal. In addition to historic sights, you will see great blue heron, kingfisher, and osprey, along with myriad wetland plant species. You can also hike or bike the historic towpath.

Location: Northbridge and Uxbridge, MA
Maps: *Massachusetts Atlas & Gazetteer*, Map 51: H17, 18, I18, J18; USGS Blackstone, Uxbridge
Length: 4 miles one way
Time: 5 hours round-trip
Habitat Type: moderate-flowing river and parallel canal with no current
Fish: largemouth, smallmouth, and calico bass; yellow perch; pickerel; northern pike (see fish advisory, Appendix A)
Information: Blackstone River & Canal Heritage State Park, mass.gov/eea/agencies/dcr/massparks/region-central/blackstone-river-and-canal-heritage-state-park.html; Slater Mill, SlaterMill.org
Take Note: limited development; current on Blackstone River below dam can be significant, inexperienced paddlers should avoid river, always wear PFD on the river

GETTING THERE
From the junction of Routes 16 and 146, go 2.6 miles (2.6 miles) east on Route 16, and turn left on Oak Street. Go 0.8 mile (3.4 miles) to the access on the right at River Bend Farm Visitor Center (42° 5.651′ N, 71° 37.396′ W).

WHAT YOU'LL SEE
Paddling on the Blackstone River and Blackstone Canal allows not just an exploration of natural history but also a tour through some of our nation's extraordinary cultural history. America's industrial revolution, in many ways, began on the Blackstone River, where the first water-powered mills began to spin cotton. The Slater Mill, America's first true factory, built in 1793, is located on the river in Pawtucket, Rhode Island, and open as a museum dedicated to the American Industrial Revolution.

The Blackstone River extends from Worcester to Providence, dropping 438 feet in its 45-mile length. Its 34 dams use 409 feet of the river's drop for the many

BLACKSTONE RIVER

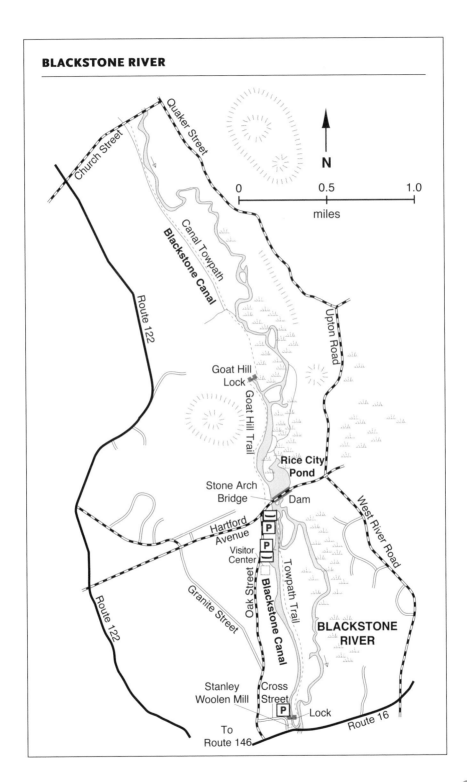

mills along here. From 1828 to 1848, a canal paralleled portions of the river, allowing horse-drawn boats and barges to carry freight and people between Providence and Worcester.

This entire stretch of the river and canal lies within the John H. Chafee Blackstone River Valley National Heritage Corridor. We address only one small segment here, but dozens of other places await exploration by canoe or kayak—as well as by foot or bicycle on the many miles of pathways created here, including on the restored towpath that paralleled the Blackstone Canal; a bicycle path will eventually connect Worcester and Providence.

The segment of river and canal covered here, both upriver and downriver from the River Bend Farm visitor center, offers one of the best places to explore this region by canoe or kayak. As you leave the visitor center, paddle to the left (north), crossing under a pedestrian bridge and into the canal. Paddling up this non-flowing canal, which will be pea green with floating vegetation by midsummer, you will quickly reach a wall and steps where you can portage either into the river, beneath the dam, or above the dam into the combined canal and river.

On a visit here on a beautiful early August day, we launched into the river, paddling north under the Hartford Avenue Stone Arch Bridge (admire the construction of the 1869 bridge with tightly fitting, precisely cut granite) into Rice City Pond, a large wetland. Be aware of the dam to the right here, keeping your distance.

A wide range of marsh plants, including cattail, bulrush, pickerelweed, arrowhead, bur-reed, *Phragmites*, and wild rice populate the pond's shoreline. In late summer, look for elderberry bushes laden with fruit. On more solid ground, you will see gray birch and red maple in profusion; looking carefully, you should find some catalpa, swamp white oak, and blackgum trees. In early August, you may smell the flowers of very common sweet pepperbush; look for elongated clusters of small white flowers.

The very shallow, muddy-bottomed water harbors huge carp; we caught glimpses of a few but saw the trails of stirred-up mud left by dozens of these large fish as they fled before us. Fishermen have caught carp of more than 30 pounds here, but consuming Blackstone fish carries risk, as this was once one of the nation's most polluted rivers. In Rice City Pond and continuing northward, we saw great blue herons, kingfishers, cormorants, and ospreys; earlier in the season, one would see more waterfowl. Moving along quietly, you should catch glimpses of many painted turtles sunning on logs before they retreat into the water as you approach.

Sticking to the western shore, you will enter the canal, and about a mile north from Hartford Avenue, you can find the remnants of the Goat Hill Lock,

The Blackstone River passes under the historic Stone Arch Bridge, constructed in 1869 of precisely fitted granite stones.

built in 1827, one of only four of the original 48 locks that remain visible.

Explore the extensive coves north of the pond—to the extent vegetation allows. Eventually, stronger current and shallow water impede your travel. We got about 2 miles upstream from the Hartford Avenue bridge before continuing our explorations southward, back to the bridge and portage around the dam. At the portage just south of the Hartford Avenue bridge, note the water level. When water goes over the spillway, the water level is too high for paddling south on the river—except by experienced whitewater paddlers. On the river, use caution and wear your PFD. Even at low water, strong current and downed trees may cause strainers that can roll or trap a boat.

With the water level down, we portaged over to the river put-in and paddled with the current about 2 miles down to a portage across to the canal and the Stanley Woolen Mill, built in 1853. Look for the portage sign fairly high on a tree to the right, marking the easy carry across a mowed field to the dam. Before getting back in your boat, consider walking down the towpath trail to look at the well-preserved Stanley Woolen Mill.

Launch your boat into the canal for an easy paddle on still water back up to the River Bend Farm Visitor Center. Duckweed can cover the fairly stagnant water here, making paddling not quite as pleasant as earlier in the season.

13 | Charles River

The upper Charles River carves a narrow, undulating path through generally wooded shores, proffering up solitude and beauty. You should see muskrats and myriad bird species. If you're quiet, you may see deer in the early morning or evening.

Location: Dover, Medfield, Millis, Natick, Norfolk, and Sherborn, MA
Maps: *Massachusetts Atlas & Gazetteer*, Map 40: O6, Map 52: A6, B5, 6, C4, 5, D5, 6, E6, F5, 6, G5; USGS Framingham, Medfield
Length: 13.4 miles one way; shorter trips possible
Time: all day
Habitat Type: meandering, slow-flowing river through mostly preserved land; marshlands
Fish: largemouth, smallmouth, and calico bass; white and yellow perch; pickerel; northern pike (see fish advisory, Appendix A)
Information: *The Charles River* (see Appendix B); The Trustees of Reservations, thetrustees.org, 508-785-0339; Massachusetts Audubon Society, massaudubon. org, 508-655-2296; Charles River Watershed Association, crwa.org
Take Note: limited development; too shallow for motors

GETTING THERE

Access points are given in order, starting upstream (south end).

Route 115 (42° 8.584′ N, 71° 20.929′ W). Use only for a one-way trip downstream. From the junction of Routes 109 and 115 in Millis, go 1.8 miles south on Route 115 to the access on the left, just over the bridge.

Forest Road (42° 9.48′ N, 71° 19.977′ W). From the junction of Routes 109 and 115, go 0.7 mile (0.7 mile) east on Route 109, and turn right on Village Street. Go 0.8 mile (1.5 miles), and turn left on Forest Road. Go 0.8 mile (2.3 miles) to the access on the left, just before the bridge.

Dwight Street (42° 10.452′ N, 71° 19.397′ W). From the junction of Routes 109 and 115, go 1.4 miles (1.4 miles) east on Route 109, and turn right on Dwight Street. Go 0.5 mile (1.9 miles) to the access on the right.

West Street (42° 11.347′ N, 71° 20.004′ W). From the junction of Routes 109 and 115, go 1.0 mile (1.0 mile) east on Route 109, and turn left on Dover Road (turns into West Street). Go 1.1 miles (2.1 miles) to the access on the left, just over the bridge.

CHARLES RIVER

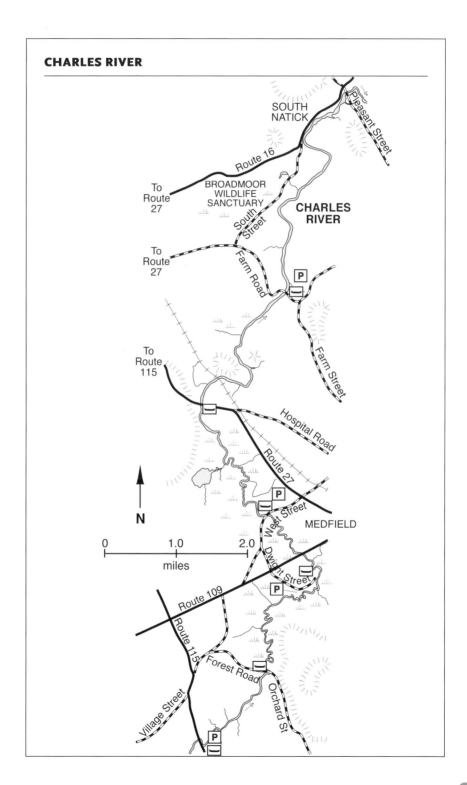

Route 27 (42° 12.591′ N, 71° 21.063′ W). From the junction of Routes 27 and 115, go 0.3 mile south on Route 27 to the access on the right, just over the bridge.

Farm Road (42° 13.965′ N, 71° 19.788′ W). From Sherborn, go south on Routes 16 and 27, and bear left onto Route 27 at the Y. Go 0.3 mile (0.3 mile), and turn left on Farm Road. Go 2.4 miles (2.7 miles) to the access on the left, just across the bridge.

Broadmoor Wildlife Sanctuary (42° 15.379′ N, 71° 20.361′ W). From the junction of Routes 16 and 27 in Sherborn, go 1.6 miles northeast on Route 16 to the visitor center on the right.

WHAT YOU'LL SEE

If you think of boating on the Charles as sailing or rowing through Cambridge, then try the upper Charles, one of the finest paddling destinations in the Northeast. It begins its 80-mile meander from Echo Lake in Hopkinton, flowing down to Boston Harbor, dropping an average of only about 4 feet per mile. We cover, more or less, the river's middle section.

When we paddled here in late June, wild grapes clung to the streamside vegetation, swamp rose bloomed in profusion, and the sweet scent of swamp azalea wafted along on the slightest breeze. Red maple dominates the shores in marshy sections, but you may also spot some stately elms and swamp white oaks, along with a variety of other trees.

In the Charles' north-flowing upper reaches, we watched the boat compass needle swing back and forth endlessly as the river meandered through low-lying red maple swamps and wet meadows. As a muskrat swam before us, towing a clump of grass, and a great horned owl eyed us from an overhead perch, we marveled at this truly wild place that lies a stone's throw from Boston suburbs.

Two very large snapping turtles dived for cover in deeper water as we glided by, and we watched a green heron and a great blue heron stalk the shallows for fish and other prey. A red-tailed hawk wheeled overhead while myriad songbirds sang from hidden perches. We listened to the beautiful, flutelike notes of a hermit thrush—normally a deep-woods resident—and thought of the similarities to northern New England. We strained to hear road noise but heard none.

Medfield State Forest, Sherborn Town Forest, The Trustees of Reservations, Massachusetts Audubon Society, and private landowners protect much of the land in this section from development. The Forest Road access marks the beginning of a river section navigable even during periods of low water. We recommend paddling upstream to start, especially in spring, and letting the light current help carry you back down. Our favorite paddle starts at Dwight Street and heads upstream (south) to Route 115, a round-trip distance of 7.5 miles through the most pristine areas.

Hiking trails abound. About a mile downstream from Farm Road, The Trustees of Reservations maintains a landing on the left bank. From there, you can hike uphill for nearly a mile to King Philip's Lookout in the contiguous Sherborn Town Forest. Foot trails meander through Peters Reservation on the right bank, just downstream from Farm Road. Also, visit the Broadmoor Wildlife Sanctuary (owned by Mass Audubon; see above for directions) with its elevated boardwalk and 9 miles of trails.

14 | Neponset River

The Neponset River, which forms Boston's southern boundary, flows lazily for about 8 miles through extensive wetlands with very limited development. Streamside trees, shrubs, and vines form an overarching canopy in many areas, making it a great place to paddle on hot, sunny days. You can find wood duck, great blue heron, beaver, and deer here.

Location: Boston, Canton, Dedham, Milton, Norwood, MA
Maps: *Massachusetts Atlas & Gazetteer*, Map 53: A18, B17, 18, C17, D16, E16; USGS Blue Hills, Norwood
Length: 8 miles one way; shorter trips possible
Time: all day
Habitat Type: meandering, slow-flowing river through mostly preserved land; marshlands
Fish: largemouth bass, pickerel (see fish advisory, Appendix A)
Information: The Trustees of Reservations, thetrustees.org/places-to-visit/ greater-boston/signal-hill.html; Neponset River Reservation, mass.gov/eea/ agencies/dcr/massparks/region-boston/neponset-river-reservation.html; Blue Hill Adventure canoe rentals, bluehilladventure-quarrymuseum.com (see Calendar)
Take Note: limited development; no motors

NEPONSET RIVER

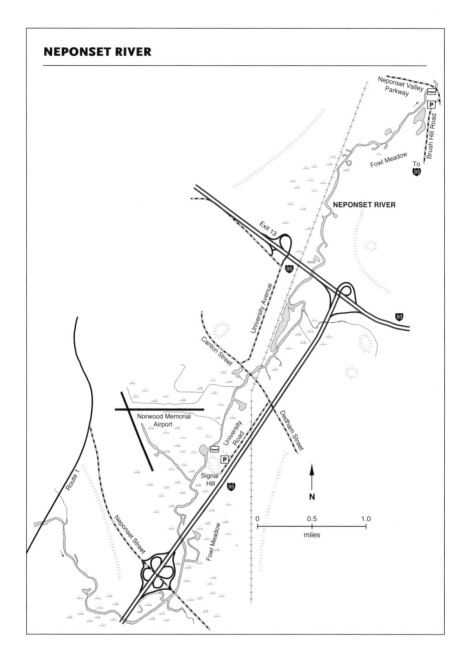

GETTING THERE
Brush Hill Road (42° 14.013′ N, 71° 7.344′ W). From I-93, Exit 2B, go 1.3 miles (1.3 miles) north on Route 138, and veer right onto Canton Avenue. Go 0.1

mile (1.4 miles), and turn left onto the connector to Brush Hill Road. Go 0.9 mile (2.3 miles) to the access on the left, just before Neponset Valley Parkway.

University Road (42° 11.115′ N, 71° 9.576′ W). From I-95, Exit 13, go 0.1 mile (0.1 mile), and turn right on University Avenue. Go 1.0 mile (1.1 miles), and turn left on Canton Street. Go 0.2 mile (1.3 miles), and turn right on University Road. Go 0.8 mile (2.1 miles) to the Signal Hill, The Trustees of Reservations, access on the right.

WHAT YOU'LL SEE

The Neponset River offers a fabulous paddling resource, especially given its location on the very edge of metropolitan Boston. It actually forms Boston's southern and Quincy's northern boundaries. This section flows for 8 lazy miles through the Fowl Meadow section of the Neponset River Reservation, from Route 1 down to Paul's Bridge (Brush Hill access). We prefer putting in at Paul's Bridge, paddling upstream, and letting the slow-flowing river help carry us back to the access. This strategy allows any length day trip; going all the way to Route 1 and back would take most of a day. You could spend even more time if you explored the many side channels that flow into the river.

Trees and shrubs line the length of the river, providing relatively shady paddling, ideal for hot, sunny days. Impressive amounts of wild grapevine drape over trees and shrubs, hanging out over the river, making it seem narrower than it is. Look for royal fern tucked under the canopy along the shore. When we paddled here in mid-August, large numbers of birds fed on the abundant fruits of shrubs and trees. We noted buttonbush, red osier dogwood, and many others.

Red maple; red, scarlet, white, and swamp white oaks; chokecherry; and quaking aspen provide a lot of the shade. Swifts cruise above for insects, while wood ducks try to hide along the shore. Beaver and storms topple an occasional tree, but you should be able to negotiate most of these without having to portage around. Look for deer in the evening or early morning.

From Paul's Bridge, you can also hike the 2.5-mile Burma Road, viewing the marshes from another angle. If you find yourself at the University Road access, be sure to climb Signal Hill to view Fowl Meadow and the Blue Hills. Maintained by The Trustees of Reservations, this site also offers a place to rent canoes on weekends and holidays from April through October.

The Neponset River salt marshes were the first in Massachusetts to be publicly owned. Since purchasing the marshes in the late 1880s, the state has acquired, protected, and rehabilitated 750 acres along the river which now make up the Neponset River Reservation.

15 | Weymouth Back River

This is a great place to paddle at or near high tide; watch out for extensive mud flats as tides recede. You should see osprey here against a wooded shore backdrop; osprey pairs nest here successfully nearly every year, sometimes fledging as many as three young. Huge numbers of what locals call herring spawn here.

Location: Hingham and Weymouth, MA
Maps: *Massachusetts Atlas & Gazetteer*, Map 41: O29, 30, Map 53: A29, 30, B30; USGS Hull, Weymouth
Length: 3.6 miles one way
Time: 4 hours round-trip
Habitat Type: tidal estuary, wooded shores
Fish: striped bass, alewife, herring, rainbow smelt (see fish advisory, Appendix A)
Information: tide charts, maineharbors.com
Camping: Wompatuck State Park
Take Note: no water-skiing or personal watercraft south of Route 3A bridge; no development; visit at or near high tide—exposed mud banks at low tide dramatically reduce paddling area

GETTING THERE

From I-93, Exit 12 southbound, go 6.8 miles (6.8 miles) southeast on Route 3A (follow signs carefully) to the stoplight at the junction of Route 3A (Bridge Street) with Green Street (right/south) and Neck Street (left/north). Directions to the three access points given from this junction.

Abigail Adams Park (42° 14.846′ N, 70° 54.019′ W). From the junction, go 0.3 mile (7.1 miles) east on Route 3A, and turn right to cross Route 3A into the park, just before the bridge.

Weymouth Public Launch (42° 15.116′ N, 70° 56.18′ W). From the junction, go 0.6 mile (7.4 miles) north on Neck Street to the access on the right. Launch fee.

Great Esker Park (42° 13.785′ N, 70° 55.65′ W). From the junction, go 1.1 miles (7.9 miles) south on Green Street, and turn left on East Street. Go 0.8 mile (8.7 miles), and turn left on Puritan Road. Go 0.5 mile (9.2 miles) to the end,

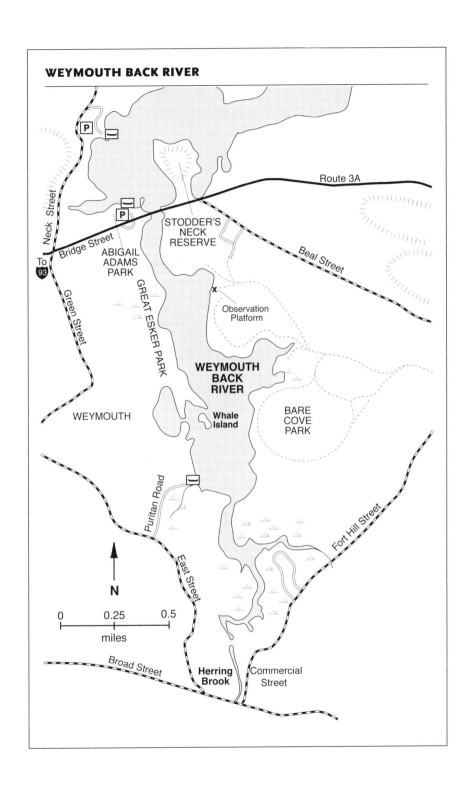

WEYMOUTH BACK RIVER

P

P

Neck Street

Route 3A

Bridge Street

STODDER'S
NECK
RESERVE

Beal Street

To 93

ABIGAIL
ADAMS
PARK

Green Street

GREAT ESKER PARK

x

Observation
Platform

WEYMOUTH
BACK
RIVER

WEYMOUTH

Whale
Island

BARE
COVE
PARK

Puritan Road

N

0   0.25   0.5
miles

East Street

Fort Hill Street

Broad Street

Herring
Brook

Commercial
Street

and park by the gate. Abigail Adams Park is the preferred access; carry over the bank to the water. Weymouth Public Launch is the easiest access but is not free. Great Esker Park does not have a developed boat launch but is a good place to launch when it's windy. It's very muddy at low tide.

WHAT YOU'LL SEE

Bounded by wildlife preserves, Weymouth Back River presents an outstanding paddling resource within the Greater Boston metropolitan area. Harbormasters from Hingham and Weymouth established the river as a no-wake zone, with no water-skiing and no personal watercraft allowed south of the Route 3A bridge. The wooded shores—the longest in the Boston Harbor area—enclose modest areas of salt marsh, standing in stark contrast to the seas of *Spartina* encountered in other estuaries.

Three active osprey nests fledged eight young in 2002. Media reported a banner year for nesting success, with many South Shore nests fledging three young. They continue to produce more young nearly every year. Researchers annually band as many as 24 young along the South Shore.

The 469 acres of Bare Cove Park harbor many species of plants, including scrub or bear oak and pitch pine growing on tree-covered dunes. Look for coyote, fox, and deer here; an observation platform provides views of the river and the surrounding woods. Hiking trails course through the park and also through 1.5-mile-long, 237-acre Great Esker Park across the way. The esker, which reaches 90 feet in height, appears as a long, winding, snakelike ridge of stratified sand and gravel, formed during the last glacial epoch about 12,000 years ago. Subglacial streams laid the deposits as they tunneled beneath the melting glacier. Also in this area, valuable archaeological finds dating back as far as 9,000 years indicate a long presence of native people along the river.

Alewives, locally known as herring, make a famous annual pilgrimage here, up the river to Whitman's Pond. From eggs laid in spring, young fish grow up to 4 inches by fall when they return to the sea. As adults, the fish return the following spring, now a silvery 12 inches long, to begin the cycle anew. As Henry Beston said in his book, *The Outermost House*:

> Somewhere in the depths of the ocean each Weymouth-born fish remembers Whitman's Pond, and comes to it through the directionless leagues of the sea. What stirs in each cold brain? What call quivers, as the new sun strikes down into the river of ocean? How do the creatures find their way? Whatever the reason, the herring are "in" at Weymouth, breasting the brook's overflow to the ancestral pond.

2 | SOUTHEASTERN MASSACHUSETTS AND CAPE COD

This section includes seven entries, extending from the Rhode Island border out onto Cape Cod. Hockomock Swamp provides the most unusual entry; the swamp and associated wetlands comprise a 17,000-acre Area of Critical Environmental Concern. Not infrequently, people paddle into and get lost in this vast swamp that also forms the headwaters of the Town River. In contrast, we include the short, narrow Bungay River. While the Hockomock Swamp harbors the largest Atlantic white cedar swamp in New England, the most important red maple swamp in Massachusetts surrounds the Bungay River.

East Head Pond lies within the Myles Standish State Forest. Look here for the extremely rare Plymouth redbelly turtle (*Pseudemys rubriventris bangsi*) amid the extensive, but rare, pitch pine–scrub oak forest that thrives only on ancient sand dunes. You may find other rare species here, as well. To the south, we include 4 miles of tidal Slocums River. Besides geography, the underlying sand strata ties together Slocums River and East Head Pond, although the river offers radically different paddling. Instead of turtles and pine-oak forest, look for shorebirds, long-legged waders, ospreys, and other aquatic birds at the river.

A more extensive salt marsh habitat awaits you at protected Nauset Marsh. Paddling here can be a challenge because of exposed mud flats at low tide, difficult currents, and wind, but we really enjoy paddling here, especially during shorebird migrations. Nearby tidal Herring River offers a real treat, partly because it's away from typical Cape Cod tourist attractions, but mostly because it's a bird-filled refuge. In this area, you will find Nickerson State Park, one of the few public camping areas in southeast Massachusetts.

16 | **Bungay River**

The narrow Bungay River undulates through what is reputed to be the most important red maple swamp in Massachusetts. Look for Atlantic white cedar, royal fern, buttonbush, and painted turtles. Watch out for poison ivy.

Location: Attleboro and North Attleborough, MA
Maps: *Massachusetts Atlas & Gazetteer*, Map 56: B8, 9, C9; USGS Providence
Length: 2 miles one way
Time: 3 hours round-trip
Habitat Type: narrow meandering river
Fish: brook and rainbow trout, largemouth and smallmouth bass, pickerel (see fish advisory, Appendix A)
Take Note: large stands of poison ivy along the shore

GETTING THERE
From I-95, Exit 5, go east on Toner Boulevard,, and turn right on Route 152/ Main Street. Go 1.0 mile (1.0 mile), and turn left on Holden Street. Go 0.5 mile (1.5 miles) to the access on the left (41° 57.244′ N, 71° 16.821′ W).

WHAT YOU'LL SEE
The Bungay River offers a pleasant morning or afternoon of paddling. When we visited on a beautiful mid-June afternoon, we saw just two kayakers during the three-hour up-and-back paddle. Leaving the hand-carry access, you initially pass a few houses on the east bank, but after that, no houses impinge on the water, and only road noise from I-95—which is about a mile to the west when you start out, but gets closer as you paddle north—reminds you of nearby civilization.

BUNGAY RIVER

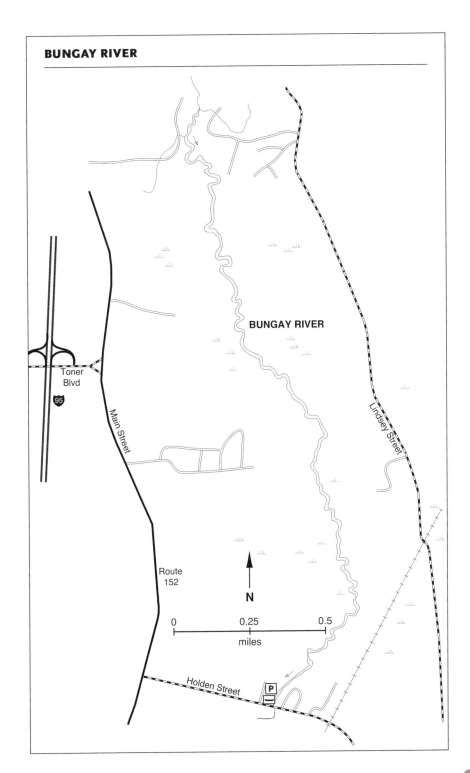

BUNGAY RIVER

Toner
Blvd

95

Main Street

Lindsey Street

Route
152

N

0   0.25   0.5

miles

Holden Street

P

The aromatic flowers of swamp azalea make paddling the Bungay River in late summer a real pleasure.

Tannins stain the water of this gently flowing river a deep brown. Its sinewy bends will test your paddling skills, especially if you're in a longer canoe, requiring lots of draw strokes by the bow paddler to make the tight turns. If paddling a kayak and wanting to push as far upstream as possible, you might want to bring a single paddle or a break-down double paddle for greater maneuverability.

Heavy vegetation straddles the river's shoreline. Shrubs include silky dogwood, sweetgale, buttonbush, alder, highbush blueberry, a wild azalea that blooms in early June, and the invasive buckthorn. Unfortunately, lush poison ivy vines also populate the banks—often reaching out into the water.

Red maple dominates the tree species; in fact, the area surrounding Bungay River is considered the most important red maple swamp in Massachusetts. Other trees include Atlantic white cedar and a few white pine and white oak. You will see lots of royal fern, pickerelweed, yellow pond-lily, and various grasses and sedges where the overhanging trees and shrubs afford them light.

While few logs occur along the shore, where you do see them you are likely to see painted turtles sunning. We saw about twenty on our up-and-back trip. These skittish turtles rarely let you get close before plopping into the water. Large snapping turtles occur here as well. You will see lots of nesting boxes along the river's lower stretch. We saw one that was clearly a wood duck nesting box but were not sure about target species for the others.

Paddling north, the river gradually narrows; if you paddle far enough, you'll have to push the brush aside as you squeeze through. Be on the lookout for poison ivy; there were places where we had to be very careful to avoid contact.

We paddled upstream for about an hour and a half, perhaps 2 miles, until several large logs across the river blocked our way. We could have pulled our boat across, but the channel had narrowed to the point that we frequently had to hold branches back as we pushed through, and we probably could not have made it much farther.

17 | Lake Nippenicket, Hockomock Swamp, and Town River

Hockomock Swamp is an extraordinary paddling resource with huge biodiversity. Take care not to get lost in the swamp's depths. Lake Nippenicket may experience significant boat traffic at times, but on a quiet morning can be pleasant—and it offers access to the swamp. You can paddle the Town River within the swamp or a separate downstream section, where you can't get lost.

Location: Bridgewater and West Bridgewater, MA
Maps: *Massachusetts Atlas & Gazetteer*, Map 53: O26, Map 57: A23, 24, B23, C23; USGS Abington, Taunton
Area/Length: Hockomock Swamp, 16,950 acres; Lake Nippenicket, 354 acres; Town River, 2 miles one way
Time: all day, unless you get lost in the depths of the swamp; shorter trips possible
Habitat Type: extensive undeveloped Atlantic white cedar swamp
Fish: largemouth and calico bass, white and yellow perch, pickerel (see fish advisory, Appendix A)
Information: Hockomock Swamp, mass.gov/dcr/stewardship/acec/acecs/l-hcksmp.htm; The Nature Conservancy interactive map, maps.tnc.org/hockomock

LAKE NIPPENICKET, HOCKOMOCK SWAMP, AND TOWN RIVER

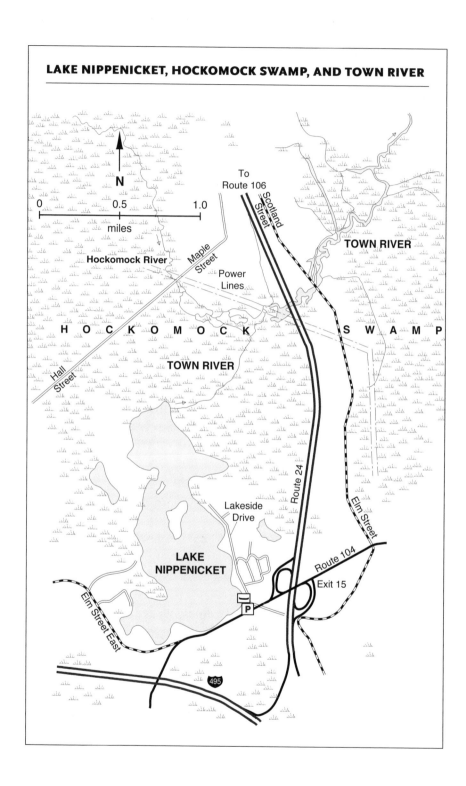

N

0   0.5   1.0

miles

To
Route 106

Scotland Street

TOWN RIVER

Hockomock River

Maple Street

Power Lines

H O C K O M O C K   S W A M P

Hall Street

TOWN RIVER

Route 24

Lakeside Drive

Elm Street

LAKE NIPPENICKET

Route 104

Exit 15

Elm Street East

P

495

GETTING THERE

Lake Nippenicket (41° 57.866′ N, 71° 2.02′ W). From Route 24, Exit 15, go 0.2 mile west on Route 104, and turn right on Lakeside Drive. Turn immediately left into the access.

Town River (42° 0.758′ N, 70° 59.612′ W). From Route 24, Exit 16, go east on Route 106 to West Bridgwater, and turn right on Route 28. Go 0.4 mile (0.4 mile), and turn left on Ash Street. Go 0.6 mile (1.0 mile), and turn left into the Reynolds Landing access.

WHAT YOU'LL SEE

Lake Nippenicket

Lake Nippenicket, locally known as "The Nip," is a modest-sized, shallow lake between Brockton and Taunton. While the lake offers pleasant paddling, don't expect solitude on the lake itself, as motorboats and personal watercraft dominate on popular weekends, and you hear a lot of road noise from Route 24 and I-495, both of which come within a half-mile of the lake.

We paddled here twice, once in late September with a fairly low water level and accompanying heavy vegetation, which limited passage. We also paddled in mid-June, following a period of heavy rain. With the heavy load of tannins in the water limiting visibility, you may not appreciate the lake's shallowness— a maximum depth of 6 feet and an average depth of just 3 feet.

Significant residential and some commercial development impinges on the southwestern cove, and houses along the eastern shore extend north to the island, but most of the shoreline is either swampy or marshy, especially along the northern half of the lake that abuts Hockomock Swamp.

Hockomock Swamp

The Hockomock Swamp, spanning parts of six towns, is the largest vegetated freshwater wetland in Massachusetts. The swamp and associated wetlands comprise a 16,950-acre Area of Critical Environmental Concern (ACEC) and form the headwaters of Town River, which drains into the Taunton River.

In the right conditions you can paddle into the swamp from Lake Nippenicket—but doing so is hard and potentially dangerous. To access The Nature Conservancy interactive map of the swamp, you have to click a liability release, which describes warnings that every year people get lost in the swamp. This even includes rescuers getting stuck trying to reach those lost.

We explored the swamp in mid-June after a wet several weeks caused significant regional flooding; in normal water, most of the swamp would likely be inaccessible by boat. If you can get in, it is an extraordinary place, the largest Atlantic white cedar swamp in New England, but we were as much struck by the large number of swamp white oaks, scattered throughout the swamp.

We entered the swamp from the northeastern tip of Lake Nippenicket. Paddling back and forth along the shoreline, looking for a way in, we weaved among the flooded trees and shrubs but were ultimately blocked. Eventually, at the far eastern tip of the north end, we found a hidden channel amid a stand of 20-foot-tall willow trees that offered a way in. Look for a modest channel in the center of that willow stand.

As we paddled generally eastward and then northeastward, the channel became somewhat easier to follow, although still a challenge, making it very clear how people get lost. You might do well here with a GPS that offers a detailed map database to be able to pinpoint your location—or a guide who knows the area intimately.

As the channel turned northward, huge power lines that cross the swamp came into view. Here, we picked up flow from the Hockomock River that merges with the slow swamp flow to become Town River. Paddling downstream, we passed under the power lines and then under Route 24—having to duck slightly with the elevated water level. We continued a short way across some broader expanses of open water to the Elm Street/Scotland Street bridge, which was too low to paddle beneath when we visited.

When we entered the Town River, we tried carefully to mark our return visually so that we could find the channel that would take us back to Lake Nippenicket. We did make some turns into the wrong cove of open water, but after exploring a bit we would find the proper channel. At one place, we had to proceed very carefully to avoid a lush growth of poison ivy extending out into the channel.

Despite the struggle to navigate the swamp—or perhaps because of it—our efforts were richly rewarded. No other place like this exists in New England. In fact, nowhere have we seen swamp white oak in such numbers in New England. We also saw Atlantic white cedar, blackgum, silver maple, red maple, ash, and myriad shrubs and both floating and emergent wetland plants.

Town River east of Route 28

We also enjoyed several miles of wonderful paddling and exploring on the Town River, putting in at the well-maintained Reynolds Landing on Ash Street in West Bridgewater. During high-water conditions, we had no trouble getting our boats into the river from the landing; later in the summer or during a dry spring, the access could be more challenging.

Alex and his wife, Jerelyn, do their best not to get themselves and their dog lost while wending their way through Hockomock Swamp.

Leaving the access, you will see a golf course immediately opposite. Paddling downstream (to the right) you follow a wide, grassy channel with lots of arrowhead amid the grasses and sedges. We saw one mute swan here and a few painted turtles, along with lots of red-winged blackbirds, tree swallows, and eastern kingbirds. Earlier in the season, we would expect to see more waterfowl.

We paddled downstream to Stanley village, reaching a small dam, then paddled back upstream, past the access, to Route 28. With the water level as high as it was, there was no way to paddle under the bridge, but doing so might be possible at lower water levels. If passage weren't hampered by low bridges, you could paddle into the Hockomock Swamp and Lake Nippenicket from the access point on Town River.

We saw a few blackgum trees along here, as well as Atlantic white cedar, red and silver maple, ash, a few white pine, and pin cherry. Closer to shore grow thick stands of swamp loosestrife, silky dogwood, alder, and other shrubs.

18 | Lake Rico and Big Bearhole Pond

In this great place for a leisurely paddle away from motorboats, expect to see mute swans, ducks, herons, and egrets. It can get crowded on busy summer weekends, and fishing pressure can get a little heavy at times, but this is still a great place to explore wooded shorelines.

Location: Taunton, MA
Maps: *Massachusetts Atlas & Gazetteer*, Map 57: H25, 26; USGS Assawompset Pond, Bridgewater, Somerset, Taunton
Area: Lake Rico, 250 acres; Big Bearhole Pond, 37 acres
Time: 4 hours
Habitat Type: wooded reservoir in a state park
Fish: largemouth and calico bass, yellow perch, pickerel (see fish advisory, Appendix A)
Information: Massasoit State Park, mass.gov/eea/agencies/dcr/massparks/region-south/massasoit-state-park.html, 508-822-7405
Camping: Myles Standish State Forest
Take Note: no motors; limited development

GETTING THERE

From I-495, Exit 5 southbound, go 0.4 mile (0.4 mile) south on Route 18, and turn right on Taunton Street/Middleboro Avenue, following signs to Massasoit State Park. Go 2.4 miles (2.8 miles) to the Lake Rico access on the left (41° 52.941′ N, 70° 59.941′ W). To reach Big Bearhole Pond, turn in to the state park (0.2 mile before Lake Rico), and follow signs to the access; it can also be accessed off Turner Street (41° 51.928′ N, 80° 50.222′ W).

WHAT YOU'LL SEE

Lake Rico and the other small ponds in Massasoit State Park provide superb quietwater paddling—some of the best in this part of the state. Though some maps show six bodies of water (Lake Rico, Kings Pond, Furnace Pond, Middle Pond, and Little and Big Bearhole ponds), Lake Rico, Kings Pond, and Furnace Pond are connected. Formerly used by cranberry growers, these separate ponds merged when the state raised the water level after acquiring the property. Some development intrudes on the western side of Furnace Pond and Lake Rico and on the eastern end of Big Bearhole Pond, but the rest of these ponds lie fully

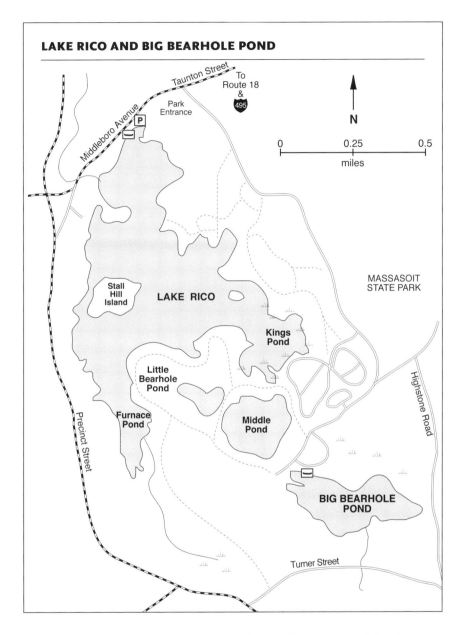

LAKE RICO AND BIG BEARHOLE POND

Taunton Street

To Route 18 & **495**

Park Entrance

Middleboro Avenue

P

N

0   0.25   0.5

miles

MASSASOIT STATE PARK

Stall Hill Island

LAKE RICO

Kings Pond

Little Bearhole Pond

Furnace Pond

Middle Pond

Precinct Street

Highstone Road

BIG BEARHOLE POND

Turner Street

within the 1,500-acre Massasoit State Park, so only recreational development occurs there.

Lake Rico offers several miles of shoreline, enough to provide enjoyable paddling for half a day. From the access on Middleboro Avenue, you can see only Lake Rico's northern cove. Paddling to the south, you leave the road noise, passing some large stands of white pine with open forest floor—quite

In the early morning light, mist rising off still waters makes Lake Rico seem almost mystical.

accessible if you want to get out for a picnic lunch or a short walk. Marshy Kings Pond presents a challenge, but you can pick your way through the abundant vegetation, paddling carefully around the bulrushes, pickerelweed, stands of cattail, and waterlilies. Near the tip of this cove, listen for the small waterfall inlet from Middle Pond (you can carry into Middle Pond). Expect to see waterfowl species, especially great blue heron, green heron, wood duck, teal, and pied-billed grebe here.

We saw two pairs of mute swan, each with two cygnets, on the more open sections of the lake. While much open water remains, invasive watermilfoil and Carolina fanwort seemed to be crowding out the bladderwort, pondweed, and other native aquatic vegetation when we paddled here. Other invasive plants—purple loosestrife and *Phragmites*—also seemed to be taking hold.

Big Bearhole Pond, a lot smaller than Lake Rico and with some houses on the eastern tip, still rates a visit. White pine dominates the shoreline vegetation, mixed with red maple, blackgum, scarlet oak, gray birch, sweet pepperbush, blueberry, winterberry, and alder. Patches of swamp loosestrife grow along the shore, and some shallow coves sport patches of yellow pond-lily and American white waterlily. Underwater vegetation includes Carolina fanwort and bladderwort.

19 | East Head Pond

This pristine pond nestles within the 14,635-acre Myles Standish State Forest. Look for endangered Plymouth redbelly turtles. Besides paddling this beautiful pond, you can also take advantage of camping and extensive hiking and mountain bike trails. The backdrop includes numerous kettle-hole ponds and trees adapted to sand barrens—pitch pine and scrub oak.

Location: Carver and Plymouth, MA
Maps: *Massachusetts Atlas & Gazetteer*, Map 58: J14, 15; USGS Wareham
Area: 92 acres
Time: 2 hours
Habitat Type: glaciated kettle hole surrounded by sand barrens
Fish: largemouth bass, yellow perch, pickerel (see fish advisory, Appendix A)
Information: Plymouth redbelly turtles, New England Herpetological Society, neherp.com/index.php/nehs-projects/red-belly-turtles; Myles Standish State Forest, mass.gov/eea/agencies/dcr/massparks/region-south/myles-standish-state-forest.html
Camping: Myles Standish State Forest
Take Note: no gasoline motors; no development

GETTING THERE

From I-495, Exit 2 southbound, go 2.5 miles (2.5 miles) north on Route 58, and continue straight on Tremont Street when Route 58 goes left. Go 0.8 mile (3.3 miles), and turn right on Cranberry Road. Go 2.7 miles (6.0 miles) to the Myles Standish State Forest. Park left of the gate, and carry your boat about 100 yards, crossing the bridge over the outlet, to the access on the left (41° 50.348′ N, 70° 41.446′ W).

WHAT YOU'LL SEE

Myles Standish State Forest—one of the largest publicly owned tracts of land in Massachusetts at 14,635 acres—harbors many rare and endangered plants and animals and contains many ecologically rich kettle-hole ponds. When the glaciers receded 12,000 years ago, they left a few large chunks of glacial ice behind, usually buried in debris. As these ice blocks melted, they left depressions in the surrounding sand that formed ponds.

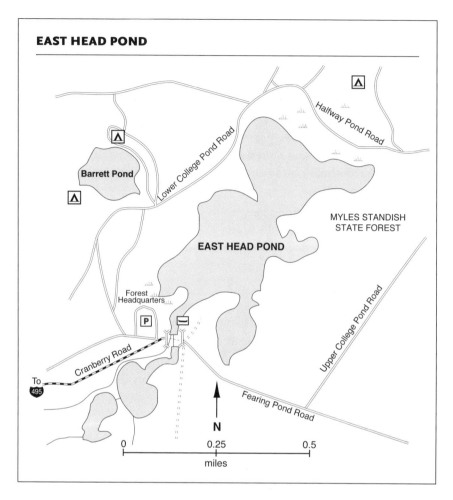

EAST HEAD POND

Barrett Pond

Lower College Pond Road

Halfway Pond Road

MYLES STANDISH
STATE FOREST

EAST HEAD POND

Forest
Headquarters

P

Upper College Pond Road

Cranberry Road

To
495

Fearing Pond Road

N

| 0 | 0.25 | 0.5 |

miles

Compared with most of New England, a quite different species set surrounds East Head Pond and the other, smaller ponds of the state forest. Dominant species include pitch pine (*Pinus rigida*) and bear or scrub oak (*Quercus ilicifolia*) in a pine barrens ecosystem. This forest community develops on acidic, sandy soil and requires frequent fires for pitch pine seed release.

Along with the dominant species—pitch pine and scrub or bear oak—red maple, gray birch, white pine, blackgum, scarlet oak, and bigtooth aspen grow along the shores of East Head Pond. A rich diversity of shrubs also lines the shore: two species of blueberries (highbush and black highbush), sweet pepperbush, leatherleaf, sweetgale, mountain laurel, wild raisin or witherod (*Viburnum cassinoides*), and inkberry, a type of swamp-loving holly (*Ilex glabra*). Pond vegetation includes watershield, American white waterlily, and bladderwort. Freshwater mussels inhabit the sandy bottom. Anglers fish for largemouth bass, pickerel, and yellow perch, and you may be lucky enough to see an osprey join the human anglers, as we did on an early September morning. If you are extraordinarily lucky, you might see one of the approximately 300 remaining endangered Plymouth redbelly turtles (*Pseudemys rubriventris*) in one of these coastal ponds. Redbelly adults are much larger than the ubiquitous painted turtle (*Chrysemys picta*), also found here, along with common snapping turtles and the rare spotted turtle.

With no gasoline-powered motors, East Head Pond provides a great spot for a morning or evening of relaxed paddling. The extremely popular campground (reservations required) provides a base for hiking on one of the many trails of the state forest. In all, the state forest boasts 90 miles of hiking, horse, and bicycle trails that crisscross the pine barrens.

Myles Standish State Forest and surrounding areas contain the largest pitch pine/scrub oak community remaining in New England and, along with those on Long Island and New Jersey, one of only three major pine barrens ecosystems remaining. Unfortunately, more economically valuable white and red pines have replaced much of the pitch pine; agriculture and development have pared away the surrounding barrens; and destructive off-road vehicles have threatened other rare and endangered plants of the community. Although ORVs have been banned for many years, rogue riders continue to degrade portions of this fragile ecosystem.

During the eighteenth century, settlers mined the ponds in this area for bog iron. After this industry petered out, cranberry production took over; many commercial cranberry bogs still dot the area.

---

20 | Slocums River

Expect to see herons, egrets, and nesting osprey as you paddle this delightful estuary. The upper reach is well-protected, but expect winds in the more open lower bay, especially in the afternoon; it's best to paddle here in the morning. Look for fiddler crabs along the shore at lower tides.

Location: Dartmouth, MA
Maps: *Massachusetts Atlas & Gazetteer*, Map 63: K25, L25, M25, 26, 27, N27; USGS New Bedford South, Westport

SLOCUMS RIVER

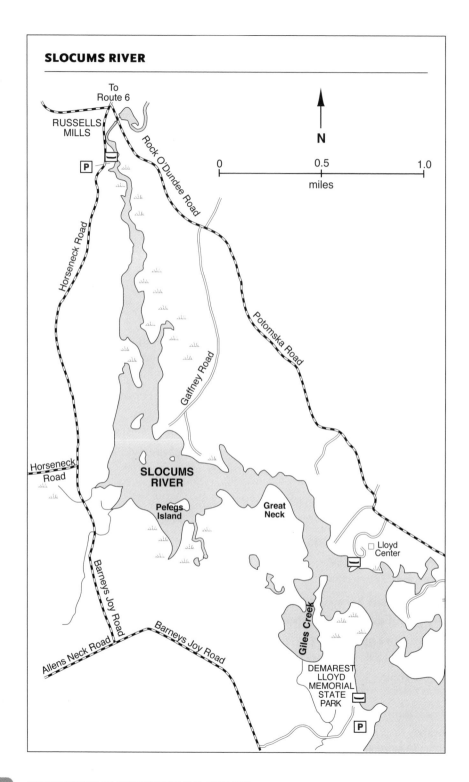

To Route 6

RUSSELLS MILLS

P

Rock O'Dundee Road

N

0   0.5   1.0
miles

Horseneck Road

Gaffney Road

Potomska Road

Horseneck Road

SLOCUMS RIVER

Pelegs Island

Great Neck

Lloyd Center

Barneys Joy Road

Giles Creek

Allens Neck Road

Barneys Joy Road

DEMAREST LLOYD MEMORIAL STATE PARK

P

Length: 4 miles one way

Time: 4 hours round-trip

Habitat Type: tidal estuary, salt marsh

Fish: striped bass, bluefish (see fish advisory, Appendix A)

Information: Demarest Lloyd State Park, mass.gov/dcr/parks/southeast/deml.htm, 508-636-3298; The Lloyd Center, lloydcenter.org, 508-990-0505; tide charts, maineharbors.com

Camping: Horseneck Beach State Reservation

Take Note: little development; motors allowed

GETTING THERE

Slocums River (41° 34.105′ N, 71° 0.304′ W). From I-195, Exit 12 southbound, go 5.0 miles (5.0 miles) south on Faunce Corner Road then Old Westport Road, veering left on Chase Road, and turn right on Russells Mills Road at the T. Go 1.0 mile (6.0 miles), and stay straight onto Horseneck Road. Go 0.2 mile (6.2 miles) to the access on the left at Russells Mills Town Park.

Demarest-Lloyd State Park. Continue south on Horseneck Road, turn left onto Barneys Joy Road, and follow it to the park.

Lloyd Center. From the junction of Horseneck and Russells Mills roads, go 2.5 miles (8.5 miles) southeast on Rock O'Dundee and Potomska roads to the entrance on the right.

WHAT YOU'LL SEE

Slocums River represents one of the best tidal rivers in New England for quiet paddling, birds, and salt marsh plants. You could easily spend a day or two exploring the river, getting to know its different personalities at high and low tide. The few houses along the river do not detract from the peace and quiet. The Slocum family originally settled this isolated corner of Dartmouth township. Joshua Slocum, a distant relative, sailed a small ketch out of nearby Fairhaven and around the world in the early 1900s in the first solo circumnavigation of the Earth in a small craft. The feat perhaps epitomizes the rigor and determination of the early Slocums: Anthony, who first cleared the land, and Giles, who founded the Society of Friends Apponegansett Meeting in 1638, still active not far from Russells Mills.

The 8-mile round-trip from Russells Mills Town Park to the Demarest Lloyd State Park at the entrance to Buzzards Bay can be paddled in half a day, but we recommend that you spend more time and explore the islands, inlets, and coves. We particularly enjoyed paddling up Giles Creek and the various inlets near Pelegs Island.

Slocums River, one of New England's most beautiful tidal estuaries, provides wonderful wildlife-watching opportunities.

Giles Creek often fills with egrets, herons, and gulls that feed amid the salt marsh grass (*Spartina spp.*). At low tide, you may see only the egrets' heads extending above the grasses. An unnamed creek off to the west of Pelegs Island offers a superb spot to learn about the salt marsh ecosystem. Paddling up this creek in early September at just about low tide, we saw literally thousands of fiddler crabs along the banks (one claw grows much larger than the other, making the critter look as if it's holding a fiddle). The exposed mud flats seemed to move as we paddled close, and the startled crabs scurried to safety—with the clickety-clack of thousands of tiny legs on the pebbles and mud.

When we paddled here in early July, some large patches of very fragrant swamp azalea diverted our attention from the legions of fiddler crabs. We also imagine that many migrating waterfowl join the resident black ducks in the fall. Out on Buzzards Bay, watch for interesting gulls and terns. Though the bay has swells, barrier islands usually keep the water fairly calm.

While here, you may want to visit the Lloyd Center for Environmental Studies, across the mouth of the river from Demarest Lloyd State Park. This highly regarded nature center, on 55 acres, offers exhibits and a wide range of educational programs, nature walks, lecture programs, and canoe trips. You can reach the center either by boat or by car.

21 | Herring River and West Reservoir

Birds abound along the Herring River and West Reservoir. Look for osprey, ducks, geese, mute swan, herons, egrets, kingfisher, and tree-top warblers. The river's protected upper portion is a gorgeous place to paddle among the cattails and streamside grasses.

Location: Harwich, MA
Maps: *Massachusetts Atlas & Gazetteer*, Map 67: D18, 19, E18, 19, F19; USGS Harwich
Area/Length: Herring River, 4.5 miles one way; West Reservoir, 47 acres
Time: 4 hours round-trip
Habitat Type: fresh- and saltwater estuary; wooded reservoir
Fish: striped bass, bluefish (see fish advisory, Appendix A)
Information: tide charts, maineharbors.com
Camping: Nickerson State Park
Take Note: limited development; motors allowed

GETTING THERE
Herring River (41° 40.108′ N, 70° 6.535′ W). From the junction of Routes 28 and 134, go 2.1 miles east on Route 28 to the access on the right, just over the bridge. From the junction of Routes 28 and 39, go 0.9 mile west on Route 28 to the access on the left, just before the bridge.

West Reservoir (41° 40.95′ N, 0° 7.589′ W). From the Route 28 bridge over the Herring River, go 0.5 mile (0.5 mile) west on Route 28, and turn right on Depot Road. Go 0.8 mile (1.3 miles), and bear right on Depot Street. Go 0.2 mile (1.5 miles), and turn right on an unmarked dirt road. Go 0.2 mile (1.7 miles) to the access by the Harwich Conservation Lands sign. The gate was locked when we visited in spring 2013; you may have to reach the access by carrying up from the river.

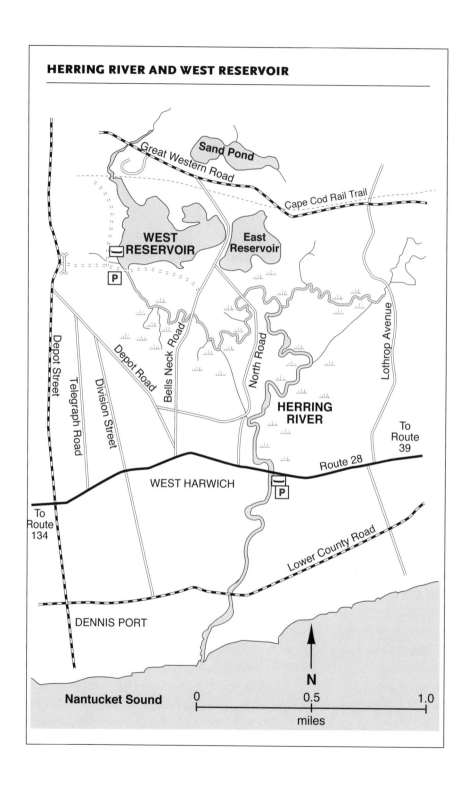

HERRING RIVER AND WEST RESERVOIR

Sand Pond

Great Western Road

Cape Cod Rail Trail

WEST RESERVOIR

East Reservoir

P

Depot Street

Telegraph Road

Division Street

Depot Road

Bells Neck Road

North Road

Lothrop Avenue

HERRING RIVER

To Route 39

Route 28

WEST HARWICH

P

To Route 134

Lower County Road

DENNIS PORT

Nantucket Sound

N

0   0.5   1.0

miles

WHAT YOU'LL SEE
Herring River

Well away from usual Cape Cod recreation destinations, the Herring River provides superb quietwater paddling through bird-filled saltwater and freshwater marshes. The best paddling occurs from Route 28 up to West Reservoir. You can also paddle south to Nantucket Sound, but houses interrupt the solitude below Route 28.

Paddling upriver from the Route 28 bridge, you will quickly leave the few houses behind and wind through a wild, broad salt marsh, a tremendous spot for birding. You might see gulls, snowy egrets, great blue and green herons, yellowlegs, Canada geese, cormorants, mallards, black ducks, mute swans, red-winged blackbirds, kingfishers, and various hawks as you paddle along. The salt marsh environment grows thick with grasses and cattails that provide nesting habitat for species of birds that you hear but rarely see: marsh wren, swamp sparrow, Virginia rail, and least bittern. Trees along the marsh's edge contain many woodland species, including northern parula, a warbler that uses the beard moss found hanging from many trees here to make its nest.

The Herring River, although tidal for its entire length, has an increasing saltwater gradient as it flows downstream. Heading upriver on an incoming tide makes for easier paddling, although the river flows gently enough that wind—a common Cape companion—usually presents a bigger obstacle than current. Near high tide you can explore numerous little canals and inlets along the river. At the West Reservoir outlet, carry up over the dike on the left by the herring fish ladder to get onto the reservoir. During the herring (alewife) spawning season, you can watch the fish swimming up the fish ladder.

West Reservoir

West Reservoir provides a great location for studying freshwater aquatic plants, birds, and other wildlife. We saw a dozen black-crowned night-herons, but the turtle life excited us even more, including literally hundreds of painted turtles sunning on logs. We also saw a good-sized snapper and two far less common stinkpot turtles (*Sternotherus odoratus*). This latter species sports a steeply humped carapace that seems undersized, a pointed "beak," and a musky smell you will probably notice if you pick one up (a defensive musky secretion released from glands on both sides of the body). The smell that emanates from the stinkpot and other musk turtles gives them their names. Generally, you see these turtles underwater, but on occasion they sun on protruding logs or rocks, even in trees—and unlike painted turtles, you can often quietly paddle right up to them for close observation. Rare spotted and box turtles also occur here,

A rarely seen Virginia rail stalks the marsh, searching for its next meal. (Photo courtesy of Michel Hersen at photographybymichel.net.)

although we've not spotted any on our trips here.

Groves of black and white oaks and pitch pine surround this fairly deep reservoir. Blackgum or black or swamp tupelo—with brilliant crimson fall foliage—grows by water's edge. The Town of Harwich Conservation Lands protect much of the land surrounding the reservoir and Herring River. A nice trail and several dirt roads begin at the reservoir. Also, the Cape Cod Rail Trail passes the reservoir's north end. This wonderful biking and hiking trail extends for 25 miles along an abandoned railway bed through the towns of Dennis, Harwich, Brewster, Orleans, and Eastham.

22 | Nauset Marsh and Salt Pond Bay

Nauset Marsh provides hours of paddling through hundreds and of salt marsh acres. Shorebirds and other birds occur in profusion. Not many people paddle here, and it can be a bit tricky. Low tide can leave you stranded, and wind often howls across the marsh unimpeded.

Location: Eastham, MA
Maps: *Massachusetts Atlas & Gazetteer*, Map 61: J28, 29, K27, 28, 29, L28, 29; USGS Orleans

Area: 1,300 acres

Time: 4 hours or more

Habitat Type: tidal estuary, salt marsh

Fish: striped bass, bluefish (see fish advisory, Appendix A)

Information: Cape Cod National Seashore, nps.gov/caco, Salt Pond Visitor Center, 508-255-3421; tide charts, maineharbors.com

Camping: Nickerson State Park

Take Note: little development; too shallow for motors in most places; check with rangers at Salt Pond Visitor Center about tide and wind conditions before venturing out; novice paddlers should avoid this area; red tide has closed the marsh to shellfishing in recent years

GETTING THERE

Salt Pond (41° 50.106′ N, 69° 58.407′ W). From Route 6 at the rotary where the limited-access highway ends, continue 2.7 miles east on Route 6, and turn right on Salt Pond Landing.

Salt Pond Visitor Center. From Salt Pond Landing, go 0.2 mile north on Route 6, turn right on Nauset Road, and go 100 feet to the visitor center on the right.

WHAT YOU'LL SEE

Salt Pond Bay in Nauset Marsh provides very enjoyable paddling in a fascinating salt marsh ecosystem, at least at high tide. Low tide exposes vast areas of mud flats that could leave you stranded. We paddled here twice on falling tides and both times had to drag our boats through rapidly retreating waters. Fortunately, the mud underfoot was quite solid. At high tide you can paddle around this area quite easily, but watch out for strong tidal currents in some channels. Also, wind can cause problems as it blows unimpeded over vast expanses of salt marsh and low-lying islands.

Cape Cod National Seashore—a 40-mile-long preserve of dunes, beach, and estuary between Chatham and Provincetown—includes Nauset Marsh. Established in 1961, the national seashore provides superb hiking, bicycling, swimming, and fishing opportunities for tens of thousands of visitors each year, though few people think of paddling here. Salt Pond, where you launch, was once a freshwater kettle pond, but the ocean broke through, and tides now feed the pond twice daily through a narrow channel connecting it to Salt Pond Bay and the large Nauset Marsh estuary.

Nauset Marsh, a classic tidal estuary, is rich in birdlife, woodland mammals, marine animals (including quahogs, oysters, mussels, and various fish), and

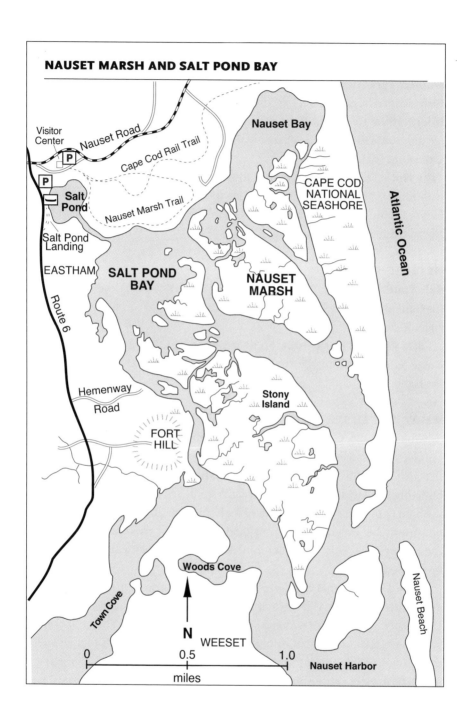

NAUSET MARSH AND SALT POND BAY

Visitor Center

Nauset Road

Cape Cod Rail Trail

P

P

Salt Pond

Nauset Marsh Trail

Salt Pond Landing

EASTHAM

Route 6

SALT POND BAY

Nauset Bay

CAPE COD NATIONAL SEASHORE

Atlantic Ocean

NAUSET MARSH

Hemenway Road

FORT HILL

Stony Island

Woods Cove

Town Cove

N

WEESET

Nauset Beach

0   0.5   1.0

miles

Nauset Harbor

A lesser yellowlegs scurries along the shore of Nauset Marsh.

the unusual plants that comprise this ecosystem. As you get out into the bay, note the thick masses of peat that gulls and sandpipers scour for food on the many islands that dot this huge marsh. On one early trip, we watched 50 harbor seals near the break between Coast Guard and Nauset beaches (harbor seals winter in this area, but most head to Maine to raise their young). Today, gray seal populations have mushroomed, making them much more common and also drawing in more great white sharks. As of this writing, the increased shark presence has not dampened beachgoer enthusiasm.

We spent many hours looking with binoculars at myriad birdlife, including skeins of cormorants and several gull species. Also look for black duck, kingfisher, great blue heron, snowy egret, semipalmated plover, black-bellied plover, lesser yellowlegs, and sanderling. Alas, we did not see the threatened piping plover that nests on the beach, of which Thoreau had this to say:

> But if I were required to name a sound, the remembrance of which most perfectly revives the impression which the beach has made, it would be the dreary peep of the piping plover (Charadrius melodus) which haunts there. Their voices, too, are heard as a fugacious part in the dirge which is ever played along the shore for those mariners who have been lost in the deep since first it was created. But through

*all this dreariness we seemed to have a pure and unqualified strain
of eternal melody, for always the same strain which is a dirge to one
household is a morning song of rejoicing to another.*

If you find yourself here at low tide, you can enjoy wonderful hiking near the Salt Pond Visitor Center or, farther north, within Cape Cod National Seashore. Nauset Marsh Trail leads from the Salt Pond Visitor Center along the east side of Salt Pond, and then along the edge of Salt Pond Bay. This mile-long trail provides a great way to learn to identify some of the more common flora here: black oak, pitch pine, black locust, eastern red cedar (juniper), beach plum, winterberry, saltmeadow cordgrass, and smooth cordgrass. Pick up a trail map at the visitor center.

Also, you can bicycle the scenic, 25-mile-long Cape Cod Rail Trail that connects the visitor center with Nickerson State Park. Occupying the bed of an abandoned railway, this ideal bicycle trail covers generally flat terrain with minimal road crossings and interruptions. You can pick up a map of the trail, plus rent bicycles, at Nickerson State Park.

3 | MARTHA'S VINEYARD

Long known for sailing, beachcombing, bed and breakfast hopping, gift shopping, and general vacationing, Martha's Vineyard also offers truly spectacular paddling. We include descriptions of six bodies of water in this guide. Most have permanent or periodic access to the sea, which renews their nutrients and fish species. Many people come here to fish for striped bass and bluefish. Most people reach Martha's Vineyard via ferry out of Woods Hole. Rates in 2013: $137 round-trip for a car, plus $16 per passenger and driver; reservations are highly recommended.

Anyone wishing to paddle on Martha's Vineyard must think about timing. The population increases from about 16,000 in winter to more than 100,000 during peak summer periods. Unless you reserve early, the ferry, inns, and campsites will be full. Many visitors scoot around on mopeds when not shopping, contributing to traffic problems. A possible solution: Schedule your visit before mid-June or after Labor Day (ferry rates drop after November 1). You might not get warm sun during off-season visits, but you will compete less for space.

The island's great salt ponds offer fabulous paddling, but we do not recommend the Vineyard to novice paddlers. Sailboarders love the Vineyard for a reason—wind—and sudden weather changes crop up often. Ponds open to the sea can suffer from extremely strong tidal currents—in some places the tidal current moves faster than you can paddle. Combined with a strong breeze, this can engender very hazardous paddling conditions. Use caution and good sense when paddling here so that you can fully enjoy what the Vineyard offers. Wear PFDs, especially with children—simply having PFDs onboard is not sufficient.

The information below pertains to all trips in this section.

Information: For ferry reservations, contact the Steamship Authority at 508-477-8800, 508-693-9130, or steamshipauthority.com. For tide charts, see maineharbors.com. Books: *Discover Martha's Vineyard* (see Appendix B).

Camping and Accommodations: One private campground: Martha's Vineyard Family Campground—in Vineyard Haven, 508-693-3772. Accommodations: American Youth Hostel, 508-693-2665; Martha's Vineyard Chamber of Commerce, 508-693-0085, mvy.com.

Take Note: motors allowed on some ponds; minimal development; wind and tide can create hazardous conditions—novice paddlers should avoid this area on windy days, wear PFD; respect private property

---

23 | Edgartown Great Pond

Edgartown Great Pond is one of our favorite paddling spots in Massachusetts. Wildlife abounds. Look for osprey, herons and egrets, and tree-top warblers. You might see otter and least tern and piping plover on the dunes. Salt-tolerant plants inhabit most of the shoreline, with occasional salt-intolerant plants in some coves, leading to high plant species diversity.

Location: Edgartown, MA
Maps: *Massachusetts Atlas & Gazetteer*, Map 69: H24, I23, 24, 25; USGS Edgartown
Area: 890 acres
Time: all day, shorter trips possible

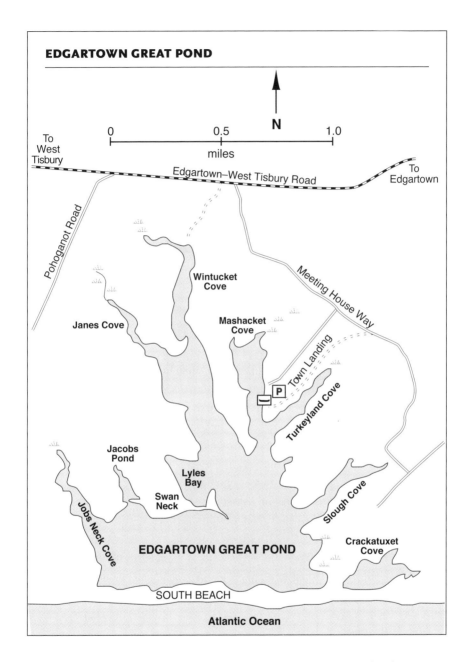

EDGARTOWN GREAT POND

Habitat Type: saltwater pond, salinity depends on how long it has been cut off from the ocean

Fish: striped bass, bluefish, white perch (see fish advisory, Appendix A)

GETTING THERE

From Main Street in Edgartown, go 1.8 miles (1.8 miles) west on Edgartown–West Tisbury Road, and turn left on Meeting House Way. Go 1.4 miles (3.2 miles) on a rough, sandy road, then take a sharp right onto a less traveled, unmarked sand road. Go 0.8 mile (4.0 miles) to the access (41° 22.006′ N, 70° 33.027′ W). Be careful not to block the access points used for loading by commercial shellfish harvesters.

WHAT YOU'LL SEE

One of our favorite paddling spots in all of Massachusetts, Edgartown Great Pond has very little development, lots of wildlife, a 10 HP limit, and more than 15 miles of shoreline to explore. The pond's south edge backs up against a barrier beach, separating it from the Atlantic Ocean, and you can hear waves crash just across the low dunes. The beach isolates the pond from the ocean, freeing it from tidal currents.

Edgartown Great Pond and Tisbury Great Pond (Trip 24) stand among the best remaining examples anywhere of great salt ponds, a geologic feature of coastal outwash plains. The rippling topography on Martha's Vineyard resulted from glacial streams depositing till as they flowed. As glaciers receded northward, meltwater flowed south off the glaciers, creating streams carrying silt and sand, eventually depositing its burden to form the outwash plains found here and on Nantucket, Cape Cod, and Long Island. Moving coastal sands then sealed off the south end of these ponds with barrier beaches.

The great salt ponds' varying salinity results in considerable plant and animal diversity. Periodically, storms open and close channels between the pond and ocean, causing fresh and salt water to mix. Hurricane Bob in 1991, for example, swept ocean water over the barrier beach, thoroughly mixing Edgartown Great Pond's water with seawater in a few hours. In recent decades, an artificial channel has been cut several times a year to maintain adequate salinity for shellfish and to allow alewives to enter, followed by the great angling prize, striped bass. But major storms can make that work difficult. In 2012, both Hurricane Sandy and a following nor'easter deposited huge amounts of sand, closing off the pond.

At the tips of some Edgartown Great Pond coves, freshwater ecosystems harbor salt-intolerant plants, such as cranberry, woolgrass, and grass pink (a type of orchid). Salt-tolerant species, such as salt marsh grasses (*Spartina spp.*), glasswort, and saline saltbush, grow along the main pond.

Piping plover, a threatened species, and least tern, a species of special concern, nest on the dunes here. Osprey nest on several platforms around the

Edgartown Great Pond, a rare great salt pond, boasts more than 15 miles of shoreline, filled with wildlife.

pond, and numerous warblers and other songbirds nest in the surrounding area. Paddling here in September, we saw many great blue herons, snowy and great egrets, black-crowned night-herons, black-backed and herring gulls, and various sandpipers and plovers. We also had the good fortune to see a family of five otters. Otter density on the Vineyard is probably the highest in Massachusetts. Look for otters early in the morning or toward dusk.

Janes Cove seems the most remote of the Edgartown Great Pond coves. We saw the otters and a pair of large snapping turtles here. Note the thick moss draped over some of the old red maples and bettlebung trees (a local name for blackgum). Jobs Neck Cove, with just one house on it, also looks great. As you paddle along the shore, watch for blue crabs scurrying away. Specimens up to 8 inches across occur here (note the bright blue claws of some individuals).

Settlers fished here as early as 1660, primarily for alewife. A school of alewives feeding at the surface of calm water looks like a mass of bubbles breaking the surface. They enter the pond through the South Beach opening in spring to spawn, leaving in fall when the barrier beach breaches. Anglers also catch yellow and white perch, eel, and occasional trapped oceanic fish such as striped bass, flounder, and bluefish. Today the primary commercial fishery in Edgartown Great Pond is shellfish: oysters and steamer clams.

Paddling the full perimeter of Edgartown Great Pond could easily take a full day, especially if you spend time studying its varied plants and wildlife. Remember to respect private property. Except for the public landing on Mashacket Neck, the entire shoreline is privately owned: no camping and no strolling along South Beach allowed.

24 | Tisbury Great Pond

Tisbury Great Pond is very similar to Edgartown Great Pond. Look here for the same species: osprey, herons and egrets, warblers, otter, least tern, and piping plover, along with high plant species diversity.

Location: Chilmark and West Tisbury, MA
Maps: *Massachusetts Atlas & Gazetteer*, Maps 69: H17, 18, 19, I18, 19, 20; USGS Tisbury Great Pond, Vineyard Haven
Area: 790 acres
Time: all day, shorter trips possible
Habitat Type: saltwater pond, brackish water
Fish: striped bass, bluefish, white perch (see fish advisory, Appendix A)

GETTING THERE

From Main Street in Edgartown, go 7.7 miles (7.7 miles) west on Edgartown–West Tisbury Road, and turn left on New Lane (coming from West Tisbury, New Lane is 0.3 mile past Old Country Road). New Lane quickly becomes Tiah Cove Road. Go 1.2 miles (8.9 miles), and turn right on Clam Point Road. Park on the left; carry your boat about 200 feet down to the water (41° 22.34′ N, 70° 38.954′ W). An access at the end of Clam Point Road has limited parking.

WHAT YOU'LL SEE

With long fingerlike coves that head away from the barrier beach, Tisbury Great Pond closely resembles Edgartown Great Pond (Trip 23), with one important difference: Tisbury suffers more from development. To get a feel for what it would be like to paddle on Tisbury, see the Edgartown Great Pond entry. Martha's Vineyard Land Bank owns property along Tiah Cove, which contains the public access. In 2013, The Nature Conservancy, along with the towns of Chilmark and West Tisbury, were in the process of developing an oyster sanctuary in the middle of the pond.

All of the Vineyard's great ponds suffer from nitrogen eutrophication, mostly from septic tanks and leach fields, but also from sewage treatment plants and fertilizer runoff. In an effort to reduce harmful algal blooms resulting from too much nitrogen, the towns have taken significant steps to reduce nitrogen pollution.

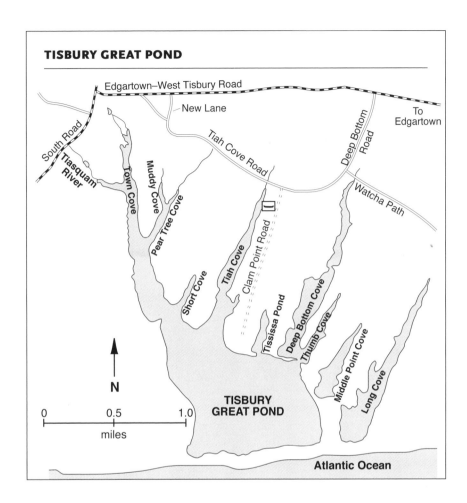

TISBURY GREAT POND

Edgartown–West Tisbury Road

New Lane

To Edgartown

South Road

Tiah Cove Road

Deep Bottom Road

Tiasquam River

Watcha Path

Town Cove

Muddy Cove

Pear Tree Cove

Clam Point Road

Short Cove

Tiah Cove

Tississa Pond

Deep Bottom Cove

Thumb Cove

Middle Point Cove

Long Cove

N

0   0.5   1.0
miles

TISBURY GREAT POND

Atlantic Ocean

25 | Pocha Pond

Perched on the northwest corner of the Vineyard, Pocha Pond offers the most remote paddling, along scenic dunes. Look for herons and egrets, and all the other birds that populate the Vineyard's ponds. For an extended trip, you can paddle up into Cape Poge Bay, at least under less windy conditions.

Location: Edgartown, MA
Maps: *Massachusetts Atlas & Gazetteer*, Map 69: H30, I30;
USGS Edgartown

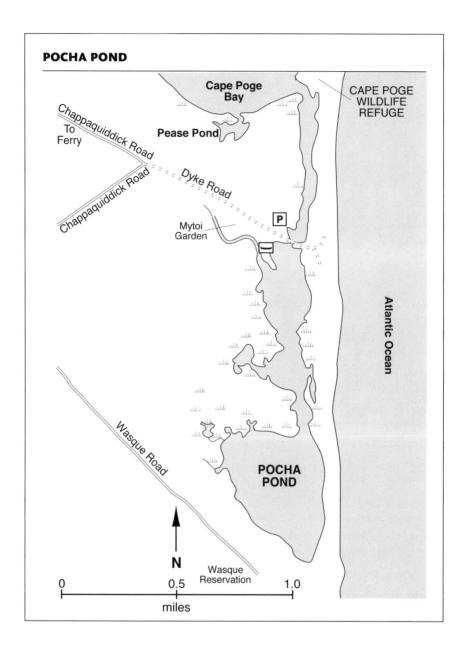

POCHA POND

Cape Poge Bay

CAPE POGE WILDLIFE REFUGE

Pease Pond

Chappaquiddick Road

To Ferry

Chappaquiddick Road

Dyke Road

Mytoi Garden

P

Atlantic Ocean

Wasque Road

N

Wasque Reservation

POCHA POND

0 0.5 1.0

miles

Area: 210 acres

Time: 2 hours, more if you paddle Cape Poge Bay

Habitat Type: saltwater pond and marsh

Fish: striped bass, bluefish (see fish advisory, Appendix A)

Pocha Pond offers some of the most remote paddling on Martha's Vineyard ponds.

Information: Long Cove, Cape Poge Wildlife Refuge, Wasque Reservation, or Mytoi Japanese-style garden: The Trustees of Reservations, thetrustees.org; Chappaquiddick Ferry, chappyferry.com

Take Note: Cape Poge Bay not recommended for novice paddlers

GETTING THERE

From Edgartown, take the ferry to Chappaquiddick Island ($12 plus $4 per passenger in 2013). Go 2.4 miles (2.4 miles) east on Chappaquiddick Road, and continue straight on Dyke Road (dirt) when the paved road curves sharply right. Go 0.6 mile (3.0 miles) to the access at Dyke Bridge (41° 22.416′ N, 70° 27.235′ W).

WHAT YOU'LL SEE

This pond and the connecting channel into Cape Poge Bay provide wonderful paddling and public access across the Cape Poge dunes to several miles of beautiful, remote ocean beach. From the access, you can paddle south into Pocha Pond. A couple of houses near the end of Dyke Road and a few at the south end represent the only development along here, amid acres of wonderful salt marsh.

Paddling here on a September morning, we saw dozens of great blue herons, great and snowy egrets, gulls, and cormorants, plus a few black scoters and kingfishers. Salt marsh plants found here include Carolina sealavender (*Limonium carolinianum*), glasswort (*Salicornia depressa*), and salt marsh cordgrasses (*Spartina patens* and *S. alterniflora*). Pocha Pond links to the sea via the Cape Poge Gut, so only plants that withstand saltwater flooding survive here. On the exposed peat at low tide, beneath the salt marsh grass, grow various seaweeds and mussels, and in the water, sponge colonies, various crabs, and mollusks (we found some very large whelk shells). Past the open marsh, you will see pitch pine, scrub and swamp white oaks, and blackgum.

Just southwest of Dyke Bridge, a narrow inlet creek invites exploration. Watch out for mollusk-encrusted rocks and shell conglomerates here, particularly near low tide. A *Phragmites* marsh inhabits the end of this little creek, along with a dense grove of blackgum, whose leaves turn brilliant crimson in early fall.

North of Dyke Bridge, the channel narrows along Toms Neck (an area called the Lagoon) but opens up into Cape Poge Bay. In a strong breeze, the bay gets quite rough. With winds from the south, you can reach Pease Pond without too much difficulty (at low tide, exposed sand banks present obstacles). You can also land on the Atlantic side of the Lagoon or Cape Poge Bay and hike the 14 miles of trails in the wildlife refuge along the beach, although four-wheeler trails preclude having a wilderness experience. Also, note that poison ivy grows in profusion amid the dunes. Waves crash the sandy shores of this beautiful beach. Surf fishing for striped bass and bluefish is considered to be among the best on the Atlantic Coast—and you may find some interesting things washed up on the beach; on a 1992 visit, we came across the remains of a whale.

---

26 | Menemsha Pond and Quitsa Pond

We prefer to paddle here late in the day to take advantage of gorgeous sunsets, with light playing on the buildings of a classic New England fishing village. Because of treacherous currents at the put-in on Menemsha Pond, we prefer starting out at Quitsa Pond.

Location: Chilmark and Gay Head, MA
Maps: *Massachusetts Atlas & Gazetteer*, Map 68: J11, 12, K11, 12; USGS Squibnocket

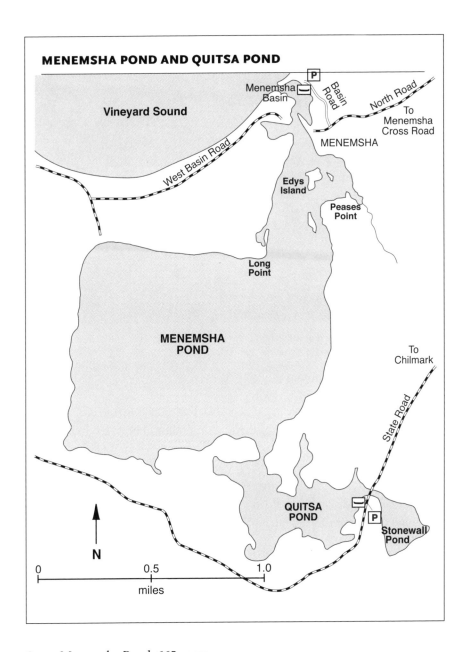

MENEMSHA POND AND QUITSA POND

Vineyard Sound

Menemsha Basin

Basin Road

North Road

To Menemsha Cross Road

MENEMSHA

West Basin Road

Edys Island

Peases Point

Long Point

MENEMSHA POND

To Chilmark

State Road

QUITSA POND

Stonewall Pond

N

0   0.5   1.0

miles

Area: Menemsha Pond, 665 acres

Time: 4 hours

Habitat Type: saltwater pond, open to ocean

Fish: striped bass, bluefish (see fish advisory, Appendix A)

Take Note: strong rip current at jetty, north end of Menemsha Pond; area not recommended for novice paddlers; significant road noise

Quitsa (or Nashquita) Pond is smaller and more protected from wind and currents than Menemsha Pond to the north; a channel connects the two.

GETTING THERE

Quitsa Pond (41° 19.722′ N, 70° 45.598′ W). From the junction of Menemsha Cross Road and State Road in Chilmark, go 1.3 miles southwest on State Road to the access at the bridge.

Menemsha Pond (41° 21.268′ N, 70° 46.004′ W). From the junction of Menemsha Cross Road and North Road northwest of Chilmark, go 0.5 mile (0.5 mile) southwest on North Road, and turn right on Basin Road. Go 0.3 mile (0.8 mile) to the parking at Dutcher Dock. Hand launch just before the jetty.

WHAT YOU'LL SEE

From the water at the north end of Menemsha Pond, you can view a classic New England fishing village, known outside the region as the backdrop for the movie *Jaws*. Some fishing boats that dock here run very large. Smaller fishing and sailing boats moor along the perimeter of both Menemsha and Quitsa ponds. Despite the development, we recommend paddling here for its scenic beauty, especially the renowned sunsets. You could use the access at the end of Dutcher Dock near the large public beach area at the north end of Menemsha Pond, but because of strong tidal currents on Menemsha Creek leading into the pond, we recommend the access on Quitsa Pond. If you paddle up to Menemsha's north end, use caution there to avoid strong tides.

27 | Sengekontacket Pond

Although this pond suffers from development and road noise, it's well worth exploring the numerous marshy coves and islands along the western shore. Look for the typical plants and birds of the Vineyard here.

Location: Edgartown and Oak Bluffs, MA
Maps: *Massachusetts Atlas & Gazetteer,* Map 69: E23, 24, F24, 25; USGS Edgartown
Area: 726 acres
Time: 5 hours
Habitat Type: saltwater pond
Fish: striped bass, bluefish (see fish advisory, Appendix A)
Information: Felix Neck Wildlife Sanctuary, Massachusetts Audubon Society, 508-627-4850 or massaudubon.org
Take Note: significant road noise; much of shoreline is conserved; wind and tide can create hazardous conditions—novice paddlers should use great care

GETTING THERE

From the junction of Edgartown and Vineyard Haven Roads in Edgartown, go 2.0 miles north on Edgartown–Oak Bluffs (Beach) Road to the access on the left. You could also hand launch from several other locations along the road (41° 25.914′ N, 70° 33.397′ W).

WHAT YOU'LL SEE

Located between Oak Bluffs and Edgartown, this large pond suffers from a fair amount of development and road noise but offers nice paddling nonetheless. Numerous marshy coves and islands along the western shore beg to be explored. On Felix Neck near the pond's midpoint (reachable from Vineyard Haven Road), the Massachusetts Audubon Society maintains the Felix Neck Wildlife Sanctuary. Fortunately, you don't have to be able to pronounce the pond's name to paddle on it.

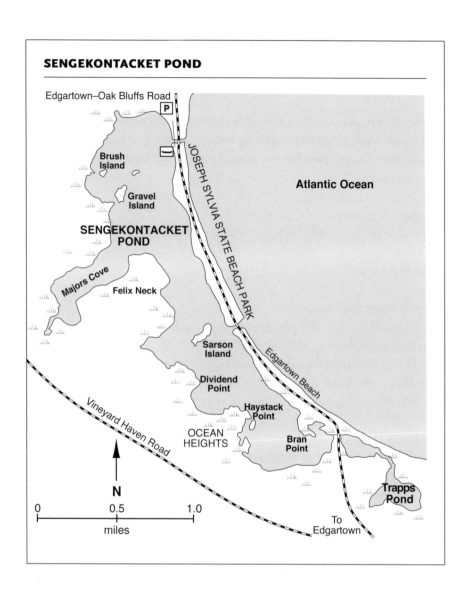

SENGEKONTACKET POND

Edgartown–Oak Bluffs Road

P

Brush Island

Gravel Island

JOSEPH SYLVIA STATE BEACH PARK

Atlantic Ocean

SENGEKONTACKET POND

Majors Cove

Felix Neck

Sarson Island

Dividend Point

Haystack Point

Edgartown Beach

OCEAN HEIGHTS

Bran Point

Vineyard Haven Road

N

0   0.5   1.0
miles

Trapps Pond

To Edgartown

4 | CENTRAL MASSACHUSETTS

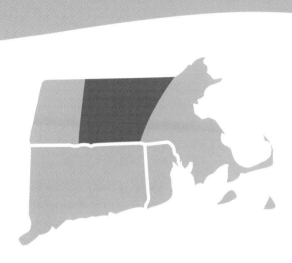

Sixteen entries comprise this section of Massachusetts and include several within fabulous wildlife refuges. The bodies of water extend from the New Hampshire border to the Connecticut border and lie between I-91 and I-495.

Many wilderness and semi-wilderness areas occur in the region. We love paddling Tully Lake and East Branch Tully River, where you're virtually guaranteed to see beaver on an evening paddle. Wildlife refuges, wildlife management areas, and state forests encompass areas of additional rivers, including the Nashua, Squannacook, Quaboag, East Brookfield, Quinebaug, Millers, Otter, and Ware rivers, making them wildlife-rich areas to paddle. Most flow lazily through extensive wetlands, backed by unbroken forest. Compared with eastern Massachusetts rivers, those here exude a more wilderness feel. We see lots of muskrats when paddling here, along with the occasional river otter. On one trip on the Ware River, we saw a great horned owl and a coyote, both close up. Sometimes we see minks. Birdlife abounds.

Though not protected by federal or state lands, Beaver Brook offers a great place to paddle through an extensive swamp. It's marshier than most other rivers and a great place to look for beaver and muskrats. Muddy Brook, which starts at Hardwick Pond, possibly attracts the fewest paddlers, particularly in its upper reaches that traverse some serious beaver swamps; we saw a beaver in the middle of the day, indicating that it probably sees few human intruders.

We also include some small ponds that you can paddle, which we sometimes use to study aquatic plants. We've seen huge blooms of eastern purple bladderwort on Eames Pond, and we travel to Moosehorn Pond to look at sphagnum mats, with their attendant pitcher plants and sundews. In June, we travel to Paradise Pond for its spectacular mountain laurel bloom. If you want to paddle through abundant floating aquatic vegetation, then by all means visit Lake Rohunta.

28 | Nashua River and Pepperell Pond

We include two sections of the Nashua River, with this, the northern one, backed up behind a dam in Pepperell. The numerous channels and coves provide hours of paddling and habitat for numerous wildlife. Look for muskrat, beaver, mink, otter, and many bird species.

Location: Groton and Pepperell, MA
Maps: *Massachusetts Atlas & Gazetteer*, Map 27: F21, G20, 21, H20, 21; USGS Pepperell
Length: 5 miles one way
Time: 6 hours
Habitat Type: dammed-up meandering river, shrubby marshlands, many islands and protected bays
Fish: largemouth, smallmouth, and calico bass; yellow perch; pickerel (see fish advisory, Appendix A)
Camping: Willard Brook State Forest, Pearl Hill State Park
Take Note: little development; motors allowed; take care to avoid getting lost

GETTING THERE
From Groton at the junction of Routes 111, 119, and 225, go 1.4 miles north on Routes 111 and 119 to the access on the right, just before the bridge (42° 37.62′ N, 71° 35.571′ W).

An alternate hand-carry access, maintained by the Pepperell Conservation Commission, is on Canal Street, 0.1 mile south of Route 113 in Pepperell (42° 39.832′ N, 71° 34.693′ W).

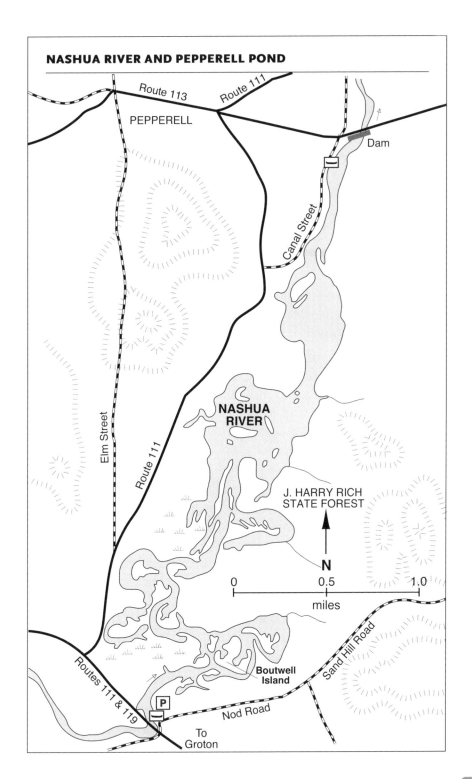

NASHUA RIVER AND PEPPERELL POND

Route 113

Route 111

PEPPERELL

Dam

Canal Street

Elm Street

Route 111

NASHUA
RIVER

J. HARRY RICH
STATE FOREST

N

0   0.5   1.0
miles

Sand Hill Road

Routes 111 & 119

**Boutwell
Island**

P

Nod Road

To
Groton

If you paddle quietly close to shore, you may be lucky enough to spot a mink searching for its next meal. (Photo courtesy of Mikelane45 and Dreamstime.)

WHAT YOU'LL SEE

This dammed-up section of the Nashua River, lying halfway between Fitchburg and Lowell, would take an entire day to explore fully. Twists and turns among the many islands, coupled with adjacent oxbows and side channels, turn this inundated marshland into a giant 5-mile-long maze. Use care to avoid getting disoriented in the maze of channels. If you have limited time and want to avoid getting lost, take along a compass and a photocopy of the map.

A shrubby, marshy shoreline provides cover for numerous ducks, geese, and other birds. We saw lots of beaver activity and several muskrats. As we paddled along, we thought we saw a beaver swimming, until it hustled out onto a 25-foot-long, horizontal dead tree and ran for shore. It turned out to be a gorgeous reddish gray mink that dived for cover into the dead tree's stump. If you sit patiently, chances are a mink will pop back into view after a few minutes to check you out, as this one did. Satisfied that we were interlopers, it dived back into the stump.

Though shrubs and cattails cover much of the marshy shoreline, a large number of majestic white pines tower overhead, especially along the eastern shore in the J. Harry Rich State Forest, giving the entire area a substantial wilderness feel. The state allows motors but limits their speed to 22 MPH.

We loved paddling here in spring, listening to the returning songbirds staking out their nesting territories and the choruses of spring peepers. Its gorgeous setting, large size, and plentiful wildlife make it one of the best places to paddle in central Massachusetts.

MUSKRAT
DENIZEN OF THE CATTAIL MARSH

Toward dusk on marshy ponds and estuaries, as you paddle past tall stands of cattails and *Phragmites*, watch for a V rippling out across still water. You can distinguish a muskrat from its larger cousin, the beaver, by the way it swims. A beaver swims with only its large, broad head above water. A muskrat swims with its head above water and with its narrow tail snaking rapidly from side to side behind it. While generally wary, muskrats may seem oblivious to their surroundings. They have bumped into our boats, and they have sat unconcerned as we photographed them from a short distance away.

The muskrat, *Ondatra zibethicus*, in the order Rodentia along with the beaver, is more closely related to voles, rats, some mice, and lemmings in the family Cricetidae. Its common name derives from the strong musky scent emitted from glands in its groin during breeding season. They grow to a foot long, have an 8- to 10-inch scaly tail, and weigh 2 to 4 pounds. Males and females look identical, except under close examination.

Using both their hind feet and their vertically flattened tails for propulsion, muskrats swim adeptly. They can remain underwater for up to 15 minutes, covering distances up to 150 feet. Like beaver, their lips split behind the four incisors, allowing them to cut stems without swallowing water. Their diet consists of cattails and other common marsh plants, such as bulrush, water-lily, pickerelweed, arrowhead, and swamp loosestrife. They supplement this vegetarian diet with mussels, crayfish, snails, tadpoles, and other aquatic animals, particularly in winter when vegetation is scarce. Being ever wary of predators, muskrats usually cut their food and take it to a safer place to eat, such as a specially constructed feeding platform or, in winter, on top of ice. Though chiefly nocturnal, they can be seen during the daytime as well. Unlike beaver, they rarely venture more than 200 feet for food.

Muskrats build two types of houses: dens and lodges, depending on local conditions. They dig dens in the bank of a pond or river and always place the entrances below water level. On reservoirs and ponds with fluctuating water levels, these underwater entrances may be exposed at certain times of year. Muskrats use tunnels and dens for many generations and develop them into elaborate labyrinths. Tunnels up to 200 yards long have been found, and these can damage earthen dams, levees, and dikes. Individual nesting chambers typically measure 6 by 8 inches and contain shredded plant material.

Muskrats build lodges in shallow open water or marsh—places where bank dens cannot be built—of vegetation and mud collected from the immediate vicinity and resembling small beaver lodges. An underwater entrance connects to the chamber, typically about a foot in diameter. Unlike beaver, muskrats build solid lodges and then tunnel them out later.

While muskrat lodges do not afford good protection from predators during warmer months, once the mud freezes in winter they become impenetrable fortresses. Muskrats use some lodges only in winter, when a large lodge may house as many as eight or nine muskrats, possibly congregating to keep warm. Most lodges last only a year, then collapse as the vegetation rots. In addition to lodges, muskrats build feeding platforms from the same materials; these smaller structures provide safe places to eat collected food.

Muskrats breed prolifically. Females typically have two or three litters in a single season and may have even more in the South, where they breed year-round. They can breed again just a few days after giving birth. After a gestation period of about 30 days, four to six nearly hairless, blind kits are born in the den or lodge. They open their eyes after two weeks, begin swimming in their third week, and become totally independent after four or five weeks. In fact, if the mother has another litter at that time, she will forcibly evict the youngsters, even injuring them in some cases to drive them away. Rapid population growth can lead to stress, competition for food, territory battles, and illnesses. Sometimes disease wipes out entire muskrat populations. Commonly, only a third of muskrat young survive into their first winter.

While muskrats may congregate in winter, they disperse in spring. During April and May, some individuals may travel as far as 20 miles overland looking for a new territory, leading to some muskrat road kills.

Trappers have long sought muskrats for their soft fur, but their prolific reproduction and lower visibility protected them from population depletion, unlike beaver. Trappers nearly drove the beaver to extinction in the late 1800s. Muskrats have proved hardy, able to survive, even prosper, in suburban and urban areas—wherever they find a bit of cattail marsh.

29 | Squannacook River

The Squannacook provides a wonderful paddling resource away from civilization and road noise. Fishermen ply the water for trout, and birds fill the trees. Look for wood duck, beaver, and muskrat.

Location: Groton and Shirley, MA
Maps: *Massachusetts Atlas & Gazetteer*, Map 27: G16, H16, 17, I17; USGS Ayer, Townsend
Length: 3 miles one way
Time: 3 hours round-trip
Habitat Type: dammed-up meandering river, extensive marshlands
Fish: brook, brown, and rainbow trout (see fish advisory, Appendix A)
Camping: Willard Brook State Forest, Pearl Hill State Park
Take Note: no development; too shallow for motors

GETTING THERE

From the junction of Routes 13 and 119 in Townsend, go 2.8 miles (2.8 miles) east on Route 119, and turn right on Townsend Road. Go 2.5 miles (5.3 miles), and turn right by the yellow fire hydrant at the West Groton Water Supply plant on the right (42° 36.893′ N, 71° 38.332′ W).

From Route 225 in West Groton, go 1.1 miles north on Townsend Road to the access on the left.

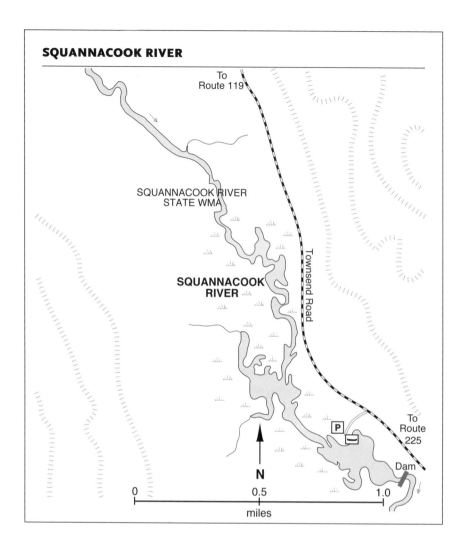

SQUANNACOOK RIVER

To Route 119

SQUANNACOOK RIVER STATE WMA

SQUANNACOOK RIVER

Townsend Road

P

To Route 225

Dam

N

0   0.5   1.0

miles

WHAT YOU'LL SEE

Paddling through Squannacook River Wildlife Management Area, you may become entranced with the peacefulness, away from the bustle of everyday life. Marshlands head off like fingers in the lower reaches, providing ample opportunity for exploration. Birdlife fills the area, and—judging by the number of anglers—trout must fill the waters. The side channels abound with American white waterlily, along with lesser amounts of yellow pond-lily, watershield, pondweed, and pickerelweed.

We found an enormous beaver lodge with winter stores of freshly cut boughs jammed butt-first into the mud. Beaver swim out under the winter ice, retrieving branches to gnaw the bark that sustains them. We watched the occasional muskrat harvest streamside grasses for winter. Great blue herons patrolled the coves, and we scared up a few flocks of wood ducks as we intruded on their territories.

Paddling upstream away from the dam, side channels disappear, and the canopy closes in over the narrow, twisting river. Besides the occasional white pine, deciduous trees hold sway. We paddled the Squannacook on a truly gorgeous, misty but balmy autumn day. Fall colors filled the air, and migrating sparrows filled the streamside vegetation. We navigated upstream through the slow current until a ledgy rapids blocked our way, then sat there soaking in the golden color of the streamside ferns and regretting our need to turn around.

30 | Beaver Brook

Beaver Brook is a heavily vegetated haven for wildlife, surrounded by suburban Westford. Expect to see cattail, pickerelweed, smartweed, and the usual assemblage of marshland birds. We saw an otter here, and you should see beaver at dusk.

Location: Littleton and Westford, MA
Maps: *Massachusetts Atlas & Gazetteer*, Map 27: K27, L27; USGS Westford
Length: 3 miles one way
Time: 4 hours round-trip
Habitat Type: meandering, slow-flowing, cattail-lined brook
Fish: trout, largemouth bass, yellow perch, pickerel (see fish advisory, Appendix A)
Camping: Willard Brook State Forest, Pearl Hill State Park
Take Note: little development; too shallow for motors

GETTING THERE
From I-495, Exit 31, go 0.7 mile (0.7 mile) west on Route 119, and turn right on Beaver Brook Road. Go 1.2 miles (1.9 miles) to the access on the right, just over the bridge (42° 34.355′ N, 71° 28.71′ W).

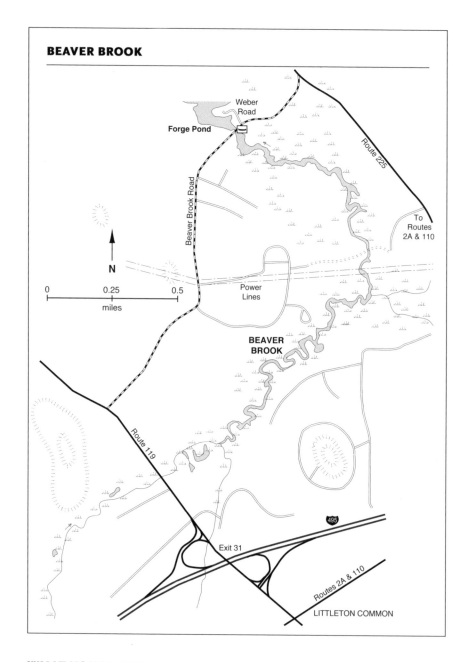

BEAVER BROOK

Weber Road

Forge Pond

Route 225

Beaver Brook Road

To Routes 2A & 110

N

0   0.25   0.5
miles

Power Lines

BEAVER BROOK

Route 119

495

Exit 31

Routes 2A & 110

LITTLETON COMMON

WHAT YOU'LL SEE

You can paddle downstream from the unimproved boat ramp (other side of the road from the access) on Beaver Brook Road a few hundred feet to the Forge Pond inlet, but we wouldn't bother paddling the pond itself because of development and because of numerous high-powered motorboats that populate these waters. Going back upstream from Forge Pond, we contemplated paddling through one of the twin culverts under Beaver Brook Road but decided against it. Debris clogged the upstream ends of both culverts, and dragging the boat over the accumulated debris while crouched—trying to dodge the dozens of spiderwebs hanging down from the culvert ceilings—did not seem too appealing.

Instead, we portaged up over the road and put in at the easy access on the northeast side of the bridge. You can avoid carrying over the road by parking at this access. Even though we paddled here in mid-September, we immediately started seeing wildlife. Look for red-winged blackbird, great blue heron, black duck, green heron, Canada goose, common yellowthroat, yellow warbler, and other marshland species. We saw dozens of painted turtles, including a surprisingly large number of young turtles.

While we did not see any of the eponymous beaver on our paddle here, we did see quite a bit of evidence of them. You should be able to see beaver here in the evening. Just south of Beaver Brook Road on our way back to the access, with the afternoon trending toward dusk, we got a glimpse of a river otter that quickly disappeared into the marsh.

While cattails dominate this brook, we also saw plenty of American white waterlily, yellow pond-lily, pickerelweed, bulrush, sensitive fern, marsh fern,

Cattails line the shore of this section of Beaver Brook. Beaver often keep channels open on narrow streams, making paddling easier.

buttonbush, and a reddish-stemmed aquatic smartweed in bloom—extensive smartweed stands gave the shoreline a pinkish blush in places. Some shoreline red maples had begun to turn red. Farther from shore, white pine dominates, interspersed with sugar maple, ash, and other northern hardwoods.

We paddled somewhat over a mile upstream from the access until thick vegetation blocked our way. In the early spring, before cattails fill the channel, you should be able to push farther upstream—although probably not all the way to Route 119.

31 | Nashua River and Oxbow National Wildlife Refuge

This protected section of river is a wonderful paddling resource, filled with ducks and other birdlife. Look for deer, muskrats, and painted and snapping turtles under the branches of silver maple that drape out over the water.

Location: Bolton, Harvard, Lancaster, and Shirley, MA
Maps: *Massachusetts Atlas & Gazetteer*, Map 27: M17, 18, N17, 18, O18, Map 39: A18, B17, 18, C17, 18; USGS Ayer, Hudson
Length: 9.5 miles one way
Time: 7 hours round-trip
Habitat Type: meandering, slow-flowing river
Fish: largemouth, smallmouth, and calico bass; yellow perch; pickerel (see fish advisory, Appendix A)
Information: Oxbow National Wildlife Refuge, fws.gov/northeast/oxbow
Camping: Willard Brook State Forest, Pearl Hill State Park
Take Note: a little development north of Route 2, too shallow for motors

GETTING THERE
From Route 2, Exit 38A, go 1.6 miles (1.6 miles) south on Routes 110/111, and turn right on Route 110 when they split. Go 2.0 miles (3.6 miles) to the sign for Oxbow National Wildlife Refuge, and turn right on Still River Depot Road. Go 0.5 mile (4.1 miles) to the access (after crossing the tracks, jog left, then right) (42° 29.758′ N, 71° 37.568′ W).

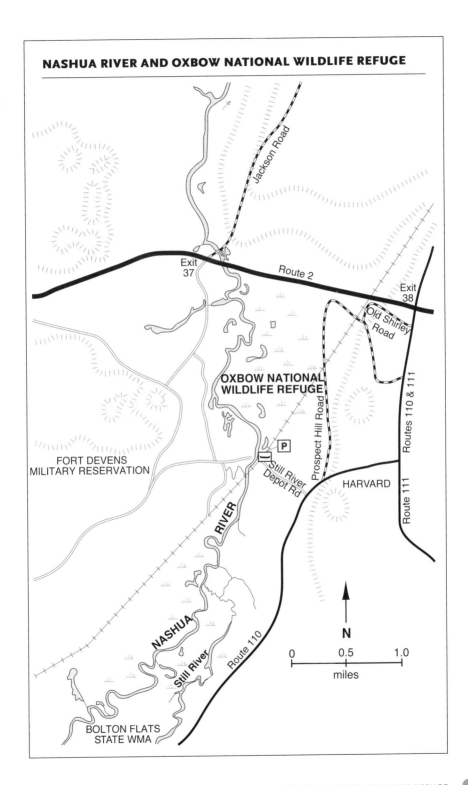

NASHUA RIVER AND OXBOW NATIONAL WILDLIFE REFUGE

Jackson Road

Exit 37

Route 2

Exit 38

Old Shirley Road

OXBOW NATIONAL
WILDLIFE REFUGE

Prospect Hill Road

Routes 110 & 111

P

Still River
Depot Rd

HARVARD

FORT DEVENS
MILITARY RESERVATION

Route 111

RIVER

NASHUA

Still River

Route 110

N

0   0.5   1.0
miles

BOLTON FLATS
STATE WMA

Dead trees populate the marsh, providing great habitat for cavity-nesting birds.

WHAT YOU'LL SEE

This Nashua River section flows from Bolton Flats Wildlife Management Area north through Oxbow National Wildlife Refuge and Fort Devens Military Reservation, and passes under the Route 2 bridge. The two natural areas, along with Fort Devens, have protected the river from development. The river has three distinct areas. Upstream from the access—up through Bolton Flats WMA—the narrow, shallow, sandy-bottomed river has many overhanging branches, lots of downed timber to negotiate, and moderate current in a few places. During times of high water, you may have to paddle the upper section in one direction. We enjoyed paddling the upper section in late summer because of reduced current and boat traffic.

The middle section between the Oxbow NWR access and Route 2 flows between Fort Devens on the west and Oxbow NWR on the east. A wooded shoreline encloses the narrow, winding river, with multiple-stemmed silver maple branches draped over the water, making it difficult to get by in a few spots. Although silver maple dominates the shore here, we also saw many sycamore and gray birch. A couple of dozen migrating wood ducks took off from a tree as we paddled near, and we also came upon a large flock of mallards. Deer came down to the water to drink; several muskrats harvested pickerelweed and streamside grasses, seemingly oblivious to passing boats. We watched a large snapping turtle feed on underwater vegetation, while dozens of painted turtles basked on branches and logs.

The section farthest downstream—north of Route 2—runs much wider and deeper than the previous sections. The banks boast greater tree-species diversity. With the sky unfettered by overhanging branches, we watched a beautiful red-tailed hawk circle overhead. A Cooper's hawk chased songbirds off through the woods, and we looked in vain for cuckoos that might be feeding on the abundant tent caterpillar nests on gray birches. On the way back to the access, we checked out a beaver dam on a bay off to the Fort Devens side that harbored huge patches of pickerelweed.

32 | Assabet River (Mill Pond, A-1 Site)

This is a great place for fishermen and for paddlers who don't mind weaving their way though a stump-filled reservoir. The wooded hillsides and scattered islands lend a scenic beauty. Look for great blue heron prowling the west-end marshes.

Location: Westborough, MA
Maps: *Massachusetts Atlas & Gazetteer*, Map 39: N16, 17, O16, 17; USGS Marlborough
Area: 333 acres
Time: 3 hours
Habitat Type: wooded, marshy reservoir
Fish: largemouth and calico bass, yellow perch, northern pike, muskellunge (see fish advisory, Appendix A)
Information: Westborough Community Land Trust, westboroughlandtrust.org
Take Note: many submerged and partially submerged stumps keep motors away, limited development

GETTING THERE
From I-495, Exit 23 southbound, go west on Route 9 for 3.2 miles (3.2 miles), and exit on Route 135 east. Go 0.7 mile (3.9 miles), and turn right on Maynard Street. Go 0.6 mile (4.5 miles), passing under the railroad tracks, and bear right on Fisher Street. Take an almost immediate left on Mill Street, and go 0.4 mile (4.9 miles) to the access on the right (42° 15.944′ N, 71° 38.034′ W).

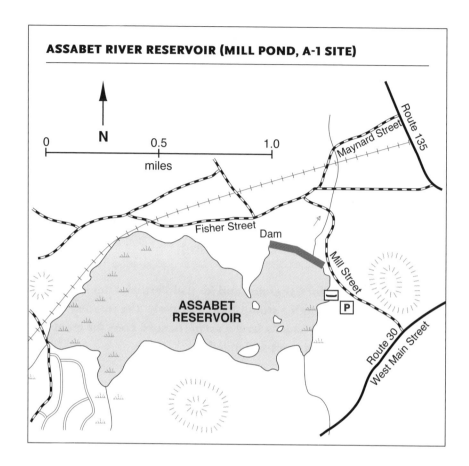

ASSABET RIVER RESERVOIR (MILL POND, A-1 SITE)

WHAT YOU'LL SEE

Assabet Reservoir, locally known as Mill Pond and also called the A-1 Site, just a few miles from busy Route 9 in Westborough, provides a wonderful place to paddle. Thousands of closely spaced tree stumps, left over from the creation of this flood-control reservoir in 1969, keep out most motorboats and make paddling here somewhat of a challenge.

Great blue herons, osprey, and tree swallows used to nest in profusion here. Unfortunately, in the last ten years the dead trees have fallen, eliminating the great blue heron rookery and the holes used by tree swallows. When we paddled here in 1992, nearly two dozen heron nests perched precariously among the spindly tops; in 2002 only nine nests remained, along with a wonderful addition, an osprey nest. By 2013, the dead trees had disappeared.

The reservoir's fairly open eastern end gives way to a forest of protruding and submerged stumps once you round the point of land extending down from

Shallow, marshy, stump-filled Assabet Reservoir is popular with fishermen and bird-watchers.

the north. In places you literally have to weave your boat around these stumps to get through. The once abundant tree swallows kept the mosquito population somewhat in check.

The shallow, stump-filled waters of Assabet Reservoir—15 feet at the deepest—provide plenty of cover for fish. Someone caught a 6-pound largemouth bass during our first trip here. Cattails and bulrush line most of the marshy perimeter, with watershield floating on open water. Looking at the reservoir, you might guess that thick muck covers the bottom; somewhat surprisingly, sand coats much of the bottom instead. Piles of freshwater mussels provide evidence of many raccoon meals. Willow, alder, red maple, red oak, and aspen surround the reservoir. A number of scattered islands add scenic beauty but offer little in the way of access for rest or a picnic. Along with swallows, great blue herons, and osprey, keep an eye out for green herons, cedar waxwings, wood ducks, and lots of painted turtles.

33 | Paradise Pond

Islands increase the amount of shoreline to explore on this small, scenic pond. Shoreline shrubs bloom throughout the spring and summer, but nothing beats the spectacular mountain laurel display in June, when the entire shoreline seems lit up with pale pink blossoms.

Location: Princeton, MA
Maps: *Massachusetts Atlas & Gazetteer*, Map 26: O4;
USGS Fitchburg, Sterling
Area: 61 acres
Time: 2 hours
Habitat Type: wooded pond
Fish: largemouth, smallmouth, and calico bass; yellow perch; pickerel (see fish advisory, Appendix A)
Camping: Willard Brook State Forest, Pearl Hill State Park, Lake Denison State Recreation Area, Otter River State Forest
Take Note: no development, no internal combustion motors

GETTING THERE

From Route 2, Exit 25, go 4.0 miles (4.0 miles) south on Route 140, and turn sharply back left on Fitchburg Road (Route 31 north). In 0.2 mile (4.2 miles) and for the next 0.5 mile (4.7 miles) after that, there are several access points on the right.

From Route 2, Exit 28, go 3.1 miles south on Route 31 to the first of several access points on the left (42° 30.38′ N, 71° 51.498′ W).

WHAT YOU'LL SEE

Bordering Leominster State Forest, undeveloped, and free of gasoline motors, Paradise Pond provides an idyllic place to paddle. With an undulating shoreline and several islands and coves to explore, you could spend a few hours on this small pond, especially in mid-June when the abundant mountain laurel puts on a spectacular display. Route 31, though not heavily traveled, occasionally intrudes on the peace and quiet.

Vegetation includes a number of species that you rarely see this far north: swamp honeysuckle, a fairly late-blooming azalea with tubular sticky white flowers; sweet pepperbush, a late-blooming shrub with clusters of small,

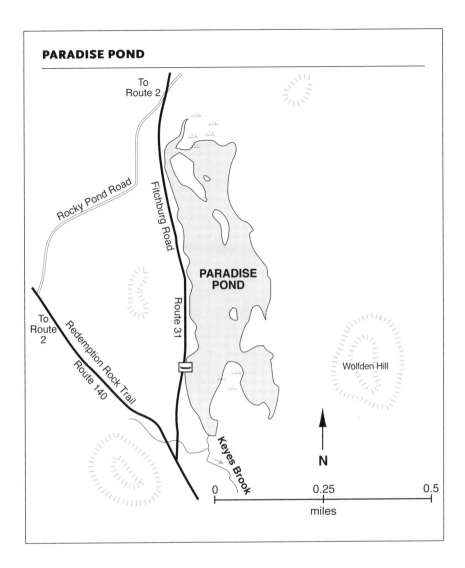

PARADISE POND

To Route 2

Rocky Pond Road

Fitchburg Road

Route 31

To Route 2

Redemption Rock Trail

Route 140

PARADISE POND

Wolfden Hill

Keyes Brook

N

0   0.25   0.5

miles

fragrant white flowers that you can still find in bloom at the end of August; and sassafras.

The islands on Paradise Pond are quite interesting and very much worth visiting. Instead of white pine and the various deciduous trees that comprise most of the woods around the pond, pitch pine—a three-needled pine with large plates of bark on older trees—dominates the islands. A thick bed of needles in the open understory provides ideal locations for a picnic lunch.

In some sections, watershield covers the surface; you can easily distinguish this from other aquatic plants because the stem extends down from the center of the oval leaves. Feel the slippery stems and the undersides of the leaves. Carnivorous plants occur here as well. In the water you will see lots of bladderwort, and if you look carefully you will find sundews on floating logs and sphagnum hummocks. We also saw a water snake here, entwined on a branch over the water.

The ruins of an old mill building stand at the southern tip of the pond; an 1870 map shows this as the E.B. Walker Saw Mill. Earlier maps show other sawmills to the northwest on the Keyes Brook branch of the Stillwater River. An old country road ran closer to this river route than the present Route 140, also known as Redemption Rock Trail. Early colonial negotiators chose Princeton as the site for a prisoner redemption at "Redemption Rock," off Route 140, less than a mile north of the junction with Route 31, deep in the woods. It was here in 1675 that Mary Rowlandson, who had been captured during the midwinter massacre at Lancaster and held in Quebec for eight weeks, was freed for twenty pounds sterling and some whiskey.

On the east side of Paradise Pond, Leominster State Forest provides some great hiking on old logging roads and trails that wind through needle-carpeted open woodland. You'll see lots of wildflowers here in spring.

34 | Moosehorn Pond

Mats of sphagnum harbor sundews and pitcher plants, along with tamarack, and lend Moosehorn the feel of northern New England ponds. Look for wood duck, mallard, great blue heron, and other aquatic birds.

Location: Hubbardston, MA
Maps: *Massachusetts Atlas & Gazetteer*, Map 37: B27, 28; USGS Sterling
Area: 67 acres
Time: 2 hours
Habitat Type: northern fen
Fish: largemouth and calico bass, yellow perch, pickerel (see fish advisory, Appendix A)
Camping: Willard Brook State Forest, Pearl Hill State Park, Lake Denison State Recreation Area, Otter River State Forest, Tully Lake

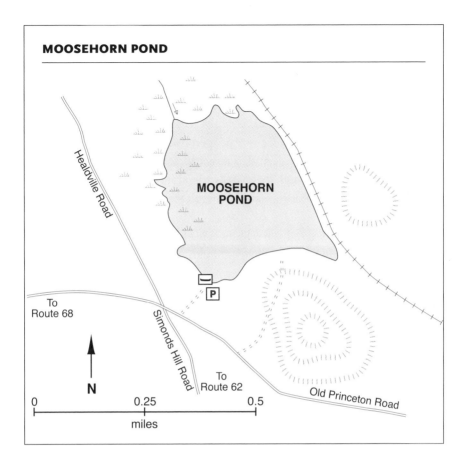

MOOSEHORN POND

MOOSEHORN POND

Healdville Road

Simonds Hill Road

To Route 68

To Route 62

Old Princeton Road

N

0   0.25   0.5

miles

Take Note: little development, hand launch limits motors, paddle quietly amid marshy islands to minimize disturbance of nesting wood ducks

GETTING THERE

From Route 2, Exit 22, go 7.5 miles (7.5 miles) south on Route 68, and turn left on Old Princeton Road (0.6 mile south of the flashing yellow light in Hubbardston). Go 1.6 miles (9.1 miles) east, less than 100 yards beyond the junction of Old Princeton Road with Simonds Hill and Healdville roads, to the access on the left (42° 27.947′ N, 71° 58.119′ W).

WHAT YOU'LL SEE

Moosehorn Pond, though small, is interesting and definitely worth a visit. Only one house, set well back from the water, interrupts the pond's otherwise pristine shoreline. Spongy mats of sphagnum and dense stands of leatherleaf, punctuated by occasional tall tamarack spires, lend a very "northern" feel to this marshy pond. Sundews, marsh ferns, and occasional pitcher plants hide amid the sphagnum.

Along with tamarack, look for red maple, white and gray birches, white pine, red oak, American chestnut, sassafras, witch hazel, blueberry, winterberry (a member of the holly genus), and sweet pepperbush. American white waterlily, yellow pond-lily, watershield, and pondweed leaves float on the water's surface. Paddle quietly through the marshy islands to minimize disturbance of nesting wood ducks; look for great blue heron stalking frogs, bass, pickerel, and yellow perch.

During most seasons you can paddle considerably farther north than the border of the pond shown on the map—though floating sphagnum mats, half-submerged logs, and grassy hillocks impede your progress. Indeed, on the pond's northern section, poling would prove far more effective than paddling. Old but still-used railroad tracks run along the pond's eastern side.

35 | Eames Pond

This heavily vegetated pond harbors acres of waterlilies, but the real treat is finding enormous amounts of eastern purple bladderwort abloom in August. Look for beaver here in the evening or early morning.

Location: Paxton, MA
Maps: *Massachusetts Atlas & Gazetteer*, Map 37: K28, 29, L28; USGS Worcester North
Area: 74 acres
Time: 2 hours
Habitat Type: shallow, marshy pond
Fish: largemouth and calico bass, yellow perch, pickerel (see fish advisory, Appendix A)
Information: Moore State Park, mass.gov/eea/agencies/dcr/massparks/region-central/moore-state-park.html
Camping: Wells State Park

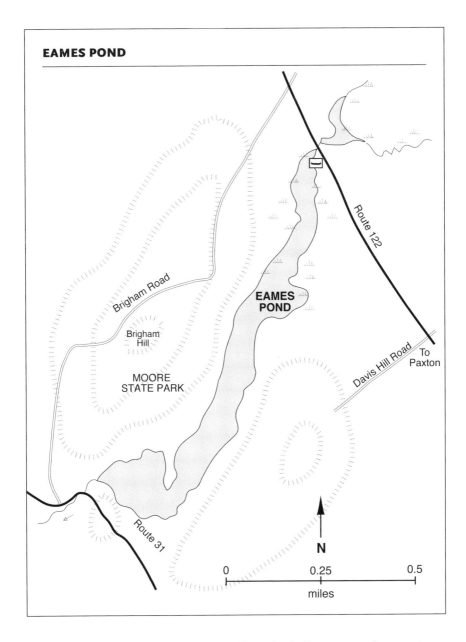

EAMES POND

Take Note: limited development; hand launch, shallowness, and vegetation keep motors out

GETTING THERE
From the junction of Routes 31, 56, and 122 in Paxton, go 1.4 miles north on Route 122 to the access on the left, just before the culvert (42° 19.541′ N, 71° 56.84′ W).

WHAT YOU'LL SEE

With much of the shoreline protected by Moore State Park, Eames Pond offers a wonderful paddling opportunity, especially if you don't mind making your way through endless seas of lily pads. Beaver maintain something of a channel—guarded by pickerelweed and arrowhead—that wends its way through what is truly a carpet of American white waterlily. As we paddled down the pond, we noticed what looked like a small island near the eastern shore; upon closer inspection, it turned out to be a massive beaver lodge at least 25 feet long, with abundant branches stored underwater as a winter larder.

In contrast to most of the American white waterlily seen on most ponds in Massachusetts, the *tuberosa* subspecies grows here. Note the huge green leaves, some spanning a foot. American white waterlily occurs as two subspecies: *Nymphaea odorata odorata* and *N.o. tuberosa*. Most guidebooks list these as separate species, but taxonomists have recently lumped them into one. The more common subspecies, *odorata*, bears much smaller leaves, with both the leaves and the flower sepals tinged with purple. *Tuberosa* produces large green leaves and green sepals.

As you paddle into the pond's southern reaches, American white waterlily gives way to watershield and pondweed. Most striking by far, though, when we paddled here in mid-August, was a truly stupendous amount of eastern purple bladderwort (*Utricularia purpurea*) in bloom, more than we had seen on all other ponds combined. The entire south end radiated a purple glow that could be seen for hundreds of yards. Paddling closer, as an incredibly sweet odor wafted toward us on a gentle breeze, floating yellow-brown pondweed leaves provided a wonderful contrast to the sea of tiny purple flowers, borne on slender 4-inch stalks. We reveled in this gorgeous setting, not wanting to paddle back to the access. We also wondered if the *N.o. tuberosa* would eventually take over the southern end, as well, crowding out the huge mats of eastern purple bladderwort.

Though few people paddle this wonderful pond, many people hike the several trails that course through Moore State Park. We prefer the paddling, especially when we see goldfinches and great blue herons among the bur-reed, joe-pye weed, sweetgale, buttonbush, wild rice, and dwarf red maples in this broad marsh. But we will never get over the sight of those purple-flowered bladderwort.

36 | Quaboag Pond, Quaboag River, and East Brookfield River

The rivers, connected by Quaboag Pond, are extraordinary paddling resources, passing through largely undisturbed habitat. Look for deer, beaver, muskrat, painted and stinkpot turtles, osprey, wood duck, and great blue heron.

Location: Brookfield, East Brookfield, Warren, and West Brookfield, MA
Maps: *Massachusetts Atlas & Gazetteer*, Map 48: A15, B14, 15, Map 49: A16, B16, 17, 18, C18, 19, 20, 21, 22, D21, 22; USGS Warren
Area/Length: Quaboag Pond, 541 acres; Quaboag River, 9 miles one way; East Brookfield River, 2 miles one way
Time: all day, shorter trips possible
Habitat Type: marshy rivers
Fish: brook, brown and rainbow trout; largemouth and calico bass; white and yellow perch; pickerel; northern pike (see fish advisory, Appendix A)
Camping: Wells State Park
Take Note: development and motors on pond; little development on rivers

GETTING THERE
Access points are given in order, starting upstream.

Quaboag Pond, North End, and East Brookfield River (42° 12.209′ N, 72° 3.777′ W). From the junction of Routes 9 and 148 in Brookfield, go 1.0 mile (1.0 mile) east on Route 9, and turn right on Quaboag Street. Go 1.4 miles (2.4 miles) to the access on the right. Because of development and water-skiers, avoid Quaboag Pond on summer weekends, except as access to the East Brookfield (or Sevenmile) River.

Route 148 (42° 12.462′ N, 72° 6.124′ W). From the junction of Routes 9 and 148 in Brookfield, go 0.6 mile south on Route 148 to the access on the left, between the two bridges.

Route 67 (42° 14.108′ N, 71° 9.717′ W). From Route 9 in West Brookfield, go less than 0.1 mile south on Routes 19 and 67 to the access and picnic area on the left.

Warren (42° 13.042′ N, 72° 11.585′ W). From Route 67 in Warren, go 0.4 mile north on Old West Brookfield Road to Lucy Stone Park on the left. This is a take-out point only (for when you have two vehicles); going downstream from here will take you into dangerous whitewater.

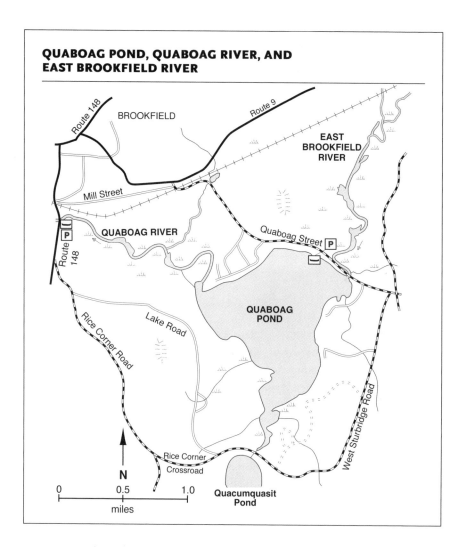

QUABOAG POND, QUABOAG RIVER, AND EAST BROOKFIELD RIVER

BROOKFIELD
Route 148
Route 9

EAST BROOKFIELD RIVER

Mill Street

QUABOAG RIVER
Route 148
Quaboag Street
P
P

QUABOAG POND

Lake Road

Rice Corner Road

West Sturbridge Road

N

Rice Corner Crossroad

0   0.5   1.0
miles

Quacumquasit Pond

WHAT YOU'LL SEE
East Brookfield River

We love paddling the inlet and outlet rivers, both of which provide an extraordinary undeveloped, wildlife-rich paddling resource. East Brookfield River flows into Quaboag Pond at the northeastern tip. Traveling upstream from the Quaboag Street bridge, the slow-flowing East Brookfield hugs the road for a few hundred yards, then turns north and east. Initially, the wide channel winds through Allen Marsh, the sides thick with pickerelweed, grasses, sedges, and buttonbush. American white waterlily, yellow pond-lily, and pondweed leaves float on the water's surface. Bladderwort and watermilfoil flow in the current beneath. Though rarely visible, freshwater mussels thrive in the sandy bottom. Look for painted turtle and the less common stinkpot turtle along here—we saw a stinkpot perched on a protruding branch well above the water's surface. Wood ducks raise their broods here, and the great blue heron patrols the shorelines. You may see muskrats harvesting streamside grasses as you paddle along.

Farther north, the channel narrows and becomes more defined, with fewer backwater ponds to explore. About 2 miles upriver, after reaching a fork, fallen trees and beaver dams impede your progress, though with perseverance you might make it to Lake Lashaway (left fork) or to East Brookfield (right fork); still, portaging over the numerous deadfalls would likely be quite an ordeal. In the upper stretches, we saw a beaver swimming midday and an osprey with a fish.

Quaboag River

At Quaboag Pond's northwestern tip, the Quaboag River rises, beginning its westward journey to its confluence with the Ware and Swift rivers, where they form the Chicopee River. Quiet, meandering flat water, through wide marshlands teeming with wildlife, marks this 9-mile section of river. Paddling down and back takes at least a full day, especially if you stop to revel in the gorgeous scenery and to watch the ubiquitous wildlife. For more than the first half of the journey, the Quaboag River winds its way through marshy Quaboag Wildlife Management Area. Thick shrub vegetation lines the banks, and underwater vegetation forms thick mats. Clumps of swamp loosestrife, some extending for hundreds of yards along the shore, arch gracefully out over the water. Along this stretch of river, trees line the higher ground, a few hundred yards across the marsh.

Paddling farther downstream one evening, where trees and taller shrubs encroach on the shores, we saw seven beaver beginning their nightly branch-gathering forays. We listened to hermit thrushes, catbirds, towhees, song sparrows, and cardinals call from the dense undergrowth, and to a veery singing off in the woods. We watched muskrats swim about and a deer come down for a drink. Swamp rose grows in profusion, and some huge swamp white oaks occur along the banks in the downstream sections.

After paddling through expansive marshes, the river narrows, and trees line the banks. When you reach the section with several large rocks in succession jutting above the surface, the current picks up. Turn around here, especially during times of high water. If you have two cars, you can paddle down to the take-out at Lucy Stone Park in Warren.

In years long past, the Quaboag River served as a major thoroughfare for the region's native people. A short portage connected Quaboag Pond to the nearby

QUABOAG POND, QUABOAG RIVER, AND
EAST BROOKFIELD RIVER

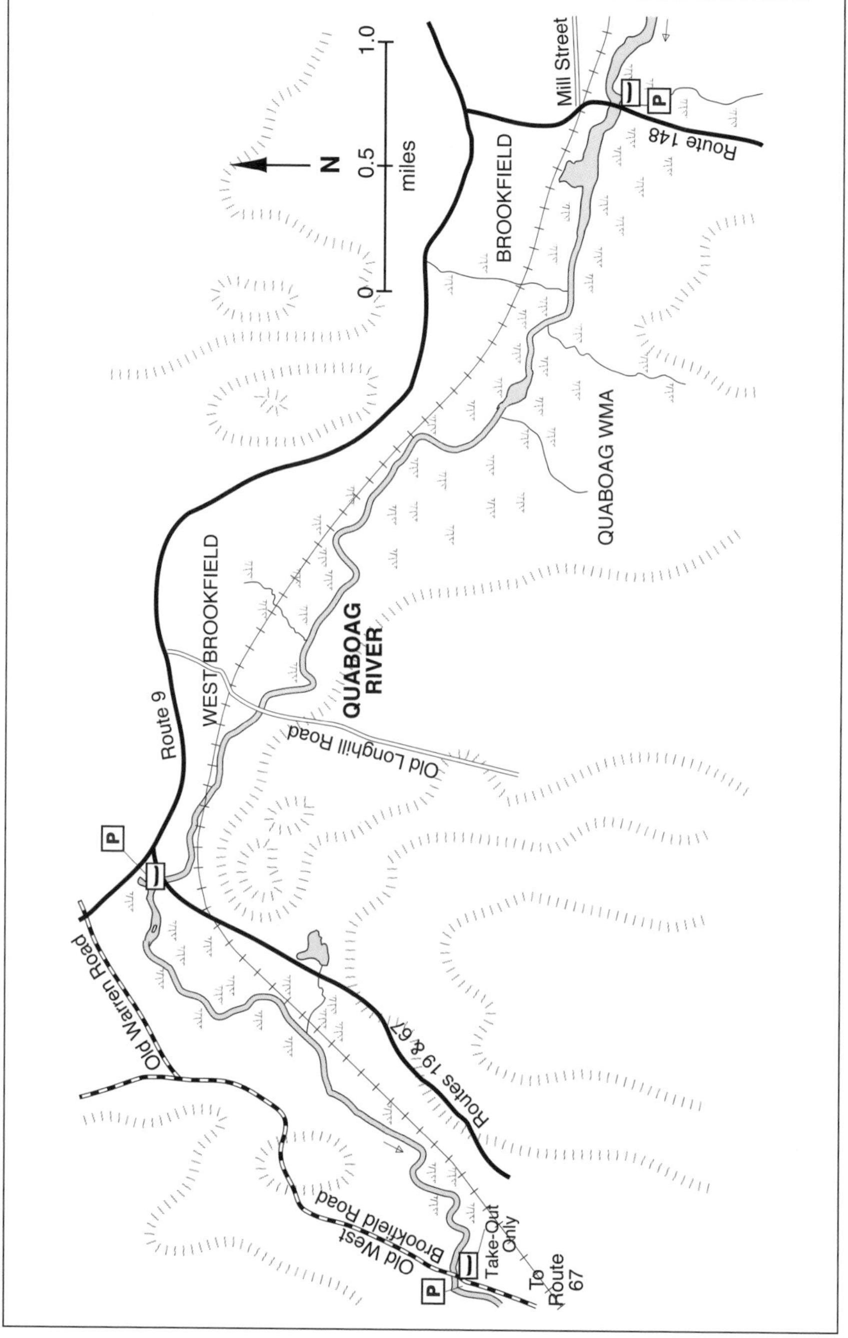

N

0   0.5   1.0
miles

Mill Street

Route 148

BROOKFIELD

QUABOAG WMA

WEST BROOKFIELD

QUABOAG RIVER

Route 9

Old Longhill Road

Old Warren Road

Routes 19 & 67

Old West Brookfield Road

Take-Out Only

To Route 67

Quinebaug River, which runs south through Nipmuk and eastern Niantic country to meet other tributaries of the Pawcatuck River system, which in turn meanders from southern Rhode Island through Narragansett country. In this way, native people of this south coastal region could communicate, trade, and journey north to Quaboag Pond, then turn west and down the Chicopee River to Connecticut country.

In the uprising known as King Philip's War, native nations along this route ravaged the more isolated English settlements. Old Brookfield, a frontier village about 8 miles to the northwest on Foster Hill, became an easy target. On August 2, 1675, Quaboag warriors ambushed an armed team of English negotiators from Boston, there to extract a pledge of neutrality amid growing warfare in southeastern New England. The retreating English took hasty refuge with Brookfield's families in their largest structure, Ayres' Tavern. Ephraim Curtis, a scout of that party, finally crept through a determined siege in which all other structures were burned, to bring about eventual rescue from Marlborough. Fifty women and children and 32 men held the tavern, while two sets of twin babies were born within. The settlers soon abandoned the town for safer and more central Hadley, in today's "Pioneer Valley" near Amherst.

37 | East Brimfield Lake, Quinebaug River, Holland Pond, and Long Pond

Quinebaug River Water Trail represents one of the finest quietwater resources in Massachusetts. With virtually no current, it wends its way for more than 4 miles through a wildlife-filled swampland. Look for deer, muskrat, beaver, otter, turtles, ducks, geese, and songbirds.

Location: Brimfield, Holland, and Sturbridge, MA
Maps: *Massachusetts Atlas & Gazetteer*, Map 49: G18, H18, I16, 17, 18, J16, K16; USGS Brimfield, Holland, Sturbridge
Area/Length: Holland Pond, 85 acres; East Brimfield Lake and Long Pond, 420 acres; Quinebaug River, 4.5 miles one way (5.5 miles one way to the East Brimfield Lake access)
Time: Quinebaug River, 5 hours round-trip; continue through East Brimfield Lake & Long Pond, all day round-trip
Habitat Type: slow, marshy, peaceful river

EAST BRIMFIELD LAKE, QUINEBAUG RIVER, HOLLAND POND, AND LONG POND

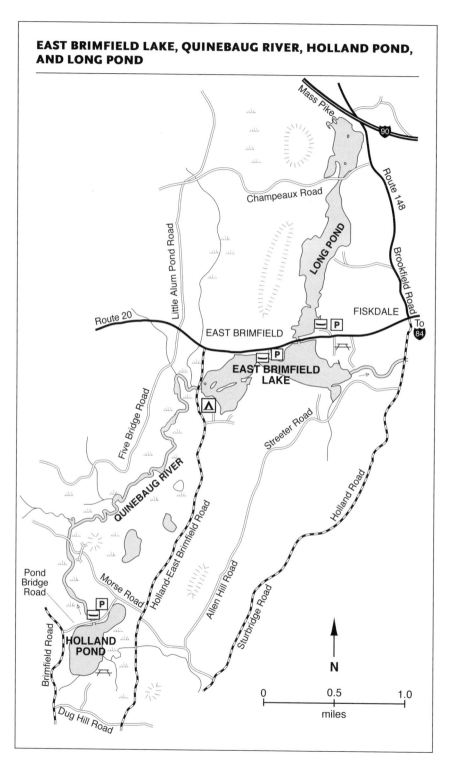

Mass Pike

90

Route 148

Champeaux Road

Brookfield Road

Little Alum Pond Road

LONG POND

FISKDALE

Route 20

EAST BRIMFIELD

To 84

EAST BRIMFIELD LAKE

Five Bridge Road

Streeter Road

QUINEBAUG RIVER

Holland-East Brimfield Road

Holland Road

Pond Bridge Road

Morse Road

Allen Hill Road

Sturbridge Road

Brimfield Road

HOLLAND POND

Dug Hill Road

N

0   0.5   1.0
miles

Fish: brook, brown, and rainbow trout; largemouth and smallmouth bass; white and yellow perch; pickerel; northern pike (see fish advisory, Appendix A)

Information: Quinebaug River Water Trail, tlgv.org/uploads/Watershed/WaterTrails/QuinebaugRiverTrailEBrimfieldLake.pdf; US Army Corps of Engineers, www.nae.usace.army.mil/Missions/Recreation/EastBrimfieldLake

Camping: Wells State Park

Take Note: no motors on river; lakes congested with motorboats, 10 MPH limit

GETTING THERE

Holland Pond/Canoe Trail (42° 4.938′ N, 72° 9.817′ W). From the junction of Routes 20 and 148 in Fiskdale, go 1.6 miles (1.6 miles) west on Route 20, and turn left on Holland–East Brimfield Road. Go 2.0 miles (3.6 miles), and turn right on Morse Road. Go 0.2 mile (3.8 miles), and turn left on the access road. Go 0.3 mile (4.1 miles) to the Canoe Trail around to the right, skirting the Holland Pond north shore.

Long Pond (42° 6.779′ N, 72° 7.901′ W). From the junction of Routes 20 and 148, go 0.7 mile west on Route 20 to the access on the right, just across from the entrance to Streeter Road Beach.

East Brimfield Lake (42° 6.622′ N, 71° 8.355′ W). Continue 0.4 mile (1.1 miles) beyond the Long Pond access to the access on the left.

WHAT YOU'LL SEE

Near historic Old Sturbridge Village you can enjoy a full day of paddling on the various bodies of water that collectively comprise East Brimfield Lake. This section of the slow-flowing Quinebaug River—part of the Quinebaug River Water Trail, a designated National Recreational Trail—connects Holland Pond to the south with Long Pond to the north. With limited time, we would paddle the quieter and less congested Quinebaug River, putting in at the Holland Pond access. With more time, we would paddle the 12-mile round-trip up to the north end of Long Pond and back to Holland Pond.

Small but very attractive Holland Pond has just a few houses on the west side, well away from and above the water. Two sandy beaches—a small one near the outlet and another larger one across the pond at the Holland Pond Recreation Area—offer a respite from the summer heat.

From Holland Pond, depending on water level, you may have to carry over the road into the Quinebaug River. The river passes some farmland near the north end but mostly winds through thick marshes filled with birdlife. Ferns grow thickly along sections of the bank, and in the few places where wooded slopes rise steeply from the water, you will see mountain laurel beneath the red oak and white oak canopy. Underwater vegetation fills the shallows. When we paddled here in July, swamp rose bloomed in profusion along the banks, while pickerelweed and waterlilies bloomed on the water. You will scarcely notice the current, because the water level drops only about 3 feet in 3 miles.

Those interested in open-water paddling can explore East Brimfield Lake south of Route 20; though a dam looms over the east end, detracting from the shoreline, the lake also includes a public beach and picnic area, a large and well-used boat ramp, and a popular private campground. For solitude, stick to the river or head immediately up to Long Pond, north of Route 20.

Long Pond extends about 1.5 miles north from the Route 20 access, almost to I-90. White pine, red and white oaks, and sugar and red maples dominate the heavily wooded shoreline. Unfortunately, invasive watermilfoil has crowded out some of the native vegetation; some development has also sprouted along the east shore. Two-thirds of the way up, you have to paddle under very low Champeaux Road bridge; marshy coves, floating pond vegetation, ferns along the banks, and lots of birds abound along the more interesting northern shoreline. A red oak and white pine grove juts out into the water, making a great picnic area on the northwestern side of Long Pond. Though shielded pretty well by trees, I-90 vehicle noise intrudes on the northern end of the pond.

While in the area, you can visit historic Old Sturbridge Village, a living museum portraying New England life in the 1830s.

38 | Millers River, Otter River, and Lake Denison

It's rare to see other paddlers on these spectacular rivers, which can be paddled both directions except during times of high water. Look for beaver, muskrat, otter, mink, snapping and painted turtles, great blue heron, ducks, geese, and lots of songbirds.

Location: Templeton and Winchendon, MA
Maps: *Massachusetts Atlas & Gazetteer*, Map 25: E20, F20, G19, 20, H19, 20; USGS Athol, Royalston, Winchendon

MILLERS RIVER, OTTER RIVER, AND LAKE DENISON

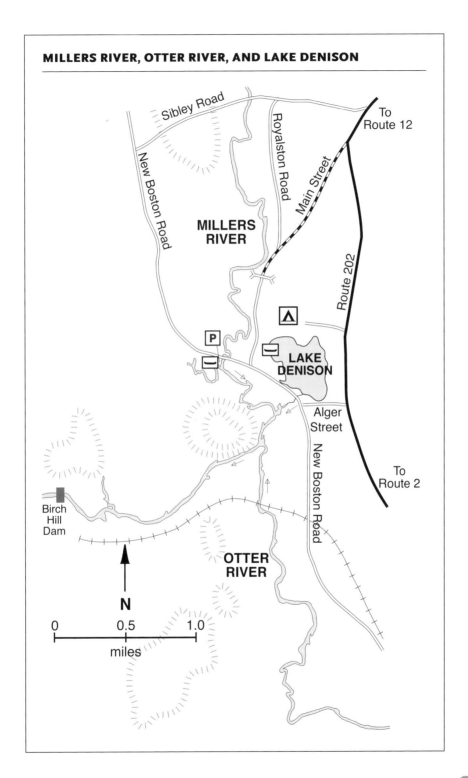

Area/Length: Lake Denison, 82 acres; Millers River, 7.5 miles one way; Otter River, 3 miles one way

Time: all day, shorter trips possible

Habitat Type: meandering unspoiled rivers, shrubby marshlands

Fish: brook, brown, and rainbow trout; largemouth, smallmouth, and calico bass (see fish advisory, Appendix A)

Camping: Lake Denison State Recreation Area, Otter River State Forest, Tully Lake

Take Note: no motors; no development

GETTING THERE

Lake Denison (42° 38.802′ N, 72° 5.547′ W). From the junction of Routes 68 and 202 in Baldwinville, go 2.2 miles (2.2 miles) north on Route 202, and turn left into the recreation area.

Millers and Otter Rivers (42° 38.731′ N, 72° 5.941′ W). After turning into the recreation area, go 0.7 mile (2.9 miles), and veer left on New Boston Road. Go 0.4 mile (3.3 miles) to the access on the left, just past the bridge.

Alternate Route. From the junction of Routes 12 and 202 in Winchendon, go 1.8 miles (1.8 miles) south on Route 202, and turn right on Main Street. Go 1.7 miles (3.5 miles) to the Lake Denison access on the left. For the rivers access, continue 0.1 mile (3.6 miles) south, and turn right on New Boston Road. Go 0.4 mile (4.0 miles) to the access on the left, just past the bridge.

WHAT YOU'LL SEE

Bounded by the Birch Hill Wildlife Management Area and the Otter River State Forest, these two rivers offer an unspoiled paddle through red maple, alder, red-willow dogwood, and buttonbush swamps. Because we love the seclusion, we have paddled here many times. In spring, the current can flow swiftly enough to make paddling upstream difficult in some places. On one trip, we paddled nearly 3 miles up the Millers River until a massive logjam blocked our way. Logjams, left over from floods, can occur anywhere on these rivers. On return trips with low water in summer and fall, several beaver dams filled the channels. Spring floods wash out the dams, followed by rebuilding in summer.

Beaver have also impounded the north-flowing Otter River, necessitating portages to reach broad upstream meadows. Many species of fern grow along the banks, including cinnamon, interrupted, royal, and marsh ferns. Marsh birds occur here in profusion. In mid-June, wood ducks, Canada geese, and mallards herded broods of young away from approaching boats. Great blue herons fed in the shallows, and killdeer nested on mud flats on the river's upper

Except during times of high water, you can paddle this section of the Millers River in both directions.

reaches. Crows mobbed a great horned owl, several snapping turtles fed just below the clear water's surface, and muskrats harvested streamside vegetation as we paddled by.

These rivers go up with rains and back down relatively quickly. Stay out of the river if you cannot paddle upstream easily. At times of high water, steer clear of trees in the water—they could cause you to capsize. Better yet, paddle Lake Denison instead. Receding glaciers formed this kettle-hole lake; a large chunk of glacier submerged in glacial till gradually melted, leaving a shallow lake with sandy shores and bottom, ideal for swimming.

39 | Tully Lake and East Branch Tully River

If you paddle the East Branch of the Tully River in the evening, you are guaranteed to see beaver in this wonderful marshland. Tully Lake, with its numerous islands, offers hours of exploration amid a wooded backdrop.

Location: Athol and Royalston, MA

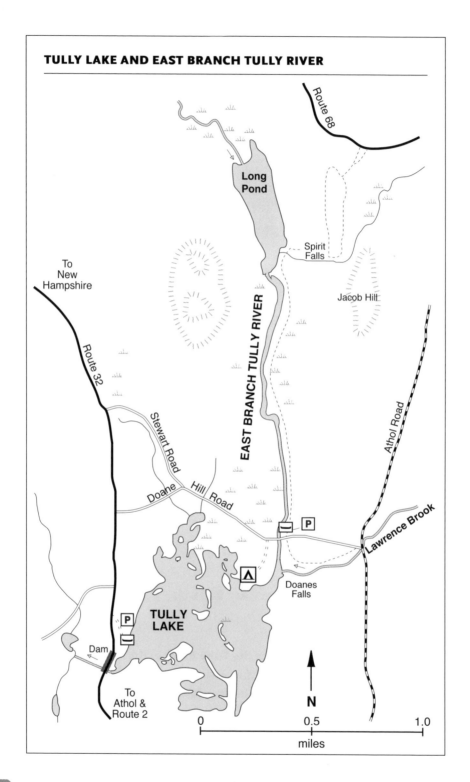

TULLY LAKE AND EAST BRANCH TULLY RIVER

Route 68

Long Pond

Spirit Falls

To New Hampshire

EAST BRANCH TULLY RIVER

Jacob Hill

Route 32

Stewart Road

Doane Hill Road

Athol Road

Lawrence Brook

P

Doanes Falls

TULLY LAKE

P

Dam

To Athol & Route 2

N

0   0.5   1.0

miles

Maps: *Massachusetts Atlas & Gazetteer*, Map 24: E13, F13, G12, 13; USGS Royalston

Area/Length: Tully Lake, 243 acres; East Branch Tully River, 3 miles one way

Time: East Branch Tully River, 3 hours round-trip; Tully Lake, 4 hours

Habitat Type: Tully Lake, dammed-up river, shrubby marshlands, many islands, protected bays; East Branch Tully River, marshlands and beaver swamps

Fish: brook and rainbow trout, largemouth and calico bass, yellow perch, pickerel, northern pike (see fish advisory, Appendix A)

Camping: Tully Lake, Lake Denison State Recreation Area, Otter River State Forest

Take Note: no development; motors allowed (with 10 HP limit) on Tully Lake; no motors on Tully River

GETTING THERE

Tully Lake (42° 38.597′ N, 72° 13.341′ W). From Route 2, Exit 17, go 5.8 miles (5.8 miles) north on Route 32 to the access on the right.

 Tully River (42° 39.054′ N, 72° 12.498′ W). From the Tully Lake access, go north on Route 32 for 0.4 mile (6.2 miles), and turn right on Doane Hill Road. Go 1.0 mile (7.2 miles) to the access on the left, just over the bridge.

WHAT YOU'LL SEE
Tully Lake

Located in north-central Massachusetts, not far from the New Hampshire border, Tully Lake is known to few people outside the immediate area. A highly varied shoreline, with dozens of islands and deep winding coves to explore, provides a wonderful paddling experience. A primitive, walk-in camping area at the north end provides an added bonus.

 Along the shore, white pine predominates, mixed with red maple, hemlock, red and white oaks, some quaking aspen, and white birch, along with a fairly dense border of shrubs, including buttonbush, various heaths, alder, blueberry, and—in places—cranberry with tiny oval leaves, dwarfed by large cranberries in late summer and fall. Farther from shore, the woods open up, providing great picnicking and hiking opportunities on 18 miles of trails. On the large island near the lake's south end, we found a few highbush blueberries absolutely covered with berries during a visit in early August. Along with the more common white pine, scrub oak—a species more common on dry, sandy hills—grows near the south end of the lake.

A camera crew films a sequence on East Branch Tully River for New Hampshire public television's *Windows to the Wild.*

East Branch Tully River

Underwater vegetation sways in the current, but otherwise you would hardly know which way the East Branch of the Tully River flows. Sweetgale, grasses, royal fern, buttonbush, and other shrubs grow thickly along the banks of this wide, gorgeous marsh. Look for American white waterlily, yellow pond-lily, pondweed, and watershield along the edges and for pitcher plant on the sphagnum hummocks.

On our paddle up and back in early June, muskrats had uprooted many of the tender shoots of pickerelweed. As hermit thrushes called from the woodlands, we saw several beaver; they had also girdled many of the streamside hemlocks, killing them, which eventually will make way for more palatable species. Beaver are especially visible here in the evening. We've seen beaver on every one of several trips here.

Rounding the last bend paddling north, the river opens up into serene Long Pond, surrounded by thick woodland. The pond marks the end of open water. You can continue on beyond the power line at the pond's north end, portaging over repeated beaver dams.

You can pull your boat up near the south end of Long Pond on the east side and hike to Spirit Falls along Spirit Brook Trail. You can also hike along another trail that starts from the Tully River access that leads both to Doanes Falls on Lawrence Brook and to Spirit Falls.

40 | Ware River and East Branch Ware River

These three sections of the Ware River offer varied paddling opportunities, with lots of wildlife. We've seen beaver, muskrat, coyote, mink, deer, great horned owl, great blue heron, bittern, ducks, geese, turtles, and lots more.

Location: Barre and Rutland, MA
Maps: *Massachusetts Atlas & Gazetteer,* Map 37: D27, 28, E24, 25, F22, 23, G22, 23; USGS Barre, Sterling
Length: East Branch, North Rutland, 2.0 miles one way; East Branch, upstream from Barre Falls Dam, 2.3 miles one way; Ware River, downstream from Barre Falls Dam, 3.0 miles one way
Time: about 3 hours for each section, round-trip
Habitat Type: marshy, slow-flowing rivers
Fish: brook, brown, and rainbow trout (see fish advisory, Appendix A)
Camping: Willard Brook State Forest, Pearl Hill State Park, Lake Denison State Recreation Area, Otter River State Forest, Tully Lake
Take Note: minor development on East Branch, North Rutland; no development on other sections; no motors

GETTING THERE

East Branch, North Rutland (42° 26.274′ N, 71° 58.257′ W). From Route 2, Exit 22, go south on Route 68. From the junction of Routes 62 and 68, continue 1.4 miles (1.4 miles) on Route 68, and turn left on River Road. Go 0.6 mile (2.0 miles) to the unmarked access on the right, just before the Pout & Trout Campground.

East Branch, Upstream from Barre Falls Dam (42° 25.426′ N, 72° 1.428′ W). From the junction of Routes 62 and 68, go 2.2 miles (2.2 miles) west on Route 62 to the Barre Falls Dam access road on the left. Go 1.1 miles (3.3 miles) to the access at the picnic area parking lot, just after crossing the dam.

From the downstream access described below, turn left on Route 122, go 0.3 mile (0.3 mile), and turn left on Coldbrook Road. Go 3.0 miles (3.3 miles) to the picnic area parking lot.

Ware River, Downstream from Barre Falls Dam (42° 23.698′ N, 72° 3.038′ W). From the junction of Routes 32, 62, and 122 in Barre, go south on

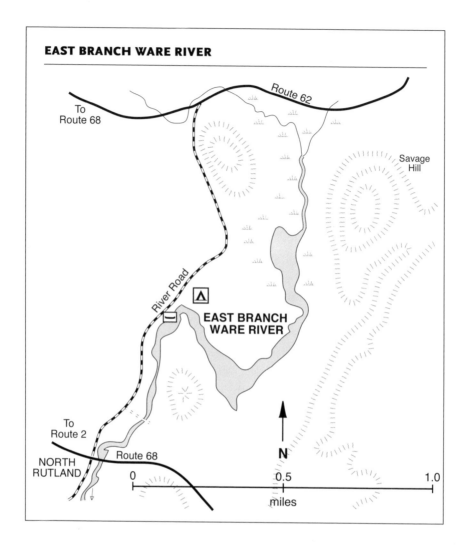

EAST BRANCH WARE RIVER

Routes 32 and 122 for 1.2 miles (1.2 miles) to the Y, and go left on Route 122. Go 3.2 miles (4.4 miles) to the access on the left, just before the bridge.

WHAT YOU'LL SEE

The Ware River presents several opportunities for quietwater paddling in areas where current allows travel in both directions. We include three nearby sections here, including one downstream of Barre Falls Dam on the Ware River and two upstream of the dam on the East Branch. We found these sections to be thick with wildlife, with very few other boaters in evidence. We cover them in order from upstream to downstream.

East Branch, North Rutland

From the access, you can paddle a short way downstream, through a few backyards, until you come to a small falls and a covered bridge. We enjoyed watching the phoebes and other birds that congregate just above the bridge, but the far more interesting section lies upstream from the access. You will encounter negligible current here as you work your away through extensive marshes, banks thick with grasses and shrubs. Red maple, white pine, and other trees line the faraway shoreline, which leads to scenic hillsides in the background.

Paddling here in the morning, you will see muskrats rooting up the ubiquitous pickerelweed; in the evening you should see beaver dragging branches for dam repair, to increase the size of their already huge lodges, or to store them, butt end stuck into the river bottom mud outside their lodges. You can paddle up beyond a series of beaver dams, but only the adventuresome will want to go very far—the streambed narrows and logjams occur with frequency.

We watched a large snapping turtle hanging lazily, fishing in the open channel, as dozens of yellow warblers sang from the streamside shrubbery. Painted turtles scrambled out onto logs to sun, as red-winged blackbirds squabbled over breeding territories. We found nesting Canada geese and mallards, and watched a red-tailed hawk circle overhead. Amazingly, we saw three bitterns, which usually stay well hidden.

A great horned owl casts a wary eye in our direction as we paddle by.

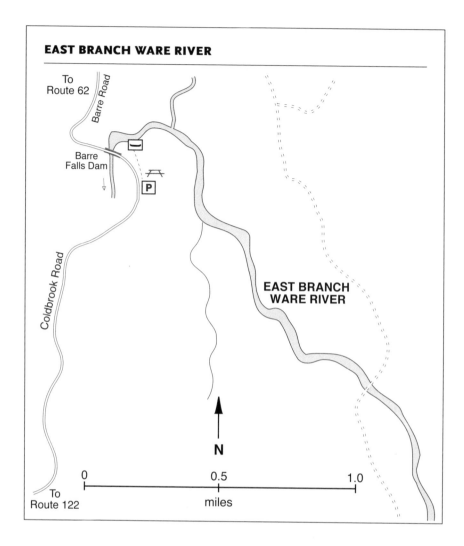

EAST BRANCH WARE RIVER

To Route 62

Barre Road

Barre Falls Dam

Coldbrook Road

P

EAST BRANCH WARE RIVER

N

To Route 122

| 0 | 0.5 | 1.0 |

miles

East Branch, Upstream from Barre Falls Dam

Do not attempt to paddle upstream from the dam unless you crave adventure. A 100-plus-yard carry down to the water from the picnic area awaits you; moreover, you have to carry back up when you may be tired from paddling. The river above the dam also can have a fair amount of current. Though we could paddle against it fairly easily, some tight, narrow turns presented a real challenge when the current pushed the bow away from our intended direction. After paddling slightly less than a mile upstream, we had to carry over a beaver dam, which gave us access to about another mile of river. By the time we finished paddling here, we knew that we had done some work.

A tiger swallowtail sips nectar from a streamside flower.

You undoubtedly will not have much company if you choose to paddle this wide, shrubby, treeless marsh. Expect to see the same marsh birds as on other sections. You will also see red and white pine plantations, sometimes red on one side and white on the other side of the river.

Ware River, Downstream from Barre Falls Dam

As we paddled through this wildlife paradise, a sphinx-type moth hover-fed on arrowwood flowers, and we studied iridescent green damselflies, tiger swallowtails, and several species of dragonflies. A great horned owl watched us warily from a streamside perch as we paddled by, and we watched a coyote burst forth from cover to chase a duck that had hidden in the pickerelweed along the shore. The Ware River also boasts the largest fish species diversity in central Massachusetts.

The pondweed and pickerelweed, with yellow pond-lily in protected coves, seem to withstand spring runoff, and we could paddle against the current, but we visited when the river was low enough that we often scraped our paddle blades on the bottom in the shallow areas. At times of high water, the current would make paddling here too much of a chore. The beaver that prune back the streamside alders burrow into the banks rather than build the typical lodge that would wash away in a flood.

WARE RIVER

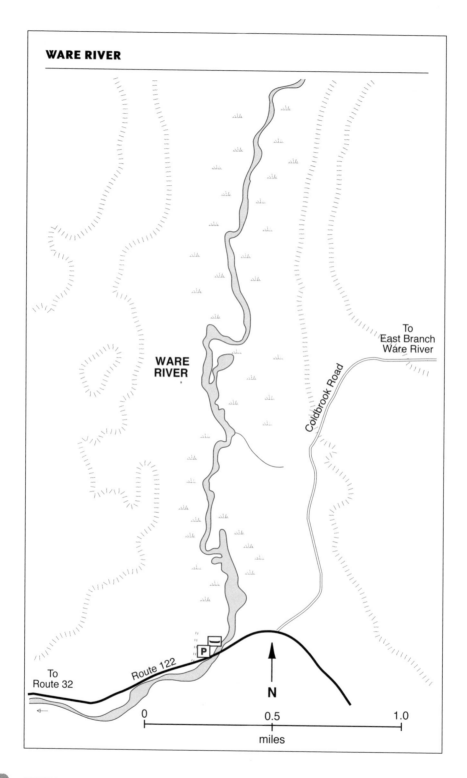

WARE
RIVER

To
East Branch
Ware River

Coldbrook Road

To
Route 32

Route 122

P

N

0   0.5   1.0

miles

OSPREY
FISH HAWK BACK FROM THE BRINK

The osprey, or fish hawk, lives near dozens of the lakes, ponds, and estuaries covered in this guide. Though we often see them on inland waterways perching or diving for fish, we see them in much larger numbers along the coast, where you may also observe them nesting.

The osprey, *Pandion haliaetus*, the sole species in the family Pandionidae, occurs on all continents except Antarctica. The bird, dark brown to almost black above and white below, soars with a characteristic M-like shape on a nearly 6-foot wingspread.

Osprey feed exclusively on fish. They soar or hover at a height of about 150 feet, using their keen eyesight to locate fish near the water's surface, then dive, crashing into the water feet first. There, they catch and grasp fish with their specially adapted feet, which have sharp, spiny projections.

They generally mate for life and return to the same nesting site each year. Males arrive first from the Gulf states or Latin American wintering grounds, followed a week later by the females. Returning males sometimes engage in a sky dance, repeatedly flying steeply up, hovering with tail fanned and talons extended, then diving down. This may be courtship behavior, a territorial display, or both.

Traditionally, osprey have nested in tall, dead trees, but more recently they have taken to hundreds of artificial nesting platforms that have been erected since the early 1970s in southern New England. The stick nest typically measures about 5 feet in diameter and 2 to 7 feet thick, depending on age. To collect sticks, the male uses an interesting technique: he alights near the end of a dead branch and breaks it off. The female collects most of the nest lining material (moss, bark, twigs, grass, and seaweed).

The female lays two or three eggs—whitish with reddish brown blotches—over a period of several days. The chicks hatch after a 34- to 40-day incubation period, during which the female does most of the sitting. Because the young hatch over several days, they vary in size. Though osprey often fledge two or three young, in a year of food shortages the larger chick will outcompete its smaller siblings and may be the sole survivor. The male osprey does virtually all the fishing during the incubation and nestling stage. Young osprey take to flight after seven or eight weeks, but they do not become fully independent for another month or two. After migrating south, the young spend two winters and the summer between in the wintering ground. Returning to the vicinity of their natal haunts the following year, they may pair up and begin nest building, but they do not breed until their third year.

The bald eagle, far less adept at fishing, often tries to steal an osprey's fish. We often spot gulls in hot pursuit as well. A far more significant enemy, however, has been humankind and its chemical warfare against insect pests.

We introduced the "miracle" insecticide DDT in 1947 and used it widely on coastal salt marshes to control mosquitoes. Over the years, DDT, an extremely long-lived chlorinated hydrocarbon, accumulated in the fatty tissue of animals. Small fish ate sprayed insects, larger fish ate smaller fish, and so on, gradually moving up the food chain to osprey. At each step, ingested DDT and its metabolites were stored in fatty tissue rather than excreted. At the top of the food chain, osprey ate many DDT-laced fish over a long lifespan and suffered from very high DDT concentrations. Those levels resulted in eggshell

thinning and, as a result, extremely high rates of nesting failure. Osprey populations plummeted. Along the Connecticut River delta, for example, the osprey population dropped from 200 nesting pairs in 1938 to 12 by 1965. By the end of the 1960s, the bird had nearly disappeared from the eastern United States. The realization that DDT caused this decline led to its ban in the early 1970s. Since that time, osprey populations have gradually recovered.

Though osprey seem to be thriving, they still face threats from dwindling habitat, high-speed boating, water pollution, and ever-increasing use of pesticides. Some evidence exists of increased competition from gulls since area landfills have closed. In addition to pesticide exposure in the US, osprey also ingest pesticides on their wintering quarters where we still apply environmentally dangerous chemicals such as DDT. With international efforts to eliminate use of such chemicals worldwide, and with better controls on water pollution here, we will be able to enjoy watching osprey hover over our waterways for many years to come.

41 | Lake Rohunta

Lake Rohunta's shallow waters harbor legions of aquatic plants, sometimes making paddling slow-going, especially on the southern reaches. Look for deer, osprey, ducks, geese, and other aquatic birds here. Blueberries grow in profusion is some places, and this is a great place to study trees, shrubs, and aquatic plants.

Location: Athol, New Salem, and Orange, MA
Maps: *Massachusetts Atlas & Gazetteer*, Map 24: L9, M9, N9; USGS Orange
Area: 383 acres
Time: 4 hours
Habitat Type: shallow pond, wooded shores
Fish: largemouth bass, yellow perch, pickerel, northern pike (see fish advisory, Appendix A)
Camping: Lake Denison State Recreation Area, Otter River State Forest, Tully Lake

LAKE ROHUNTA

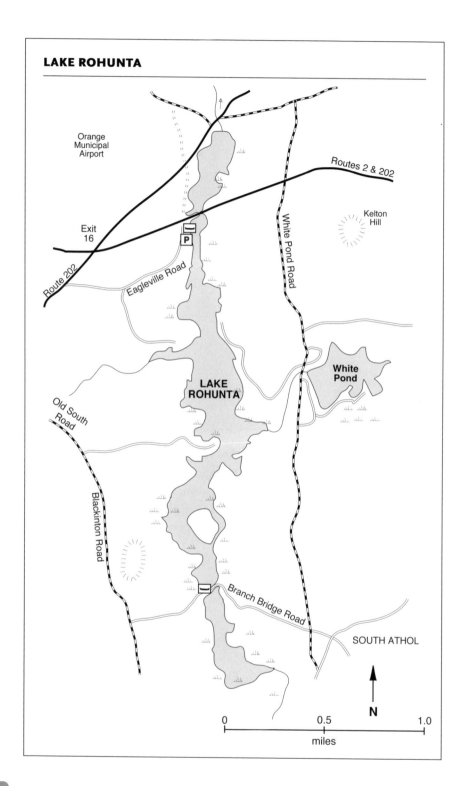

Orange Municipal Airport

Routes 2 & 202

Kelton Hill

White Pond Road

Exit 16

Route 202

Eagleville Road

LAKE ROHUNTA

White Pond

Old South Road

Blackinton Road

Branch Bridge Road

SOUTH ATHOL

N

0   0.5   1.0
miles

Take Note: shallow water and abundant aquatic vegetation limit motors; limited development

GETTING THERE

Northern Access (42° 33.65′ N, 72° 16.489′ W). From Route 2, Exit 16, go 0.2 mile (0.2 mile) south on Route 202, and turn left on Eagleville Road. Go 0.7 mile (0.9 mile) to the access

Southern Access (42° 32.09′ N, 72° 16.354′ W). From Route 2, Exit 16, go 1.0 mile (1.0 mile) south on Route 202, and turn left on Old South Road/ Blackinton Road. Go 1.5 miles (2.5 miles), and turn left on Branch Bridge Road. Go 0.4 mile (2.9 miles) to the access before the culvert. Note the very large solar photovoltaic array across from the turn to Old South Road.

WHAT YOU'LL SEE

Anyone who drives across central Massachusetts on Route 2 has probably wondered about Lake Rohunta. We had driven by it many times before taking the time to check it out thoroughly. From the highway, the main lake appears to extend north from Route 2, but far more water actually lies to the south. While some houses occur along the lake at its widest sections, few motorboats ply these shallow, weedy waters. The surrounding woods may entice you to spread out a picnic lunch—particularly on the east side of the lake north of Route 2. The quite open pine and hemlock woods harbor dense carpets of needles and acid-loving laurels and blueberry bushes along the shore.

Our first time here, we spent a wonderful half day paddling the north end of the lake and the southern section down as far as Branch Bridge Road (where a small culvert blocks passage to the lake's southernmost section), exploring the diverse aquatic vegetation, watching painted turtles bask in the sun, and gorging ourselves on plentiful blueberries in July's waning days. We paddled through acres of American white waterlily, yellow pond-lily, watershield, pickerelweed, pondweed, and two types of bladderworts, with buttonbush along the shores. In the most protected coves, the remains of trees killed during the lake's creation jutted above the water's surface. On the mossy tussocks around these stumps, we found two species of sundews, round-leaved and spatulate-leaved. On the upper side of their leaves, these tiny carnivorous plants sport sticky hairs that catch small insects. Enzymes in the leaves digest the insects to help nourish the plant.

The farther south you paddle, the shallower and weedier it gets. When we visited here in late April, an osprey fished the clear water as aquatic vegetation

Highbush blueberries, which ripen in late summer along Lake Rohunta's shores, can seriously slow down the paddling.

just began to emerge, and we paddled unfettered. But by midsummer, floating vegetation, which covers more than 90 percent of the water's surface, impedes paddling. Near the south end, we worked our way around a large, heavily wooded island. Though staying right presents an easier path, we found thicker stands of blueberry on the left.

While plowing through the pickerelweed and yellow pond-lilies requires some work, you may see some exciting wildlife. We saw black ducks, Canada geese, a pair of broad-winged hawks (which may nest on the island), and a few wood ducks flying to safety as we paddled near. Early in the morning, look for mink or even a river otter here.

Local historians believe that the name Rohunta comes from one Rodney Hunt, who operated a hydropower facility at the waterway's south end in the late 1800s. The area also has a bit of postcolonial history: in 1787 Daniel Shays led a straggling band of rebellious farmers along this way in retreat from Springfield. It marked the last desperate hurrah of "Shays' Rebellion," when farmers in western Massachusetts, suffering under post-Revolution economic depression, protested the imprisoning of debtors by occupying the Springfield courthouse—an action that alarmed even President Washington. The uprising was quickly quelled, and Shays, a reluctant leader, escaped to Vermont, where he was eventually pardoned.

42 | Muddy Brook and Hardwick Pond

Hardwick Pond and Muddy Brook offer a great place to paddle for intrepid explorers. Fully exploring Muddy Brook requires portaging over beaver dams, but it's worth the effort to reach pristine beaver meadows filled with wildlife.

Location: Hardwick, MA
Maps: *Massachusetts Atlas & Gazetteer*, Map 36: J11, 12, K11, L11; USGS North Brookfield
Area/Length: Hardwick Pond, 66 acres; Muddy Brook, 1.6 miles one way
Time: 3 hours round-trip
Habitat Type: reservoir and slow-flowing, marshy river through beaver swamp
Fish: rainbow trout, largemouth and calico bass, yellow perch, pickerel (see fish advisory, Appendix A)
Take Note: limited development and motors on Hardwick Pond only; no personal watercraft

GETTING THERE
From the North. From the junction of Routes 32 and 32A in Petersham, go 9.6 miles (9.6 miles) south on Route 32A, and turn right on Greenwich Road. Go 0.3 mile (9.9 miles), and turn left on Patrill Hollow Road. Go 3.2 miles (13.1 miles), and turn left on Greenwich Road. Go 1.2 miles (14.3 miles), and turn sharply left on Hardwick Pond Road. Go 0.3 mile (14.6 miles) to the access on the left (42° 18.011′ N, 72° 14.495′ W). (Note: In 2013, a bridge was out, eliminating this route.)

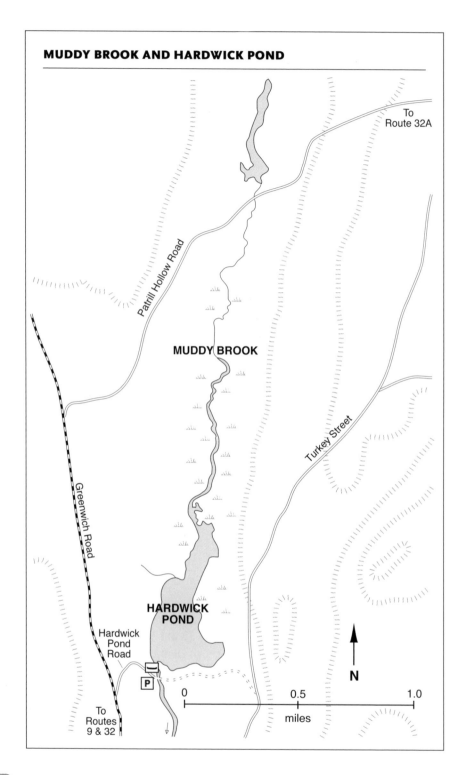

MUDDY BROOK AND HARDWICK POND

To
Route 32A

Patrill Hollow Road

MUDDY BROOK

Turkey Street

Greenwich Road

HARDWICK
POND

Hardwick
Pond
Road

P

To
Routes
9 & 32

N

0   0.5   1.0

miles

From the South. From Route 9 in Ware, go 1.3 miles (1.3 miles) north on North Street (traffic light), At the T, turn right on Greenwich Road. Go 2.4 miles (3.7 miles), and turn right on the second Hardwick Pond Road. Go 0.3 mile (4.0 miles) to the access on the left.

WHAT YOU'LL SEE

After exploring Hardwick Pond, paddle north up slow-flowing, picturesque Muddy Brook through a broad beaver marsh, a valley filled with shrubs and songbirds. Cardinals, catbirds, yellowthroats, and yellow warblers call from dense undergrowth, and scores of red-winged blackbirds sing from the marshes in early June. Shrubs line the banks and cover the islands and hummocks along the side channels of the marsh, with an occasional red maple sprouting up here and there.

At high water, you can paddle over drowned-out beaver dams, but you should be prepared to portage over some dams. One dam had a thick growth of swamp rose on and around it. Another had a beaver working on the dam at 4:15 in the afternoon. The beaver climbed off the dam, swam over to us, gave us the hairy eyeball, slapped its tail on the water, and dived for cover—strong evidence that the brook's upper reaches receive few visitors.

After we had paddled a mile or more up the brook, we came to a 5-foot-high beaver dam. We portaged through open woods around the right side of the dam onto a shrub-filled lagoon with standing dead trees, nesting wood ducks, great blue herons, snapping turtles, red-tailed hawks, and cedar waxwings. We also saw a relatively rare yellow-billed cuckoo here. We found the main channel above the lagoon with some difficulty and had to bushwhack through shrubs as we paddled and pulled ourselves along, noting the beauty of fern-clad banks. We spotted patches of royal, interrupted, cinnamon, and hay-scented fern. Though you can paddle up to Patrill Hollow Road, most of us will get tired of portaging over logjams and beaver dams and pulling our way through shrubs long before reaching the road.

From the pond, you can also paddle down the outlet a ways. You will undoubtedly have to lie down in your boat to make it under the bridge. Try not to disturb the phoebe nesting under there.

43 | Swift River

The outlet of the Quabbin Reservoir, Swift River provides a wildlife-filled paddling experience. Look for muskrat, beaver, deer, wild turkey, ducks and geese, and songbirds galore.

Location: Belchertown and Ware, MA
Maps: *Massachusetts Atlas & Gazetteer*, Map 36: N5, 6, O5, Map 48: A5, B5; USGS Palmer, Winsor Dam
Length: 4.5 miles one way
Time: 4 hours round-trip
Habitat Type: slow-flowing wooded river
Fish: brook, brown, and rainbow trout; smallmouth bass (see fish advisory, Appendix A)
Camping: Swift River lean-tos, Wells State Park, Tully Lake
Take Note: some development; shallow water and hand launch limit motors; no personal watercraft

GETTING THERE

From the junction of Routes 9 and 202 in Belchertown, go 3.8 miles (3.8 miles) east on Route 9, and turn right on East Street. Go 2.1 miles (5.9 miles), and turn left on Cold Spring Road. Go 0.1 mile (6.0 miles) to the access on the right, just before the bridge (42° 14.564′ N, 72° 20.112′ W).

WHAT YOU'LL SEE

Though clusters of houses impinge somewhat on the Swift River, most of the section included here has a very wild feel to it. Swift River's clear water, outlet for the mighty Quabbin Reservoir, meanders along slowly with a very modest low-flow volume mandated by law. Shallow water, masses of aquatic vegetation, and occasional downed trees and logjams limit motors. We watched muskrats harvest grasses and pickerelweed and saw evidence of beaver in the pruned-back streamside alders.

What we reveled in most, though, was the huge number of birds of many species. We saw wild turkey, tufted titmouse, grackle, blue jay, flicker, kingfisher, veery, eastern kingbird, eastern wood-pewee, red-winged blackbird, robin, catbird, cardinal, song sparrow, yellow-rumped warbler, yellowthroat, northern waterthrush, goldfinch, crow, mourning dove, and great blue heron. We also

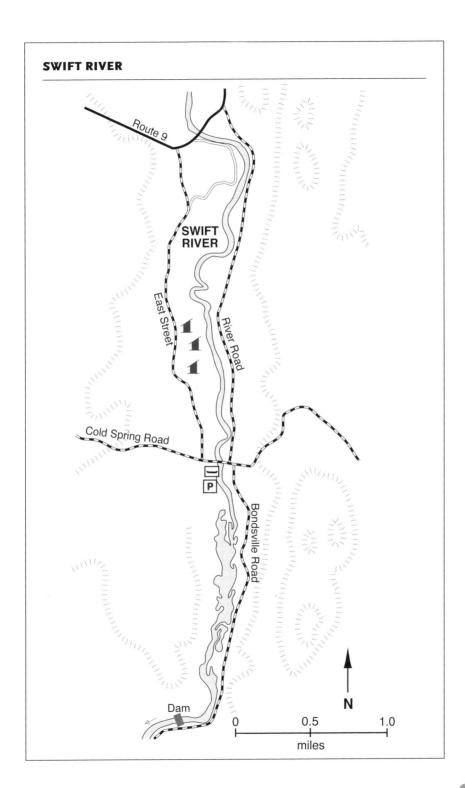

saw broods of mallards and Canada geese and treetop Baltimore orioles singing their melodious songs.

The river contains lots of aquatic vegetation, especially in late summer, which shows that high water rarely scours the channel. Pickerelweed, pondweed, and American white waterlily grow in profusion against the wooded shoreline. Downstream from the access in the section backed up by a dam, lots of inlets, islands, and coves beg to be explored. Upstream from the access, the Department of Fisheries and Wildlife maintains four lean-tos along the river within the Herman Covey Wildlife Management Area that you can use for free but must reserve in advance.

5 | WESTERN MASSACHUSETTS

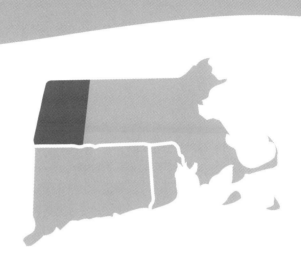

The eleven entries in Western Massachusetts offer varied paddling opportunities. One out-of-the-way pond—Upper Highland Lake—though small, is a recreation destination for paddling, camping, and hiking and a great place to bring kids to learn about the outdoors. Bog and Burnett ponds, lying within the Savoy Mountain State Forest, have much to offer, including the best locations in the state to look for moose, high elevation for cooler summer temperatures, and northern fen habitats, characteristic of northern New England.

We include both a 10-mile section of the Housatonic River and a 5-mile section of the East Branch Housatonic River for those who wish to paddle lengthy slow-flowing streams filled with wildlife. The East Branch requires portaging over numerous beaver dams; paddle here in the evening if you want to see beaver. One could also paddle tiny West Branch Farmington River through a beaver swamp, requiring beaver dam portages, giving a feel for what most small streams looked like in New England before European settlers arrived.

Mostly small ponds comprise the rest of the bodies of water. We're most intrigued by Thousand Acre Swamp and remote East Indies Pond, with its spectacular late June mountain laurel bloom from plants reaching as much as

20 feet high. Swampy Threemile Pond warrants a visit; although paddling its circumference takes little time, we have seen fabulous wildlife there, including osprey, broad-winged hawk, barred owl, wild turkey, and more.

Other ponds also occur at higher, and therefore cooler, elevations on the Berkshire Plateau. You can study many plant species at Upper Spectacle Pond and drink in the scenic hillsides surrounding Buckley-Dunton Lake, with the Appalachian Trail traversing nearby hillsides. Plainfield Pond also offers a scenic backdrop, along with rafts of little floatingheart, a relatively rare and delicate floating aquatic plant. At Littleville Lake, you may see beaver and deer in the evening, especially on the lake's north end.

44 | Bog Pond and Burnett Pond

These small mountain ponds are a great place to paddle when the surrounding valley floors suffer from summer heat. They lie within the Savoy Mountain State Forest, the best place to look for moose in Massachusetts.

Location: Savoy, MA
Maps: *Massachusetts Atlas & Gazetteer*, Map 21: G23, H23, I23; USGS Cheshire (Burnett Pond) and North Adams (Bog Pond)
Area: Bog Pond, 40 acres; Burnett Pond, 30 acres
Time: 1 hour for each pond
Habitat Type: swampy fen in state forest
Fish: largemouth bass, yellow perch, pickerel (see fish advisory, Appendix A)
Camping: Savoy Mountain State Forest, Clarksburg State Park, Mount Greylock State Reservation, Mohawk Trail State Forest
Take Note: no motors; no development

GETTING THERE
Bog Pond (42° 38.44′ N, 73° 1.991′ W). From the junction of Routes 2 and 8 in North Adams, go 4.4 miles (4.4 miles) east on Route 2, and turn right on Central Shaft Road, at the sign for Savoy State Forest. Go 5.8 miles (10.2 miles) south on Central Shaft Road (changes to Florida Road, then Burnett Road), following state forest signs, veering left on Burnett Road at the T. As Burnett

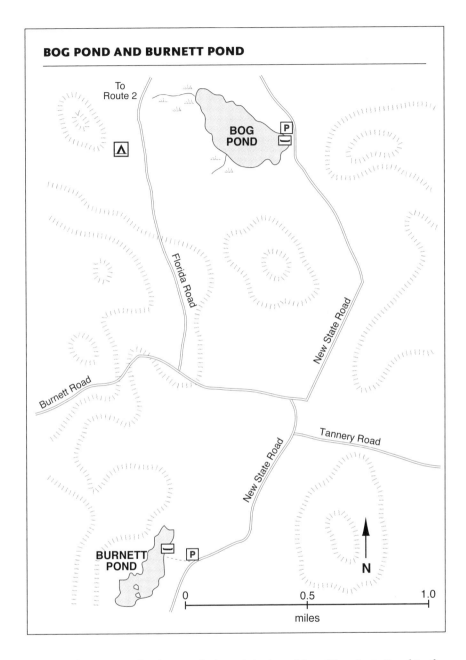

BOG POND AND BURNETT POND

Road ends, go 1.2 miles (11.4 miles) straight (north) on New State Road to the access on the left.

From the east from Whitcomb Summit, go 1.9 miles west on Route 2, turn left on Central Shaft Road, and follow directions as above.

A gorgeous, terrestrial, yellow-flowered bladderwort, *Utricularia cornuta*, bloomed in profusion when we paddled here in mid-July.

Burnett Pond (42° 37.003′ N, 73° 2.525′ W). From the junction of Burnett Road and New State Road, go 0.8 mile south on New State Road to the unmarked access on the right at a gate. Hike 100 yards down to the pond.

WHAT YOU'LL SEE

Savoy Mountain State Forest, one of the best places to see moose in Massachusetts, certainly warrants a visit, particularly during the heat of summer. Bog Pond, at an elevation of 1,858 feet, and nearby Burnett Pond are both nearly 1,300 feet higher than nearby valleys. Consequently, they can be several degrees cooler because of the so-called adiabatic lapse rate. The sun's heating of valley floors sends warm air masses skyward, expanding as they rise. Because the rising mass's heat content remains constant, as it does work expanding against adjacent air masses, it cools. Dry air masses cool at the rate of 5.4 degrees Fahrenheit per 1,000 feet, while more humid air masses cool at 3.6 degrees. So, depending on humidity, on sunny days the shores of Bog Pond should be between about 5 and 7 degrees cooler than the surrounding lowlands. In addition, cooling breezes often flow strongly across Bog Pond because no mountains lie to the west.

Bog Pond lies in a gorgeous setting, with lots of boggy islands to explore at your leisure. American white waterlily, watershield, and American eelgrass cover the water's surface, while hemlock, balsam fir, and red maple cover the shoreline. A large beaver lodge perches on a sphagnum-covered island, along with three carnivorous plants: purple pitcher plant, round-leaved sundew, and large patches of a beautiful terrestrial, yellow-flowered, horned bladderwort (*Utricularia cornuta*) that blooms in mid-July. The pond's shores—covered with ostrich fern, leatherleaf, sweetgale, sheep laurel, and several other shrubs—also provide habitat for a host of marsh birds, including yellowthroat, yellow warbler, cedar waxwing, song sparrow, black-capped chickadee, Canada goose, and great blue heron.

When we paddled here, beaver had dammed the spillway, raising the water level by more than a foot. Even with the added depth, this small, shallow pond demands that you paddle it slowly, savoring the marsh's plants and animals.

Nearby Burnett Pond, with its higher proportion of conifers, has a more northern boreal feel to it, perhaps explaining the frequent moose sightings there.

45 | Plainfield Pond

This pond perches high on the Berkshire Plateau, surrounded by gorgeous forests. This is a great place to study trees, shrubs, and aquatic plants. Large granite slabs on the pond's north end add a scenic quality.

Location: Plainfield, MA
Maps: *Massachusetts Atlas & Gazetteer*, Map 21: M28; USGS Ashfield
Area: 65 acres
Time: 2 hours
Habitat Type: shrubby wooded pond
Fish: largemouth bass, yellow perch, pickerel, northern pike (see fish advisory, Appendix A)
Camping: Savoy Mountain State Forest, Clarksburg State Park, Mount Greylock State Reservation, Mohawk Trail State Forest
Take Note: no motors; limited development

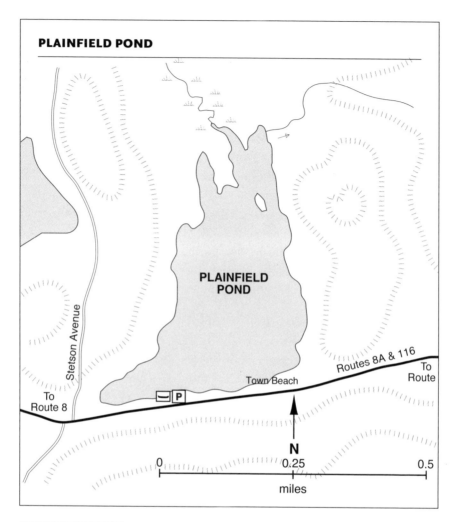

PLAINFIELD POND

PLAINFIELD POND

Stetson Avenue

Routes 8A & 116

To Route

Town Beach

P

To Route 8

N

0   0.25   0.5

miles

GETTING THERE

From Charlemont at the junction of Routes 2 and 8A, go 9.4 miles (9.4 miles) south on Route 8A, and turn right on Routes 8A/116. Go 0.9 mile (10.3 miles) to the access on the right, just past the town beach (42° 32.38′ N, 72° 57.522′ W). From Adams, go east on Route 116 to the junction with Route 8A south. Stay straight on Routes 8A/116, and go 4.9 miles to the access on the left.

From Pittsfield, go east—and from Northampton, go west—on Route 9, turn north on Route 8A, and go 9.3 miles to the access on the left.

WHAT YOU'LL SEE

At the access, very tame mallards with broods greeted us, a sure sign that residents using the town beach feed these birds. Massive quantities of little float-

Young mallards congregate near the access, a sure sign that people feed them.

ingheart (*Nymphoides cordata*), with tiny white flowers and heart-shaped leaves less than 2 inches across, also greeted us as we paddled out from the access. Rarely do we see these delicate aquatic plants growing in such profusion. Thick stands of shrubs layer the shoreline, with a profusion of highbush blueberry and mountain laurel, as well as lesser quantities of swamp azalea and arrowwood. When we paddled here in mid-July, arrowwood's umbel-like purple berries and blueberry's urnlike white flowers lent color to the shore, but we wished that we had visited earlier when the mountain laurel and swamp azalea bloomed.

Plainfield Pond perches high on the Berkshire plateau, surrounded by forests of spruce, paper birch, white pine, red maple, and hemlock. These trees populate some large, gorgeous, fractured granite slabs, some posing as islands, on the pond's north end. The pond's very clear water, harboring lots of freshwater mussels, gives way to yellow-brown water as you enter the marshes on the north end. Sweetgale, with lesser amounts of leatherleaf and swamp rose, lines the low banks, and beaver keep a channel open through the pickerelweed, watershield, a yellow-flowered bladderwort, and yellow pond-lily.

Beaver had gnawed away the bark of some hemlocks, killing them, a phenomenon that we have seen in several other locations. Apparently, if you run out of the good stuff, you kill off the bad stuff in the hope that more palatable species will replace them. Next time you see a dense stand of hemlock, take a good look at the understory. Few hardwoods—preferred beaver food—take root under hemlocks. This phenomenon is called negative allelopathy, where plants produce chemicals that inhibit seedling growth.

46 | Upper Highland Lake

Nestled in the Daughters of the American Revolution (DAR) State Forest, Upper Highland Lake is a recreation destination with camping, hiking, and paddling available. A beautiful stand of hemlock graces this site, but how long it can withstand the hemlock woolly adelgid onslaught is an open question.

Location: Goshen, MA
Maps: *Massachusetts Atlas & Gazetteer*, Map 34: C7, 8; USGS Goshen
Area: 56 acres
Time: 2 hours
Habitat Type: wooded pond
Fish: brook and rainbow trout, largemouth and smallmouth bass, yellow perch (see fish advisory, Appendix A)
Camping: DAR State Forest
Take Note: no internal combustion motors; limited development

GETTING THERE

From the South. From Northampton, go west on Route 9, turn right on Route 112, and go 0.7 mile (0.7 mile) north to the DAR State Forest entrance (Moore Hill Road) on the right. Go 0.4 mile (1.1 miles) to the access on the left (42° 27.441′ N, 72° 47.511′ W).

From the North. Go west from Greenfield or east from North Adams on Route 2, turn south on Route 112 in Shelburne Falls, and go 13.7 miles to the DAR State Forest entrance on the left. Go 0.4 mile (14.1 miles) to the access on the left.

WHAT YOU'LL SEE

Nestled within the DAR State Forest in the Berkshires, Upper Highland Lake offers a great getaway spot for a relaxed weekend of camping, paddling, and hiking. Groves of gorgeous hemlocks, with streams of light filtering through the canopy, await hikers on the many trails that traverse the 1,020-acre DAR State Forest. The 52 campsites, including some that are wheelchair accessible, fill up well before the weekend, so we recommend reservations. This small lake, with no development on it other than recreational facilities and Camp Holy Cross

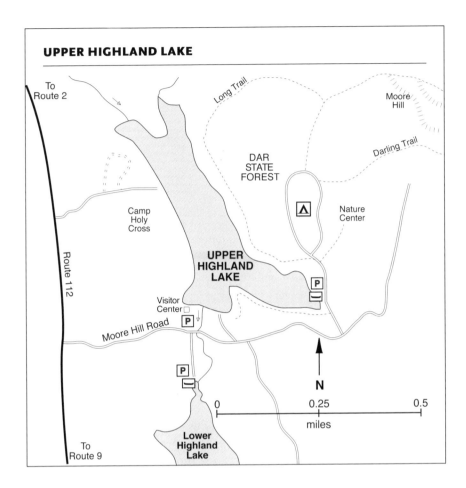

UPPER HIGHLAND LAKE

To Route 2

Long Trail

Moore Hill

Darling Trail

DAR STATE FOREST

Nature Center

Camp Holy Cross

Route 112

UPPER HIGHLAND LAKE

Visitor Center

Moore Hill Road

N

0   0.25   0.5

miles

Lower Highland Lake

To Route 9

near the northwest corner—a private youth camp—offers quiet paddling in scenic surroundings.

The shoreline vegetation consists primarily of deciduous trees—birch, maple, beech, and some oak—with many white pine and hemlock mixed in. The hemlock woolly adelgid, an Asian import that has gradually marched northward, threatens the eastern hemlock here and in the rest of New England. The hemlock may not go the way of the chestnut, as some success in controlling the adelgid has been achieved through two imported beetles from the Northwest and one from Japan. However, while the chestnut continues to sprout from stumps, once a hemlock dies, that's it, no stump sprouting. Time is running out, so a lot is riding on biological control of the adelgid. Robert Frost, the eminent New England poet, penned the following poem, "Dust of Snow," about the hemlock.

The way a crow
Shook down on me
The dust of snow
From a hemlock tree

Has given my heart
A change of mood
And saved some part
Of a day I had rued.

Highbush blueberry, mountain laurel, and other shrubs grow along the shore. An inlet and a cove extending to the northwest await exploration. A beaver lodge perches between the cove and inlet, which you might want to visit around dusk or dawn to look for beaver.

Just to the south and also largely within DAR State Forest lies the somewhat larger Lower Highland Lake. The state prohibits gasoline-powered motorboats here as well, but considerable development crowds the southern shores.

A ranger recalled finding a World War II photograph showing the boot-shaped Upper Highland Lake from the fire tower atop Moore Hill (on the east side of the lake and accessible by road or trails). Spotters used the tower, like others throughout southern New England in this uneasy time, to watch for war-planes. The photo shows a nearly bare summit with young growth of hemlock and pine, reminders that much of this area had once been cleared for raising sheep. Enlargement of the dams by the Civilian Conservation Corps increased the size of both lakes, turning these small reservoirs—used for powering silk mills at Goshen—into the lovely paddling lakes we find today.

47 | Littleville Lake

This is a great place for fishermen and for paddlers who don't mind weaving their way though a stump-filled reservoir. The wooded hillsides and scattered islands lend a scenic beauty. Look for great blue heron prowling the west-end marshes.

Location: Chester and Huntington, MA

Maps: *Massachusetts Atlas & Gazetteer*, Map 34: M2, N2, 3, O3; USGS Chester
Area: 275 acres
Time: 3 hours
Habitat Type: long, narrow, wooded reservoir
Fish: brook, brown, and rainbow trout; largemouth bass; yellow perch (see fish advisory, Appendix A)
Camping: Chester-Blandford State Forest, DAR State Forest
Take Note: no development; boats must be at least 12 feet long; motors allowed, 10 HP limit

GETTING THERE

Southern Access, from Northampton (42° 16.133′ N, 72° 52.798′ W). Go about 13.6 miles (13.6 miles) west on Route 66 (initially West Street), and turn left on Route 112. Go 2.2 miles (15.8 miles), and just after crossing the Westfield River, turn right on Littleville Road at the sign for Littleville Lake. Go 0.7 mile (16.5 miles), and veer right on Goss Hill Road. Go 0.7 mile (17.2 miles) to the access on the left.

Southern Access, from the South. At the junction of Routes 20 and 112 in Huntington, go 1.4 miles north on Route 112, and turn left just before crossing the Westfield River, at the sign for Littleville Lake. Follow directions as above.

Northern Access (42° 17.613′ N, 72° 53.975′ W). From the junction of Routes 20 and 112, go north on Route 112 for 0.1 mile (0.1 mile), and turn sharply left onto Basket Street (main road becomes Old Chester Road), just after crossing the bridge. Go 1.5 miles (1.6 miles), and turn right on Skyline Trail. Go 2.5 miles (4.1 miles), and turn right on East River Road. Go 2.0 miles (6.1 miles), turn right on Kinne Brook Road, and go 0.8 mile (6.9 miles) to the Dayville access.

WHAT YOU'LL SEE

Created in 1965 when the U.S. Army Corps of Engineers built a flood-control dam on the Middle Branch of the Westfield River to stem serious flooding that had occurred since the 1600s, Littleville Lake offers superb paddling, fishing, and picnicking in a scenic valley. To build the dam, a local fairground had to be relocated, but today's Littleville Fair continues to be a local high point in late summer. The lake doubles as a backup water supply for Springfield, about 30 miles downstream, but has yet to be drawn upon since its completion.

The wooded hills of the 1,567-acre area contain typical woodland tree species, including sugar and red maples, white ash, red oak, black and gray

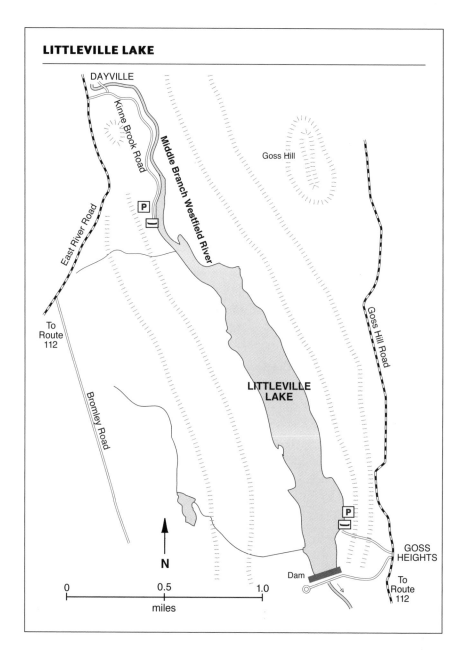

LITTLEVILLE LAKE

DAYVILLE

Kinne Brook Road

Middle Branch Westfield River

Goss Hill

East River Road

P

To Route 112

Goss Hill Road

Bromley Road

LITTLEVILLE LAKE

P

GOSS HEIGHTS

Dam

To Route 112

N

0   0.5   1.0

miles

birches, quaking aspen, white pine, ironwood, and sycamore. The rocky shore-line leads to fairly steep wooded banks. A few marshy areas occur at the north end, along with the inlet. Signs of an abandoned farm appear about two-thirds of the way up the lake: old apple trees, stone walls, and pastures growing up into woodland. We found beaver and other wildlife to be more plentiful near the north end. You can paddle up the crystal-clear inlet river a short distance, but it becomes shallow fairly quickly with a lot of exposed rocks.

Anglers ply these waters for largemouth bass, yellow perch, and rainbow trout. Paddling around early one evening with the light just right, we saw about a dozen foot-long bass lurking beneath the surface along the west shore.

Despite the general lack of inlets and coves to explore, Littleville Lake offers a pleasant morning or afternoon of paddling, with plenty of places to stop for a picnic. The Corps prohibits swimming, wading, and camping.

48 | Housatonic River

The Housatonic River is a deservedly popular place to paddle. It meanders through the eponymous valley, loaded with wildlife, backed to the east by the scenic October Mountain State Forest. Look for deer, otter, muskrat, beaver, herons and egrets, ducks and geese. We would not bring children here, for the reasons cited below.

Location: Lee, Lenox, Pittsfield, and Washington, MA
Maps: *Massachusetts Atlas & Gazetteer,* Map 32: E11, F11, G11, H11, I11, J11; USGS Pittsfield East
Length: 10 miles one way
Time: all day, shorter trips possible
Habitat Type: dammed-up meandering river, shrubby marshlands, forested hillsides, some farmland
Fish: the river holds 45 species of fish but cannot be eaten from this portion of the river because of PCB contamination (see fish advisory, Appendix A)
Information: PCBs, epa.gov/region1/ge/understandingpcbrisks.html
Camping: October Mountain State Forest, Beartown State Forest, Tolland State Forest, Pittsfield State Forest
Take Note: little development; electric motors allowed; we recommend that children not come in contact with the water because of huge PCB contamination

GETTING THERE

New Lenox Road (42° 23.62' N, 73° 14.539' W). From the junction of Route 7 and Route 20 west to Albany in Pittsfield, go 3.4 miles (3.4 miles) south on Route 7, and turn left on New Lenox Road. Go 1.4 miles (4.8 miles) to the John F. Decker canoe access on the right.

Lenox Station (42° 20.985' N, 73° 14.628' W). From the junction of East Street and New Lenox Road, go 2.9 miles (2.9 miles) south on East Street, and turn left on Housatonic Street. Go 0.9 mile (3.8 miles) to the access at the footbridge at the junction of Housatonic Street, Willow Creek Road, and Crystal Street.

WHAT YOU'LL SEE

This very popular canoeing and kayaking stream teems with paddlers on busy summer weekends, making wildlife viewing more difficult. We recommend paddling here in spring or fall or during the week in summer months. You can escape the crowds somewhat by paddling off into the numerous, very large oxbows, leaving behind the troops of paddlers intent on just making it down the river.

Though the current barely flows by midsummer, paddling here during spring high water may necessitate a one-way trip. At times of high water, you can paddle upstream from Lenox Station/Woods Pond; myriad bays and side channels sheltered by scenic hillsides beg to be explored. With limited time, we would paddle upstream from Lenox Station rather than downstream from New Lenox Road.

The relatively tame mallards that greeted us at the access did not seem to mind the paddlers, and we did manage to see abundant birdlife—the usual marshland species, including several broods of wood ducks. Though we did not paddle here in the evening, judging from the size and number of lodges, beaver must be a routine evening sight. While the Housatonic Valley Wildlife Management Area protects the river valley marshlands, the October Mountain State Forest protects the gorgeous forested hillsides to the east.

Except for farmland near New Lenox Road, trees cover the shoreline, arching out over the water and over the abundant, diverse shrubs and vines lining the shore. Silver maple dominates in some areas, its branches serving as launch pads for deerflies (a sight predator). We also saw willow, basswood, box elder, and many others. Thick patches of ostrich fern waved in the slight breeze, and wildflowers bloomed in profusion. As we listened to song sparrows calling from the underbrush and watched a phoebe bob its tail from a streamside perch, we understood why this is such a popular area. We had a hard time understanding,

HOUSATONIC RIVER

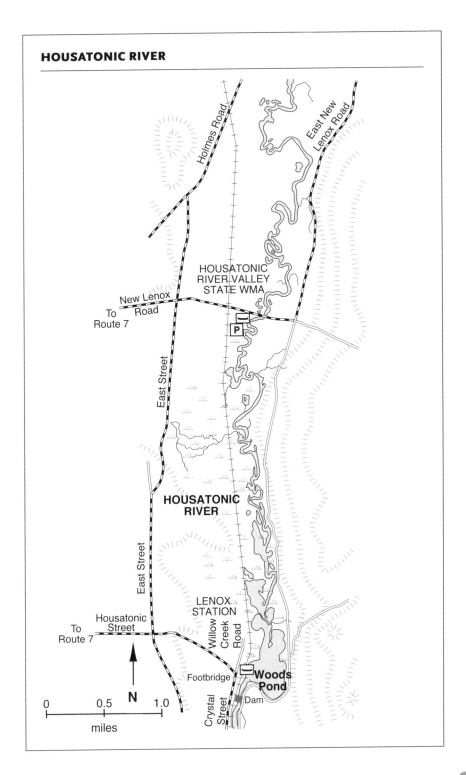

We saw many pairs of Canada geese raising their broods along the banks of the Housatonic River.

however, how so much trash could accumulate behind the numerous deadfalls; perhaps it had washed downstream from Pittsfield after heavy rains.

Paddling upstream from New Lenox Road, after about a mile you will reach several power lines and a complex of buildings on the right, a research station of the Electrical Power Research Institute (EPRI). Several years ago we visited this facility to talk with researchers about their work with electromagnetic fields (EMF) for an article that Alex was writing for his publication *Environmental Building News* on the effects of EMF on human health. EPRI had an entire house set up using different code-compliant wiring configurations to see how much EMF each produced.

Another electrical complex, however, was not so benign. For years, a General Electric (GE) plant making transformers dumped huge quantities of polychlorinated biphenyls (PCBs) into the Housatonic River. GE acknowledged dumping 20 tons into the river; the U.S. Environmental Protection Agency (EPA) says that it was between 50 and 300 tons. This is an astounding amount for a poison that acts lethally in animal species at parts per million concentrations. The highest concentrations are found in the river's sediments for the 10 miles of the river included here. Eating fish or waterfowl from this area is taboo, as is swimming. Here are the findings from a 1998 EPA report:

- Young children and teenagers playing in and near portions of the river face noncancer risks that are 200 times greater than EPA considers safe. Noncancer effects from PCBs may include liver and nervous system damage and development abnormalities, including lower IQs.
- Teenagers growing up near portions of the river face a 1 in 1,000 cancer risk due to exposure to contaminated riverbank soils.
- Fish collected in the river had PCB concentrations of up to 206 parts per million, among the highest levels ever found in the United States and 100 times higher than the limits set by the U.S. Food and Drug Administration.

Because it would take hundreds of years for the PCBs to degrade, the EPA is overseeing GE's clean-up of the river sediments.

49 | East Branch Housatonic River

The little-traveled East Branch Housatonic River meanders through an extensive series of wild beaver marshes. Look to the east to enjoy the scenic October Mountain State Forest. Look for deer, otter, muskrat, herons and egrets, ducks and geese. You should see beaver in the evening.

Location: Hinsdale, MA
Maps: *Massachusetts Atlas & Gazetteer*, Map 33: D18, E18, 19, F19, G19; USGS Peru
Length: 5 miles one way
Time: 5 hours, shorter trips possible
Habitat Type: meandering stream dammed by beaver, shrubby marshlands, forested hillsides
Fish: trout (see fish advisory, Appendix A)
Camping: October Mountain State Forest, Beartown State Forest, Tolland State Forest, Pittsfield State Forest
Take Note: no development; too shallow for motors

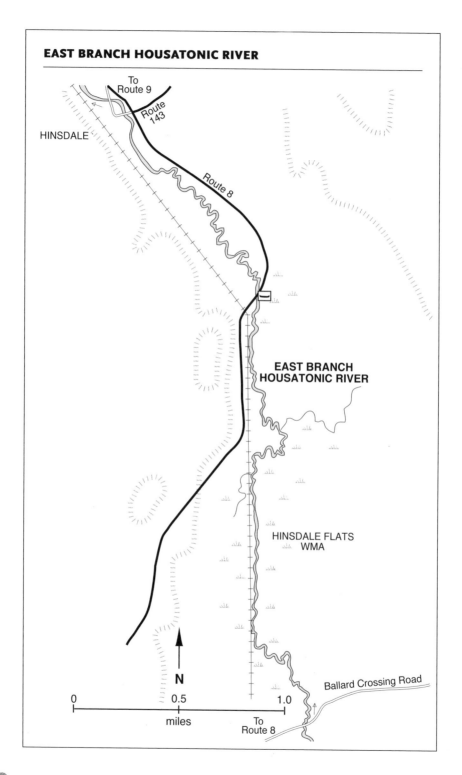

EAST BRANCH HOUSATONIC RIVER

To Route 9

Route 143

HINSDALE

Route 8

EAST BRANCH
HOUSATONIC RIVER

HINSDALE FLATS
WMA

N

Ballard Crossing Road

0   0.5   1.0

miles

To
Route 8

GETTING THERE

From Pittsfield, go east on Route 9 and Route 8 when it joins Route 9. When the roads split, go south on Route 8. From the junction with Route 143, go 1.0 mile south on Route 8 to the access on the left, just before the bridge (42° 25.59′ N, 73° 6.715′ W).

WHAT YOU'LL SEE

In contrast with the Housatonic River, few venture onto the East Branch, which intrepid explorers who don't mind getting in and out of their boats would love. When we paddled upstream (south) from the access in early June, we had to portage over thirteen beaver dams to get to the upper meadow just south of Ballard Crossing Road. We recommend that you paddle here in shorter boats and only when high water has drowned out at least some of the beaver dams.

A railroad embankment parallels the East Branch for more than a third of the distance covered here, reducing its scenic value to paddlers, although the entire area falls within the confines of the Hinsdale Flats Wildlife Management Area. We found the area alive with wildlife, particularly in the evening when beaver become active. We saw lots of waterfowl and all the usual marsh birds, including kingbirds on the nest; beaver, muskrats, painted and snapping turtles, mussels, and crayfish; and many species of shrubs and aquatic plants. We particularly enjoyed the broad expanse of meadow with a meandering stream just north of Ballard Crossing Road.

The stretch between the access and Hinsdale offers no respite from beaver dams. We have to admit that we tired of beaver-dam portages—we had just done thirteen up and thirteen back!—and did not have the patience to paddle and portage all the way to Hinsdale.

---

50 | Buckley Dunton Lake

Buckley Dunton Lake, because of its higher elevation, is a good place to paddle when the lowlands get hot. Surrounding Berkshire hillsides lend a scenic quality, with high tree-species diversity. Mountain laurel blooms in profusion in June, and large patches of blueberry ripen in August.

Location: Becket, MA

Maps: *Massachusetts Atlas & Gazetteer*, Map 33: K17, L17, 18;
USGS East Lee
Area: 195 acres
Time: 3 hours
Habitat Type: wooded reservoir
Fish: largemouth bass, pickerel (see fish advisory, Appendix A)
Camping: October Mountain State Forest, Beartown State Forest, Tolland
State Forest, Pittsfield State Forest
Take Note: barely submerged stumps, rocks, and poor access limit motors;
limited development

GETTING THERE

From I-90, Exit 2, go 4.0 miles (4.0 miles) east on Route 20, and turn left on
Becket Road (becomes Tyne Road as it ascends Becket Mountain and crosses
the Appalachian Trail). Go 1.9 miles (5.9 miles), and veer left on Yokum Road
as Tyne Road goes right. Go 0.6 mile (6.5 miles), and turn left at the hidden
access road, just before a garage (the turn is across from Leonhardt Road). Go
0.4 mile (6.9 miles) to the put-in (42° 18.335' N, 73° 7.723' W).

WHAT YOU'LL SEE

Buckley Dunton Lake nestles amid the Berkshires in the southeast corner of
October Mountain State Forest, Massachusetts's largest tract of publicly owned
land, which includes a 9-mile Appalachian Trail segment that passes over
nearby scenic peaks. The damming of Yokum Brook in the 1800s to provide
power for downstream mills created the lake.

Trees and shrubs typical of the moderately high Berkshire mountains dot
the lake's heavily wooded shoreline, including hemlock, white pine, spruce, red
and sugar maples, black cherry, ash, gray and yellow birches, and alder. Look for
large patches of mountain laurel in bloom in late June and blueberries in fruit
in late July or August. Large boulders that jut out into the water invite picnic
stops, but thick vegetation makes most of the shoreline quite impenetrable.

Rotting logs and tree stumps in the shallow, marshy north end force you to
meander along carefully. Yellow pond-lily, American white waterlily, pondweed,
blue flag, and cattail grow here. Also, look carefully for diminutive carnivorous
sundews on mossy hillocks. Listen for bullfrogs in spring, and in the evening or
early morning you may see the lake's resident beaver. We also saw ruffed grouse
here. On nice weekends you may see and hear heavy use of trails by off-road
vehicles and see a fair number of people out fishing on the lake.

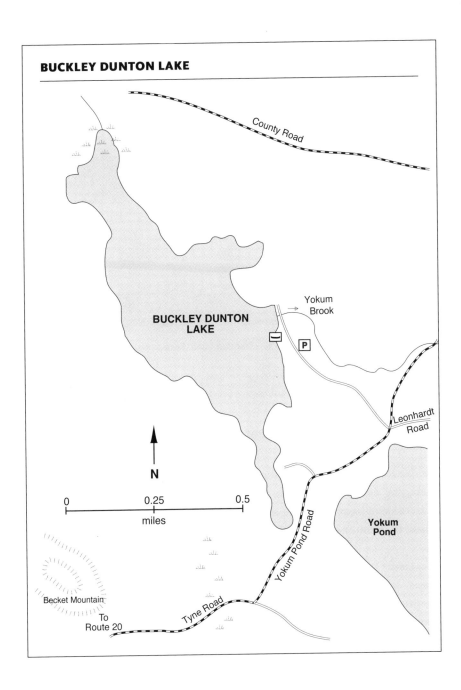

BUCKLEY DUNTON LAKE

County Road

BUCKLEY DUNTON
LAKE

Yokum
Brook

P

Leonhardt
Road

N

| 0 | 0.25 | 0.5 |

miles

Yokum Pond Road

Yokum
Pond

Becket Mountain

To
Route 20

Tyne Road

The heavily wooded hillsides of October Mountain State Forest surround Buckley Dunton Lake.

51 | West Branch Farmington River

The West Branch is a great place to explore if you don't mind portaging over beaver dams. This small stream meanders through an extensive beaver marsh; most New England streams undoubtedly would look much like this if beaver were allowed unfettered access.

Location: Otis, MA
Maps: *Massachusetts Atlas & Gazetteer*, Map 45: B19, C19; USGS Otis
Length: 1.3 miles one way
Time: 3 hours round-trip
Habitat Type: meandering, slow-flowing stream through broad beaver marsh
Fish: trout (see fish advisory, Appendix A)
Camping: Tolland State Forest, Beartown State Forest, Granville State Forest, October Mountain State Forest, Chester-Blanford State Forest
Take Note: no motors; no development

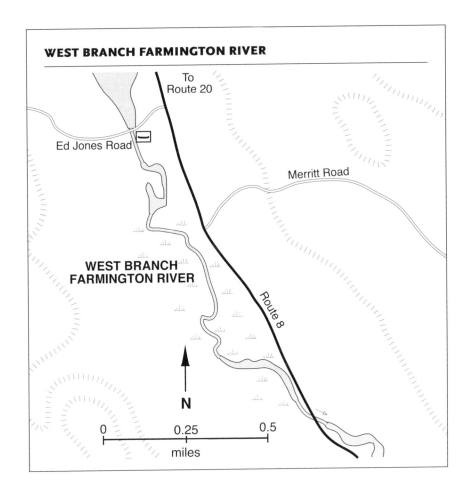

WEST BRANCH FARMINGTON RIVER

To Route 20

Ed Jones Road

Merritt Road

WEST BRANCH FARMINGTON RIVER

Route 8

N

0   0.25   0.5

miles

GETTING THERE

From I-90, Exit 2, go 6.9 miles (6.9 miles) east on Route 20, and turn right on Route 8. Go 2.8 miles (9.7 miles), and turn right on Ed Jones Road, just after the chicken farm. Go 0.2 mile (9.9 miles) to the access on the left, just before the bridge (42° 13.782′ N, 73° 6.678′ W).

WHAT YOU'LL SEE

This stretch of the West Branch Farmington River downstream from Ed Jones Road represents what most small streams must have looked like before our ancestors wiped out the beaver in the Northeast in the 1800s. From releases of a few animals in the early 1900s, beaver have reclaimed much of their original habitat. We love paddling through this broad beaver marsh, but paddle here only if you don't mind portaging over beaver dams. When we visited in early

We startled a great blue heron that took flight.

June, high water allowed us to paddle over several drowned-out dams, but we still had portages, one over a dam at least 3 feet high. We paddled by a huge beaver lodge with many succulent branches stored underwater for winter food; on the backside, a large northern water snake sunned itself.

Few trees, other than a few red maples, grow in this marsh because of raised water levels behind the beaver dams. Shrubs and ferns grow in profusion, with high species diversity, including royal and marsh ferns, sweetgale, alders, and swamp azalea in bloom in early June. In the water, look for yellow pond-lily and pickerelweed throughout and clumps of arrowhead and streaming leaves of American eelgrass in the lower reaches.

BEAVER
WETLANDS ENGINEER

The beaver, *Castor canadensis*, is one of the most remarkable animals found in New England's waters. Unlike most other animals, beaver actively modify their environment. The sole representative of the family Castoridae, this 30- to 100-pound rodent—largest in North America—descends directly from a bear-sized ancestor that lived a million years ago.

Quietwater paddlers frequently see beaver dams and lodges, especially on more remote lakes and ponds. This industrious mammal uses branches pruned from streamside trees or downed timber to construct dams and lodges. Beaver now work mostly under cover of darkness, especially in areas heavily frequented by humans. In more remote, wild areas, however, many beaver work away in broad daylight. We mention in our descriptions where we have seen beaver abroad during the day.

Beaver build dams to raise water levels, providing the resident colony with access to trees growing farther away. The deeper water also allows beaver to cache branches underwater for later retrieval, even when thick layers of ice cover their winter stores. They also dig small canals through marsh and meadow to transport branches from distant trees. Just as we find paddling easier than carrying a boat, beaver prefer swimming with a branch—taking advantage of water's buoyancy—to carrying it overland. They usually prune off leafy twigs to reduce drag.

Studies show that the sound of flowing water guides beaver in their dam building—they jam sticks into the dam where they hear the gurgle of water. In one experiment, researchers played a tape of gurgling water; beaver responded by jamming sticks into locations that emanated sound, even though no water actually flowed there. Beaver dams can be more than 10 feet high and hundreds of feet long. The largest dam ever recorded, near the present town of Berlin, New Hampshire, spanned 4,000 feet and created a lake with 40 lodges!

Beaver dams benefit many species, providing important habitat for waterfowl, fish, moose, muskrat, and other animals. Plus, the dams provide flood control, minimize erosion along streambanks, increase aquifer recharge, and improve water quality, both by allowing silt to settle out and by providing biological filtration through aquatic plants. We credit beaver with creating much of America's best farmland by damming watercourses, thus allowing nutrient-rich silt to accumulate over many years. As the ponds fill in, meadows form.

The beaver lodge includes an underwater entrance and usually two platforms: a main floor about 4 inches above the water level and a sleeping shelf another 2 inches higher. Beaver may construct the lodge in a pond's center but more commonly site it on the edge. Before the onset of winter, beaver cover much of the lodge with mud, which they carry on their broad tails while swimming. The mud freezes to provide an almost impenetrable fortress. The river otter—the only predator that can get in—can swim through the underwater entrance. Beaver leave the peak more permeable for ventilation.

Near the lodge, in deep water, beaver store up a winter's worth of branches in an underwater food cache. They jam branches butt-first into the mud to keep them under the ice and then swim out under the ice to bring back branches to eat.

The beaver has adapted remarkably well to its aquatic lifestyle. It has two layers of fur: long silky guard hairs and a dense woolly underfur. By regularly grooming this fur with a special comblike split toenail and keeping it oiled, the beaver ensures that water seldom totally wets its skin. Special valves keep the beaver's nose and ears shut underwater, and special skin folds in the mouth enable it to gnaw underwater and carry branches in its teeth without getting water down its throat. Back feet have fully webbed toes to provide propulsion underwater, and the tail provides rudder control, helping the beaver swim in a straight line when dragging a large branch. Both the respiratory and circulatory systems have adapted to underwater swimming, enabling a beaver to stay underwater for up to 15 minutes. Finally, as with other rodents, its teeth grow constantly and remain sharp through use.

Beaver generally mate for life and maintain an extended family structure. Young stay with their parents for two years, so both yearlings and the current year's kits live with the parents in the lodge. Females usually bear two—sometimes three—kits between April and June. Born fully furred with eyes open, they can walk and swim almost immediately, although they rarely leave the lodge until at least a month of age. Yearlings and both parents bring food to the kits, as well as help with dam and lodge construction.

The demand for beaver pelts, more than any other factor, prompted the early European exploration of North America. Trappers nearly exterminated the beaver by the late 1800s, but last-minute legislative protection in the 1890s

saved it from extinction. Trappers extirpated them in Connecticut in the mid-1800s, and the state began reintroducing them in 1914 as part of a restocking program. Then began what certainly must be the most successful endangered species reintroduction program ever. By 1955, beaver had repopulated the entire state.

As you paddle the shoreline of lakes or quiet rivers, keep an eye out for telltale beaver signs, including gnaw marks on trees, distinctive conical stumps of cut trees, canals leading off into the marsh, alder branches trimmed back along narrow passages, and well-worn paths leading away from the water's edge where beaver have dragged more distant branches to the water.

We see beaver most often in late evening or early morning. Paddle quietly toward a beaver lodge around dusk. Wait patiently, and you will likely see the animals emerge for evening feeding and perhaps construction work on a dam or lodge.

52 | Upper Spectacle Pond

This out-of-the-way mountain pond offers a short, pleasurable paddle between wooded hillsides. A stand of majestic hemlock and white pine greets you at the access. Expect to see Canada geese; this is also a great place to study aquatic vegetation. Mountain laurel puts on a spectacular display in June.

Location: Otis and Sandisfield, MA
Maps: *Massachusetts Atlas & Gazetteer*, Map 45: D18, E18; USGS Otis
Area: 72 acres
Time: 2 hours
Habitat Type: wooded, mountain pond
Fish: pickerel (see fish advisory, Appendix A)
Camping: Tolland State Forest, Beartown State Forest, Granville State Forest, Chester-Blanford State Forest
Take Note: hand-carry access limits motors; no development

GETTING THERE

From I-90, Exit 2, go 6.9 miles (6.9 miles) east on Route 20, and turn right on Route 8. Go 5.5 miles (12.4 miles), and turn right on Route 23. Go 3.4 miles (15.8 miles), and turn left on Cold Springs Road. Go 0.8 mile (16.6 miles), and veer left on unmarked dirt Webb Road. Go 1.0 mile (17.6 miles) to the access on the right fork (42° 10.632′ N, 73° 7.082′ W).

From Great Barrington, go east on Route 23 to Monterey. From the church, general store, and post office, go 3.7 miles, turn right on Cold Springs Road, and follow as above.

WHAT YOU'LL SEE

Passing through a deep hemlock woods, you end up at the access amid a noble stand of large hemlock and white pine. If the hemlock does not withstand the hemlock woolly adelgid onslaught, the area surrounding Spectacle Pond would be substantially diminished. (See Trip 46 for more information on the woolly adelgid.)

Although white pine occurs along the pond's shore, deciduous trees predominate here and on scenic hillsides, with mountain laurel the dominant shrub. The pond and its coves—including a beautiful island wooded with

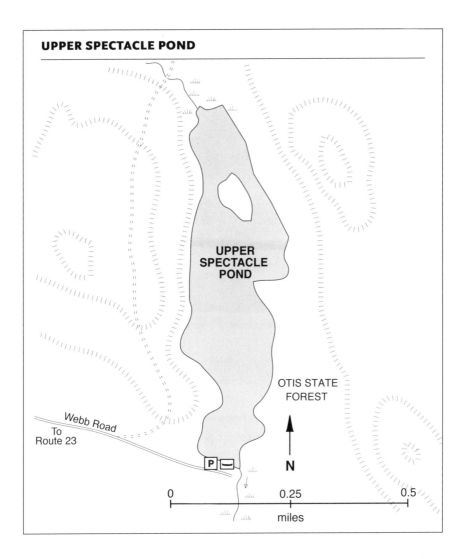

UPPER SPECTACLE POND

UPPER
SPECTACLE
POND

OTIS STATE
FOREST

N

Webb Road
To
Route 23

P

0   0.25   0.5
miles

oaks—require only an hour or two to explore fully. If geese haven't covered the granite slabs on the northeast with excrement, these slabs make an excellent picnic stop.

Water smartweed (*Polyganum amphibium*) and pondweed (*Potamogeton spp.*)—both featuring elongated, floating leaves and small, vertical puffs of flowers—grow in profusion side by side. They bear a superficial resemblance, but looking closely, note the leaf veination. Smartweed veins radiate out at roughly right angles to the midvein, whereas pondweed side veins start with the midvein at the stem and remain roughly parallel to the midvein all the way to the tip.

Water smartweed blooms abundantly on Upper Spectacle Pond.

Lots of a yellow-flowered and eastern purple bladderwort occur here, notable because invasive watermilfoil has not inundated this pond and crowded out native species yet. Gelatinous bryozoa colonies, also susceptible to crowding, occur on many submerged logs and branches along the shore. As we paddled along, an immature bald eagle soared overhead, possibly from the nest at nearby Colebrook Lake to the south.

53 | Threemile Pond

This remote pond generally provides good opportunities to see wildlife. We saw an osprey, wild turkeys, a broad-winged hawk, Canada geese, wood ducks, and heard a barred owl on our trips here. Look for beaver here in the evening.

Location: Sheffield, MA
Maps: *Massachusetts Atlas & Gazetteer*, Map 44: G7; USGS Sheffield
Area: 81 acres
Time: 2 hours

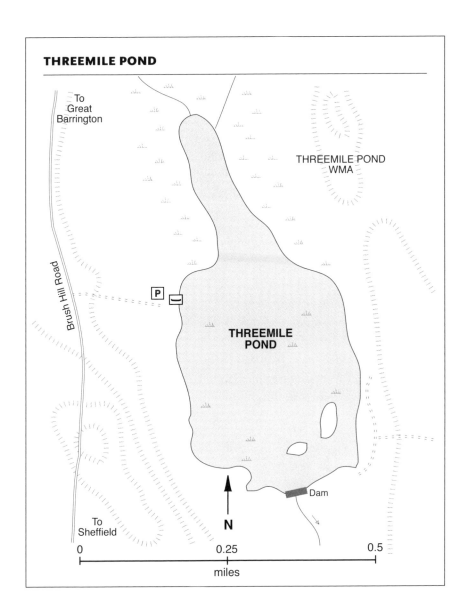

THREEMILE POND

To Great Barrington

THREEMILE POND WMA

Brush Hill Road

P

THREEMILE POND

Dam

To Sheffield

N

| 0 | 0.25 | 0.5 |

miles

Habitat Type: wooded pond, forested hillsides

Fish: largemouth bass, pickerel (see fish advisory, Appendix A)

Information: Threemile Pond Wildlife Management Area, mass.gov/eea/ docs/dfg/dfw/habitat/maps-wma/western/threemilepondwma.pdf

Camping: Beartown State Forest, Tolland State Forest, Granville State Forest, October Mountain State Forest

Take Note: too weedy and shallow for motors; limited development; most lies within Threemile Pond Wildlife Management Area

GETTING THERE

From Great Barrington. From the junction of Routes 7, 23, and 41, go 0.9 mile (0.9 mile) south on Route 7, and turn left on Brookside Road (becomes Brush Hill Road, then Home Road). Go 4.0 miles (4.9 miles), and turn left on a different Brush Hill Road. Go 1.1 miles (6.0 miles) to the access on the right; watch for ruts and mud (42° 8.785′ N, 73° 18.824′ W).

From Sheffield. From Route 7, go 1.6 miles (1.6 miles) east on Maple Avenue (which becomes County Road), and turn left on Home Road. Go 1.7 miles (3.3 miles), turn right on Brush Hill Road, and go 1.1 miles (4.4 miles) to the access on the right.

WHAT YOU'LL SEE

A broad-winged hawk soared overhead and dozens of tree swallows darted from their nest boxes as we worked our way carefully down the rutted road to the access in early May. Spring peepers beckoned to us while an osprey dived for fish. When we ventured onto the northern section of this shallow, weedy pond, wood ducks flew off into the marsh, and Canada geese paddled out of sight. On another May trip several years later, a flock of wild turkeys greeted us at the access while a barred owl called from the surrounding woods.

On a late June return trip, the osprey had vanished, no doubt because dense rafts of invasive watermilfoil clogged the waterway, leaving precious

A white-tailed skimmer, *Plathemis lydia*, soaks up the sun on a dead tree on Threemile Pond.

little open water. Though we had to slog through this sea of vegetation, we still enjoyed forging our way down to the large island off the southeast shore. Densely foliated, the island harbors quite a few tall, thin tamaracks—a tree that withstands saturated soil—along with sphagnum mats, pitcher plants, cranberries, and a large beaver lodge.

As we gazed back up the pond, with clumps of blooming mountain laurel here and there, we drank in the scenic beauty of unspoiled, undulating, deciduous tree-covered hillsides that harbor a section of the Appalachian Trail. A couple of cabins on the southeast shore and a low earthen dam on the south end provide the only evidence of civilization except, of course, for the invasive watermilfoil.

Returning to the access, we studied the several species of dragonflies that patrol the shallows and searched for frogs among the cattails. While you could paddle the entire perimeter of this pond in an hour, you could also linger, studying the myriad plants and wildlife in this picturesque spot.

54 | Thousand Acre Swamp and East Indies Pond

Thousand Acre Swamp offers a 1- to 2-hour leisurely paddle on a weed-filled pond surrounded by Cookson State Forest. While we enjoy the swamp, we much prefer the secluded East Indies Pond, especially in late June with its spectacular mountain laurel bloom. Look for beaver here in the evening, along with typical marsh species.

Location: New Marlborough, MA
Maps: *Massachusetts Atlas & Gazetteer*, Map 44: K13, 14, L13, 14; USGS South Sandisfield
Area: Thousand Acre Swamp, 155 acres; East Indies Pond, 69 acres
Time: 4 hours to paddle both ponds
Habitat Type: shallow, marshy, tree-lined ponds
Fish: largemouth bass, yellow perch, muskellunge (see fish advisory, Appendix A)
Camping: Beartown State Forest, Tolland State Forest, Granville State Forest
Take Note: few motors; no development

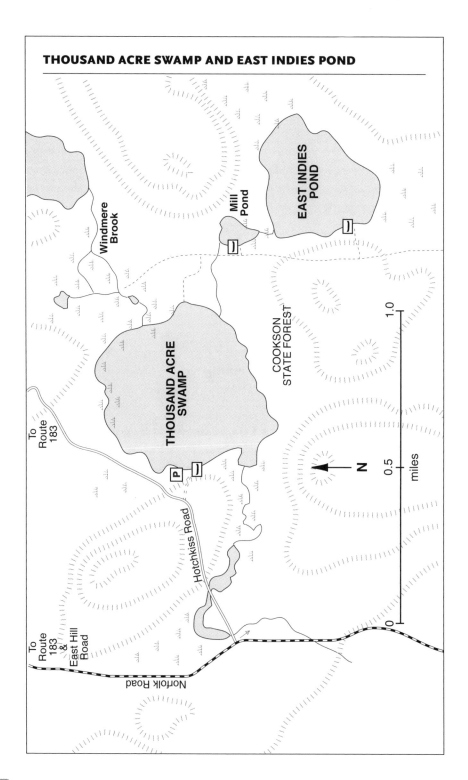

THOUSAND ACRE SWAMP AND EAST INDIES POND

EAST INDIES POND

Mill Pond

Windmere Brook

COOKSON STATE FOREST

THOUSAND ACRE SWAMP

To Route 183

Hotchkiss Road

To Route 183 & East Hill Road

Norfolk Road

N

0   0.5   1.0
miles

GETTING THERE

Thousand Acre Swamp (42° 4.222′ N, 73° 12.661′ W). From Great Barrington, go east on Routes 23 and 183; when they divide, go 5.7 miles (5.7 miles) on Routes 57 and 183, and turn right on New Marlborough–Southfield Road. Go 1.3 miles (7.0 miles), and turn left on Norfolk Road. Go 2.9 miles (9.9 miles), and turn left on Hotchkiss Road. Go 0.6 mile (10.5 miles) to the access on the right.

    East Indies Pond (42° 4.039′ N, 73° 11.792′ W). From the Thousand Acre Swamp access, paddle straight across the pond toward a grove of tall white pine, to the trailhead for East Indies Pond. The half-mile trail begins here. Go about 600 paces to a T, turn right, go about 160 paces (cross the outflow stream at about 60 paces), and turn left on an obvious trail (look for a large rock) that leads to Mill Pond. Go about 100 paces to Mill Pond. Alternatively, from the stream crossing, go about 1,000 paces, and take the left fork downhill for about 400 paces to a fire grate and East Indies Pond.

WHAT YOU'LL SEE

Thousand Acre Swamp

This out-of-the-way, scenic pond offers wonderful paddling within the borders of Campbell Falls State Park. Interestingly, Campbell Falls itself lies well outside the park, which has no development or conveniences. Although we enjoyed paddling through the abundant vegetation of this stump-filled pond, we noted luxuriant growths of invasive watermilfoil starting to crowd out the native watershield, American white waterlily, yellow pond-lily, and pondweed. While some mountain laurel bloomed along the southern shore, it paled in comparison to the growth at East Indies Pond.

    Mallard and Canada goose nest here, and if you visit in the evening, you may see some of the resident beaver as they work over the wooded shores. In the woodland during a mid-June visit, we watched a wild turkey hen herding her brood of six young. Though we did not paddle it, the outlet stream where it crosses Hotchkiss Road south of the pond looks like a wonderful area to explore. We found loads of mussels on the sandy bottom, and we watched a great blue heron—up to its nithers in yellow pond-lily—hunting fish and frogs. In early summer you may notice shallow depressions in the pond's sandy bottom, where calico bass keep their eggs aerated and protected from predators. You can paddle back into Windmere Brook about 150 feet, past a large beaver lodge to a beaver dam 3 feet high.

The northwest entrance to East Indies Pond is secluded and marshy.

East Indies Pond

Launch your boat on East Indies Pond only if you crave adventure. Branches hang low over the trails, making portaging a challenge. A wheeled portaging cart would help. After reaching the access on Mill Pond, you have to portage over some swampy beaver dams to get to East Indies Pond.

We were not prepared for what greeted us upon reaching the pond in late June—probably the most spectacular mountain laurel bloom we had ever seen. Mountain laurel, with stems reaching 15 to 20 feet tall, all in electric bloom, formed dense stands along much of the shoreline. Cruising the shoreline in this gorgeous setting, we hardly noticed the little floatingheart, American eelgrass, pondweed, waterlilies, or the complete lack of invasive watermilfoil. We expect that you would see beaver here in the evening, judging by the size of the lodges on the two ponds. A few clearings along the west shore looked pretty enticing, as did some large granite boulders—perfect for an afternoon rest or picnic.

6 | RHODE ISLAND

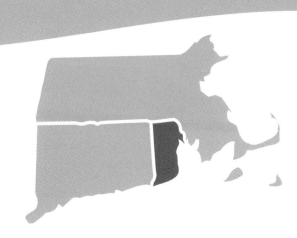

Rhode Island, although our smallest state—30 Rhode Islands would fit within Maine's borders—offers truly spectacular paddling, and lots of it. It's known for its rivers that, although short in length, flow with relatively large volumes, mostly through unspoiled habitat. Wood River is the premier paddling destination. Expect to see large numbers of birds and other wildlife as the river meanders through marshes on its way to join the Great Swamp's Charles River as the major tributaries of the Pawcatuck River.

The placid, relatively untrammeled Big River flows north through a broad marsh rich with wildlife; look for deer, great blue heron, osprey, muskrat, and beaver. We include two very different branches of the Pawtuxet River. The exceptionally clear water of the North Branch flows out of Scituate Reservoir, water supply to 60 percent of Rhode Island's population; check out the bloom on the extensive stand of mountain laurel in the upper reaches. The South Branch flows through an urban area, but the river corridor, besides some road noise, remains relatively untouched. While here, you can use the 14-mile Washington Secondary Bike Trail.

Olney Pond is a beautiful little wooded pond just minutes from downtown Providence. Because of that proximity, hikers, joggers, and bicyclists abound, especially on weekends. You can expect to find beauty here but not solitude. Shallow Brickyard Pond is a bird-watching paradise; despite the urban environment and the pond's small size, you can see osprey fishing here.

Highly productive Belleville Pond produces good fishing and great water-fowl habitat. We've watched fishermen pull good-sized bass out of the pond. Small kettle Tucker Pond harbors an impressive stand of rosebay rhododen-dron, the largest member of the heath family. Because the pond has no major inlet, water level varies with rainfall.

Bowdish Reservoir sits on the site of an ancient bog whose substrate now floats on parts of the lake, adding a northern fen character. Its large campground makes it a recreation destination. Watchaug Pond is also a recreation destination, with camping at Burlingame State Park, hiking on trails of the Kimball Wildlife Refuge, and paddling on the pond and its outflow stream.

Ninigret Pond, Rhode Island's largest coastal pond, offers great opportunities for plant and wildlife viewing. Nineteen rare or endangered plant species inhabit the pond's shores and the Ninigret National Wildlife Refuge, and more than 250 bird species have been recorded there.

55 | Bowdish Reservoir

Bowdish Reservoir is a recreation destination, with camping, bicycling, hiking, and paddling available. The reservoir has some development and suffers from road noise, but an unusual plant assemblage graces some floating islands. Plants here include black spruce, Atlantic white cedar, leatherleaf, bog laurel, bog rosemary, and more.

Location: Glocester, RI
Maps: *Connecticut/Rhode Island Atlas & Gazetteer*, Map 64: H2, 3; USGS Thompson
Area: 226 acres
Time: 4 hours
Habitat Type: shallow reservoir
Fish: largemouth and calico bass, pickerel (see fish advisory, Appendix A)
Camping: George Washington Camping Area
Take Note: motors limited to 10 HP; limited development; use caution in wind

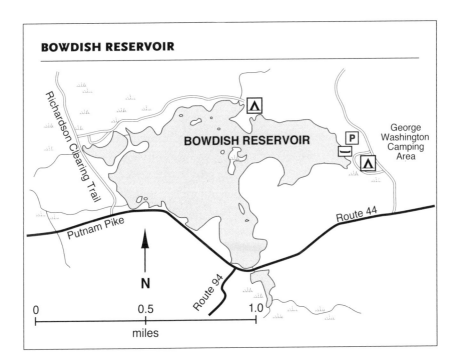

BOWDISH RESERVOIR

BOWDISH RESERVOIR

George
Washington
Camping
Area

Richardson Clearing Trail

Putnam Pike

Route 44

N

Route 94

0   0.5   1.0
miles

GETTING THERE

From the junction of Routes 44, 100, and 102 in Chepachet, go 4.4 miles (4.4 miles) west on Route 44, and turn right at the George Washington Camping Area. Go 0.3 mile (4.7 miles) to the third left, which leads to the access (41° 55.409′ N, 71° 45.508′ W).

WHAT YOU'LL SEE

A large bog stood at this site before Bowdish Reservoir flooded it out. Today a few floating sphagnum islands, the only remnants of the bog, appear near the reservoir's center. When the water level rose, these mats broke loose and floated to the surface. Tree roots anchor them in the reservoir's shallow waters. On these islands, look for rare bog plants usually seen much farther north, including black spruce (an extremely short-needled conifer), Atlantic white cedar, leatherleaf, bog laurel, bog rosemary, sundew, pitcher plant, and—rarest of all—a dwarf mistletoe that lacks roots and always grows in association with black spruce. These islands appear larger on older maps and may be disappearing.

Bowdish Reservoir does not exude wilderness, but it offers a great place to get some exercise in your boat or on foot or bicycle. The southwestern edge, bounded by heavily traveled Route 44, supports some development. Even at the far eastern end, by the George Washington Camping Area, you can still hear cars and trucks. A mammoth private campground that caters to RVs extends along most of the northern shore, although quite a bit of space extends between heavily wooded sites.

Huge slabs of granite extend down into the water in places, and the small, private island in the reservoir's southern extension appears to be mostly solid rock. The forested land of the George Washington Management Area along the reservoir's eastern end remains readily accessible to hikers and picnickers. Several very nice trails, accessible from the boat launch area, course through the surrounding oak-hemlock forests for several miles. Dominant species include hemlock; white, red, and scarlet oaks; black birch; white pine; and mountain laurel. At the water's edge you will also find lots of highbush blueberry and sweet pepperbush, which has very fragrant, late-blooming, white flower spikes.

The reservoir itself supports quite a bit of vegetation. Underwater plants include watermilfoil, Carolina fanwort, and bladderwort. Floating plants include watershield and yellow pond-lily. Though the abundant aquatic vegetation damps waves somewhat, in a strong wind large waves build up across the open water, so use caution paddling here.

56 | Olney Pond

Olney Pond is a beautiful little wooded pond just minutes from downtown Providence. Because of that proximity, hikers, joggers, and bicyclists abound, especially on weekends. You can expect to find beauty here but not solitude.

Location: Lincoln, RI
Maps: *Connecticut/Rhode Island Atlas & Gazetteer*, Map 65: J22, 23; USGS Pawtucket
Area: 120 acres
Time: 2 hours
Habitat Type: wooded pond
Fish: rainbow and brown trout, largemouth bass, pickerel (see fish advisory, Appendix A)

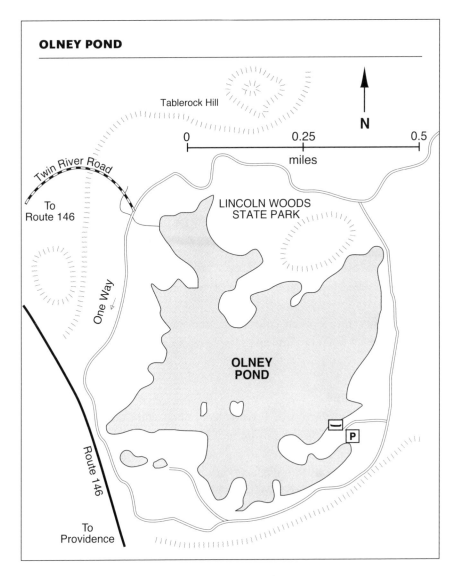

OLNEY POND

Tablerock Hill

N

0   0.25   0.5

miles

Twin River Road

To Route 146

LINCOLN WOODS STATE PARK

One Way

OLNEY POND

P

Route 146

To Providence

Information: Lincoln Woods State Park, riparks.com/Locations/
LocationLincolnWoods.html

Camping: George Washington Camping Area

Take Note: no motors weekends and holidays, otherwise 10 HP limit;
recreational development only

GETTING THERE

From Route 146, about 4.0 miles north of I-95, take the Twin River Road exit
for Lincoln Woods. Turn left at the end of the exit ramp, go 0.3 mile (0.3 mile),

Huge granite boulders lend scenic character to Olney Pond's shores.

and turn right at the stop sign, entering the one-way, 2.6-mile loop road around the pond. Go 1.4 miles (1.7 miles) to the access on the left (41° 53.364′ N, 71° 25.676′ W).

WHAT YOU'LL SEE

Just minutes from downtown Providence, Olney Pond offers surprisingly pleasant paddling. Gorgeous granite boulders—some striated with bands of quartz or blazoned with clusters of polypody fern—dot the heavily wooded shoreline. Only Lincoln Woods State Park recreational facilities occur along the pond—and herein lies the problem: Olney Pond abounds with recreational users on weekends and particularly nice days. Hikers, joggers, and bicyclists, many of whom come from nearby offices for a break during the day, fill the pond's perimeter road, removing any semblance of solitude.

Many sheltered coves beg to be explored, especially a particularly beautiful one at the pond's northern tip, where you must wend your way around huge boulders extending from the water. Red oak dominates the surrounding woods; other species include white oak, dogwood, white ash, hickory, and close to shore, red maple.

At a trail junction near the pond's northernmost cove, a marker describes the Zachariah Allen Woodlot, planted in 1820. About 0.3 mile from here, to the northwest on Quinsnicket Hill, Allen took ownership of a 40-acre worn-out pasture and planted acorns and chestnuts in an early silviculture experiment.

Today, more than 170 years later, a marker by an old spring describes this unusual businessman/botanist and his investment through planting acorns and chestnuts in plowed soil. Even before the area became a state park, city folk from nearby Providence visited the woodlot via steam cars to Lonsdale or "electrics" from Pawtucket. Wildflowers and ferns, including such uncommon species as maidenhair spleenwort and smooth yellow violet, fill the Quinsnicket Hill woods.

57 | Brickyard Pond

This small, shallow urban pond is a bird-watching paradise. Expect to see osprey, mute swan, Canada goose, wood duck, great blue heron, spotted sandpiper, catbird, cardinal, goldfinch, and more.

Location: Barrington, RI
Maps: *Connecticut/Rhode Island Atlas & Gazetteer*, Map 68: G10, 11, H10; USGS Bristol
Area: 102 acres
Time: 2 hours
Habitat Type: shallow wooded pond
Fish: rainbow and brown trout, largemouth bass, yellow perch, pickerel (see fish advisory, Appendix A)
Take Note: motors allowed; limited development

GETTING THERE
From I-195, Exit 7, in East Providence, go south on Route 114 to the first stoplight. Turn right on Federal Road, go 0.6 mile (0.6 mile), and turn left on Middle Highway. Go 1.0 mile (1.6 miles), and turn left on Legion Way. Go 0.2 mile (1.8 miles), and turn left to the access (41° 44.121′ N, 71° 19.153′ W).

WHAT YOU'LL SEE
Brickyard Pond, in an urban area that abounds with housing developments and a golf course, offers a surprisingly wild place to paddle. An abandoned railroad bed converted into a beautiful hiking and biking trail borders the northern shore, and a few houses dot the southern shore. But a wooded shoreline and

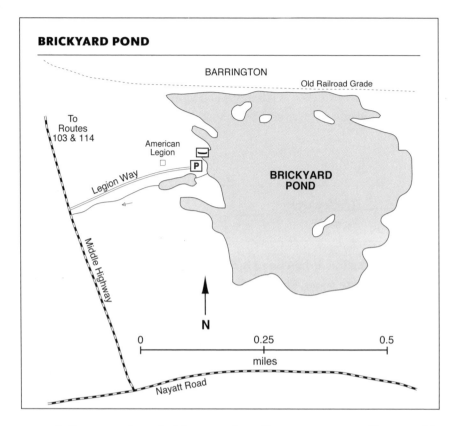

BRICKYARD POND

BARRINGTON

Old Railroad Grade

To Routes 103 & 114

American Legion

P

Legion Way

BRICKYARD POND

Middle Highway

N

0   0.25   0.5

miles

Nayatt Road

many shallow coves draped with grape arbors, Virginia creeper, and honeysuckle vines beg to be explored. Several islands provide more shoreline to investigate, making the pond seem much larger than its 102 acres.

Dozens of catbirds skulked among the dense grapevines and Virginia creeper in the fingerlike western coves, while goldfinches and gnatcatchers gleaned seeds and insects from shoreside vegetation. A downy woodpecker pulled apart heads of narrow-leaved cattail, probing for insects, while a diving osprey came up with a fish. Families of Canada geese fed in the shallows, two brightly colored male wood ducks took off in front of us, and we counted 23 mute swans. While beautiful, mute swans, introduced from Europe, aggressively compete with native species.

Four oak species—red, pin, white, and swamp white—grace the shoreline, along with willow, sassafras, cottonwood, red and Norway maples, gray birch, and alder. We saw many other bird and plant species here and could have spent several hours exploring. As a spotted sandpiper fled before us, we reveled in the rich number of species harbored by this urban wildlife paradise.

A downy woodpecker pecks apart a cattail, looking for insects.

58 | North Branch Pawtuxet River

The North Branch, with its exceptionally clear water, offers an exceptional paddling resource amid many interesting plant species. Extensive stands of mountain laurel, especially in the upper reaches, put on a glorious show, typically in mid-June.

Location: Scituate, RI
Maps: *Connecticut/Rhode Island Atlas & Gazetteer*, Map 67: G19, H20; USGS Crompton, Kent
Length: 5 miles round-trip
Time: 3 hours
Habitat Type: narrow, meandering river with shallow coves, thick with emergent vegetation
Fish: trout, smallmouth bass, pickerel, northern pike (see fish advisory, Appendix A)
Take Note: motors allowed; limited development; avoid dam at access

GETTING THERE
From I-95, Exit 16, or I-295, Exit 4, go west on Route 12 (from I-295, west on Route 14 to Comstock Parkway south to Route 12). From the junction of Routes 12 and 116, go 2.3 miles south on Route 116, and turn right on Hope Furnace Road. Go 200 feet, and turn right onto the access road (41° 43.865' N, 71° 33.923' W).

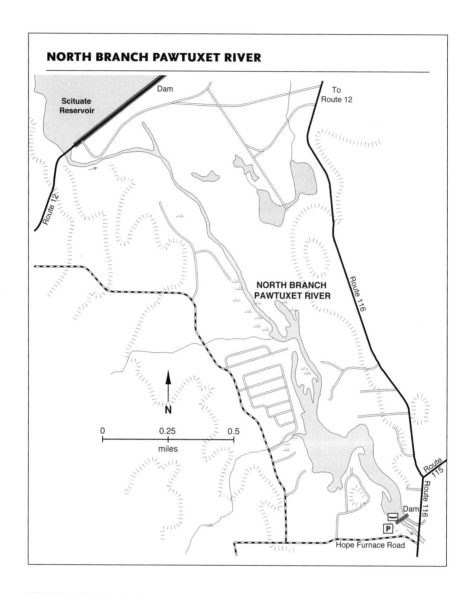

NORTH BRANCH PAWTUXET RIVER

Dam

Scituate
Reservoir

To
Route 12

Route 12

NORTH BRANCH
PAWTUXET RIVER

Route 116

N

0   0.25   0.5
miles

Route 115

Route 116

Dam

P

Hope Furnace Road

WHAT YOU'LL SEE

The North Branch Pawtuxet River is unlike any river we've paddled in Rhode Island in one major respect: it has extremely pure water. While most Rhode Island rivers suffer from heavy industrial pollution that began as far back as the 1700s, that's not the case here. The North Branch flows out of the Scituate Reservoir, the rigorously protected water supply for 60 percent of the state's population. Upper sections flow with exceptionally clear water that lacks any chemical smell. Some development occurs along the shore, particularly in the river's lower portions, but somehow it doesn't seem too intrusive.

You will see some relatively unusual vegetation along the river. Keep an eye out for sassafras (*Sassafras albidum*), with its varied leaf shape—some oval, some with a rounded lobe on left or right, and some with both lobes; crush a leaf to smell the characteristic sassafras odor. Look also for blackgum (*Nyssa sylvatica*), with its horizontally layered branch structure, swamp white oak (*Quercus bicolor*), American hornbeam or ironwood (*Carpinus caroliniana*), and red pine (*Pinus resinosa*), along with more common species, such as white pine, red maple, gray birch, alder, and red oak.

Shrubs along the winding shoreline are a highlight of this trip. Mountain laurel (*Kalmia latifolia*) grows prolifically, particularly in the upper reaches, making this a spectacular place to paddle during the laurel bloom—typically mid-June. Laurel has developed an unusual pollination scheme. Tiny sacs hold tightly the ten pollen-containing anthers of unopened buds. As the buds open, the elastic filaments connected to the anthers bend backward, developing tension. Then, when a bumblebee—the plant's main pollinator—lands on flowers, the anthers release, and the filaments spring them forward to slap the pollen load against the bee's underside. When the bee visits the next flower, its pollen load rubs against the stigma, causing pollination. This method nearly eliminates self-pollination. It would be interesting to see whether natural selection has favored bees that fly off to the next plant after visiting just one flower, maximizing out-crossing, helping to support genetic diversity.

When we paddled here later in the season, we saw lots of sweet pepperbush (*Clethra alnifolia*) in bloom, with its wonderfully sweet-smelling flower clusters. We also saw witch hazel (*Hamamelis virginiana*), a fall-blooming shrub whose seed pods mature in early August, getting ready to sling their seeds through a unique spring action as the seed pods open.

Extensive stands of yellow pond-lily and American white waterlily populate the shallow coves, accompanied by lesser amounts of little floatingheart (*Nymphoides cordata*), with small white flowers in early August, pondweed (*Potamogeton epihydrus*), yellow and purple bladderwort (*Utricularia spp.*), soft-stemmed bulrush (*Schoenoplectus tabernaemontani*, formerly *Scirpus validus*), and pickerelweed (*Pontederia cordata*). We spotted a single cardinal flower (*Lobelia cardinalis*) along the shore, with its brilliant red flower spike.

Farther north, the river narrows, the current becomes more rapid in places, and you have to dodge rocks. But the prodigious amount of mountain laurel here, along with the exceptionally clear water, make paddling the upper reaches worth the effort. Eventually you reach the looming dam of Scituate Reservoir and the fencing and No Trespassing signs that help to keep the North Branch's water so pure.

59 | South Branch Pawtuxet River

The South Branch flows gently for a mile and a half between dams in Coventry. Surprisingly little development impinges on the river. Explore marshy areas here, especially in the spring. While here, you can also take advantage of the 14-mile Washington Secondary Bike Trail.

Location: Coventry, RI
Maps: *Connecticut/Rhode Island Atlas & Gazetteer,* Map 67: J18, 19, 20, 21; USGS Crompton, Kent
Length: 3 miles round-trip
Time: 2 hours
Habitat Type: narrow, meandering river with extensive marsh areas
Fish: trout, smallmouth bass, pickerel, northern pike (see fish advisory, Appendix A)
Information: Washington Secondary Bike Path, dot.ri.gov/bikeri/wash_secondary_bike_path.asp
Take Note: motors allowed; limited development; avoid dam at access

GETTING THERE

From I-95, Exit 10, go 4.0 miles (4.0 miles) west on Route 117 (jog right, then left at 2.6 miles; turn left at 3.3 miles), and turn left on Laurel Avenue. Go 0.1 mile (4.1 miles), and turn right on Pilgrim Avenue. Go 150 feet, and turn right into the access (41° 41.678' N, 71° 32.853' W).

WHAT YOU'LL SEE

This section of the South Branch Pawtuxet River, which can be explored in a few hours, flows gently between a dam at Laurel Avenue and another at South Main Street. Massive Anthony Mill, built in 1872 and converted into apartments in 2013, lies at the lower terminus of this trip. Although large amounts of development extend in every direction, little of it impinges on the waterway. You will hear a fair amount of road noise, however.

By midsummer, Carolina fanwort (*Cabomba caroliniana*)—an aquatic plant native to the Southeast that has become invasive in the Northeast—grows thickly here, filling the water column with its lacy filaments. Like Eurasian watermilfoil, Carolina fanwort chokes waterways, as it is doing here.

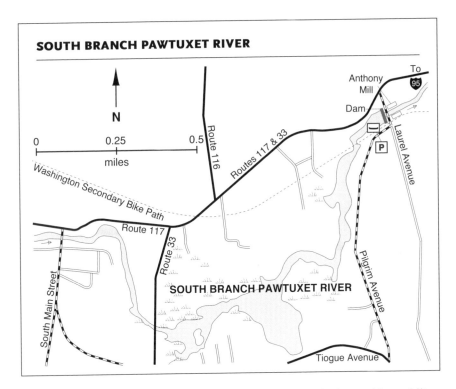

SOUTH BRANCH PAWTUXET RIVER

From the Pilgrim Avenue access, paddle to the left, fairly quickly paddling under a trestle carrying the well-maintained rail trail, known as the Washington Secondary Bike Path. The 14-mile trail, named for a Hartford, Providence & Fishkill Railroad spur, extends from Cranston to Central Coventry. The hope is that it will eventually extend 25 miles from the Connecticut state line nearly into Providence, connecting to the Blackstone River Bikeway and East Bay Bike Path. After the trestle, the river continues south and west, passing some development and a large marsh extending to Tiogue Avenue.

In early spring, you should be able to explore down to Tiogue Avenue, but by midsummer the thick floating and emergent vegetation makes paddling difficult. A fairly large stand of wild rice sways in the breeze here, along with pickerelweed, bulrush, arrowhead, bur-reed, yellow pond-lily, American white waterlily, watershield, and various grasses and sedges.

Most of the South Branch shoreline is thickly wooded with such species as blackgum, white oak, pin oak, red maple, gray birch, white pine, ironwood, and alder. Along the shore you will see sweet pepperbush, blueberry, and lots of other shrubs. Continuing upstream, the river passes under Sandy Bottom Road, narrows, and turns more to the north, passing behind strip malls. The current picks up and you have to watch out for rocks here.

This surprisingly wild marshy section of the South Branch Pawtuxet River flows through Coventry.

After the river curves around to the west and with the concrete arch of the South Main Street bridge just visible through the trees, you will find a place where you can get out, climbing the steep bank to some commercial buildings on Main Street. Look out for the not terribly inviting mounds of trash and broken glass here. If you scramble up to Main Street, walk to the left then turn left on South Main Street; from the bridge over the river you can see the large dam just upstream.

60 | Big River

Big River flows north on an imperceptible current through a broad marsh rich with wildlife. Look for deer, great blue heron, osprey, muskrat, and beaver. Many species of aquatic plants fill the water column, making for slow paddling outside the main channel.

Location: Coventry and West Greenwich, RI
Maps: *Connecticut/Rhode Island Atlas & Gazetteer*, Map 67: L16, Map 70: A12; USGS Coventry Center, Crompton
Length: 2.3 miles one way

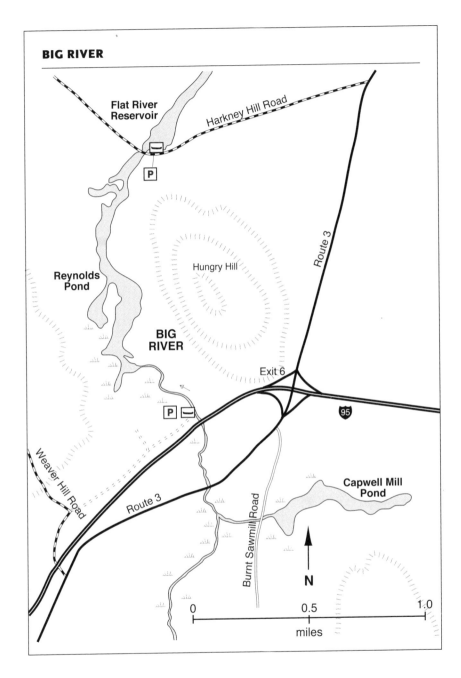

BIG RIVER

Flat River Reservoir

Harkney Hill Road

P

Reynolds Pond

Hungry Hill

Route 3

BIG RIVER

Exit 6

95

Weaver Hill Road

P

Route 3

Capwell Mill Pond

Burnt Sawmill Road

N

| 0 | 0.5 | 1.0 |

miles

Time: 3 hours round-trip

Habitat Type: slow-flowing river through broad marsh

Fish: brook, rainbow, and brown trout; largemouth and smallmouth bass; yellow perch; pickerel; northern pike (see fish advisory, Appendix A)

Camping: George Washington Camping Area; walk-in camping, Arcadia Management Area

Take Note: most motors stay north of Harkney Hill Road; limited development

GETTING THERE

Northern Access (41° 39.135′ N, 71° 37.133′ W). From I-95, Exit 6 southbound, go 1.2 miles (1.2 miles) north on Route 3, and turn left on Harkney Hill Road. Go 1.0 mile (2.2 miles) to the Zeke's Bridge Fishing Access on the right, just before the bridge.

Southern Access (41° 38.962′ N, 71° 36.865′ W). From I-95, Exit 6 southbound, go 1.3 miles (1.3 miles) south on Route 3, and turn right on Weaver Hill Road. Go 0.3 mile (1.6 miles), and turn right on the access road. Go 0.7 mile (2.3 miles), and veer right at the fork, which leads to the access.

WHAT YOU'LL SEE

Most boaters here venture out from the northern access into Flat River Reservoir; a low bridge and abundant aquatic vegetation keep most motors out of Big River's southern section. The river courses through a broad marsh, filled with aquatic vegetation and birdlife. Tons of Carolina fanwort and purple- and yellow-flowered bladderworts fill the water column, while pickerelweed, arrowhead, American eelgrass, American white waterlily, yellow pond-lily, pondweed, little floatingheart, and watershield crowd the water's surface, borne on an imperceptible current.

Along the shore, stands of Atlantic white cedar and white pine intermingle with the predominant deciduous trees. Stunted red maples, *Phragmites*, cattail, buttonbush, royal fern, sweetgale, alder, and other shrubs hang out over the water. Paddling south, you can explore a couple of large coves before the river channel narrows just before the culverts that slice through the I-95 embankment. Noise from the roadway far overhead does not intrude too much on the solitude. After passing under the Route 3 bridge, the riverbed narrows further through tight twisting turns. About 0.25 mile south of Route 3, narrow passageways block further progress.

We saw a couple of anglers in motorboats in the northern reaches, but as you progress upstream to the south, you should pretty much have the place to yourself. We spent most of our time identifying and photographing the various bladderwort species, but we also enjoyed seeing many of the marsh birds that congregate here.

61 | Belleville Pond

Highly productive Belleville Pond boasts good fishing and great waterfowl habitat. We've watched fishermen pull sizable bass out of the pond, and during fall migration, we've seen many species of waterfowl. Marshy islands on the north end provide plenty of opportunity for exploration.

Location: North Kingstown, RI
Maps: *Connecticut/Rhode Island Atlas & Gazetteer*, Map 71: E19, 20, F19, 20; USGS Wickford
Area: 159 acres
Time: 3 hours
Habitat Type: shallow, marshy pond
Fish: largemouth and calico bass, yellow perch, pickerel (see fish advisory, Appendix A)
Camping: Burlingame State Park; walk-in camping, Arcadia Management Area
Take Note: motors limited by vegetation; no development

GETTING THERE

From Route 4, Exit 5A, go 2.6 miles (2.6 miles) east on Route 102, and turn right on Route 1. Go 0.7 mile (3.3 miles), and turn right on Oak Hill Road. Go 0.6 mile (3.9 miles), and turn right at Ryan Park. Stay left on the loop road to the access (41° 33.626′ N, 71° 28.541′ W).

WHAT YOU'LL SEE

Belleville Pond boasts some of the best inland marsh habitat that we've seen. Waterfowl abound, and its shoreline provides hours of quiet exploration. The shallow water, highly productive biologically, supports the waterfowl populations, which draw in hunters in fall.

During an October visit—with both summer residents and migrants present—we saw many species, including pied-billed grebe, mallard, black duck, bufflehead, wood duck, American coot, green-winged teal, Canada goose, mute swan, cormorant, great blue heron, and marsh wren. During the warmer months, many painted turtles sun on logs. Marsh plants include cattail, *Phragmites*, swamp loosestrife, bulrush, pickerelweed, yellow pond-

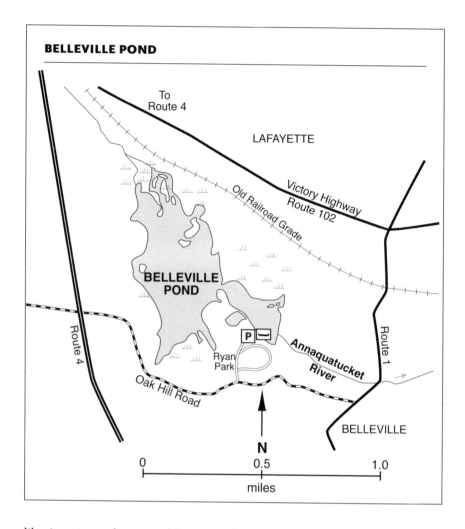

BELLEVILLE POND

To
Route 4

LAFAYETTE

Victory Highway
Route 102

Old Railroad Grade

BELLEVILLE
POND

Route 4

P

Ryan
Park

Annaquatucket
River

Route 1

Oak Hill Road

BELLEVILLE

N

| 0 | 0.5 | 1.0 |

miles

lily, American white waterlily, watershield, duckweed, Carolina fanwort, and bladderwort. The pond's water column used to harbor large quantities of bladderwort, but that is being crowded out by invasives, including Carolina fanwort, twoleaf watermilfoil, and water chestnut. The abundant underwater vegetation provides good habitat for chain pickerel, largemouth bass, and yellow perch. A fish ladder at the outlet (Annaquatucket River, which flows 3 miles into Narragansett Bay) enables alewife to swim upstream into Belleville Pond to spawn.

At the pond's poorly defined north end, marshy islands abound. Quietly exploring around these islands and the increasingly narrow channels of open water between them, you should see lots of birds.

Around the less marshy sections of the pond, deciduous trees dominate: red, white, and scarlet oaks; red maple; aspen; gray birch; and blackgum. On the more solid sections of shoreline, highbush blueberry, sweet pepperbush, and alder provide shelter and food for a wide variety of songbirds. You can hear Route 4 through the trees, but it doesn't detract too much from the solitude.

62 | Worden Pond, Great Swamp, Chipuxet River, and Charles River

This and the Wood River are the two premier paddling destinations in Rhode Island. Stick to the rivers on windy days. Expect to see large numbers of birds and other wildlife, along with diverse trees and shrubs. The narrow rivers meander through Great Swamp on their way to join the Wood River as the major tributaries of the Pawtucket.

Location: South Kingstown, RI
Maps: *Connecticut/Rhode Island Atlas & Gazetteer*, Map 70: L12, Map 71: I16, J16, K14, 15, L13, 14, 15, Map 74: A11, 12, Map 75: A13, 14, 15, B13, 14, 15; USGS Kingston
Area/Length: Worden Pond, 1,075 acres; Chipuxet and Charles rivers, 9 miles one way
Time: all day, shorter trips possible
Habitat Type: marshy, meandering rivers with overhanging shrubs and trees
Fish: largemouth and calico bass, pickerel, northern pike (see fish advisory, Appendix A)
Camping: Burlingame State Park; walk-in camping, Arcadia Management Area
Take Note: no development; no motors on rivers; little development on Worden Pond, but watch out for motors and treacherous wind; beware of poison ivy and tight curves on the Charles River

GETTING THERE
Chipuxet River (41° 28.955′ N, 71° 33.075′ W). From the junction of Routes 1 and 138, go 5.2 miles west on Route 138, through the Route 110 intersection, cross the Chipuxet River, and take an immediate left on Liberty Lane to the parking area for Taylor's Landing.

Charles River (41° 27.05' N, 71° 36.951' W). From the junction of Routes 2 and 138, go 4.1 miles (4.1 miles) south on Route 2/South County Trail, and turn left on the access road. Go 0.1 mile (4.2 miles) to the access. To reach the Charles River, paddle downstream under the railroad bridge. At the Charles, a left turn (upstream) leads to Worden Pond.

Worden Pond (41° 25.77' N, 71° 34.07' W). From the junction of Routes 110 and 138, go 3.8 miles (3.8 miles) south on Route 110, and turn right on Wordens Pond Road. Go 0.5 mile (4.3 miles) to the access on the right.

WHAT YOU'LL SEE

Worden Pond and its inlet and outlet rivers through the 3,350-acre Great Swamp vie with Wood River as the best paddling in Rhode Island. From the public boat access point at Worden Pond's south end, you can reach all the areas covered in this section. When the wind blows across Worden Pond, we would put in on either of the rivers. You can also paddle one-way from the Taylor's Landing access down the Chipuxet River, across Worden Pond, and down the Charles River to the Route 2 access, a distance of about 6 miles.

Thirty Acre and Hundred Acre Ponds

We would only paddle here during times of high water. From Taylor's Landing, paddle upstream into Thirty Acre and Hundred Acre ponds. You may encounter beaver dams that require portaging. Brush and low water may also block access up the narrow channel. Above the beaver dam, the Chipuxet widens into Thirty Acre Pond—a gorgeous pond rich in wildlife. Woodland and University of Rhode Island agricultural research fields surround the pond—you may notice irrigation pumps along the shore. Only one house occurs on the pond, although you may also see (and hear) a small brick pump house near the south end that pumps drinking water from an underground aquifer (beneath the shallow pond) for the town of South Kingstown.

We saw many pied-billed grebes amid the pond's thick vegetation (water-lilies, Carolina fanwort, pickerelweed, bur-reed, swamp loosestrife), as well as great blue herons, kingfishers, and painted turtles. An occasional train speeds past the pond's north end. Also at the north end, paddle under the cavernous, arched-stone and concrete railroad bridge and a second much lower bridge to get into Hundred Acre Pond. Though marked by some development, Hundred Acre Pond still offers wonderful paddling on a quiet morning in spring or fall. Along the perimeter, look for blackgum, whose leaves turn crimson in early fall. Mountain laurel, highbush blueberry, and sweet pepperbush grow thickly along the less developed eastern shore. The state-record northern pike, at 37 pounds, was caught here in 1987.

Paddle through the pond's marshy northern end, following the winding Chipuxet River on up through the dense swamp of red maple, cedar, alder, and swamp loosestrife, full of songbirds. The channel narrows, and the vegetation converges from the sides until it finally blocks further progress near Wolf Rocks Road. Paddling from Taylor's Landing up to here takes a couple of hours if you allow time for watching birds and investigating the ponds' vegetation.

Chipuxet River

More commonly, people paddle from Taylor's Landing downstream into Worden Pond—a distance of about 3 miles. The narrow river tightly twists through Great Swamp. The current, though noticeable, allows paddling in both directions. Along here, you pass through a red maple swamp, with patches of cattail, bulrush, and *Phragmites* on the oxbow curves, with thick stands of sweetgale, dogwood, winterberry, and sweet pepperbush. Wild rice also grows sparingly along here—look for the tall delicate grass in early fall, when the tasty grain can be shaken from the fruiting heads.

When you reach 1,000-plus-acre Worden Pond, take note of the wind conditions. Strong winds, typically from the south in summer, send up sizable waves across more than a mile of open water. If possible, try to reach Worden Pond before 10 A.M. to improve your chances of avoiding windy conditions.

Because development impinges on the eastern and southern shores and Wordens Pond Road traverses the southern shore, you will likely find more enjoyment in the northern shore. Pass a privately owned island on your left, used as a hunting and fishing camp, and then aptly named Stony Point on the right—which makes a great picnic stop. Large, seemingly out-of-place granite boulders extend out into the pond. On higher ground, beech, white oak, red oak, and sassafras grow, along with more water-tolerant red maple and blackgum found throughout Great Swamp. At one point, state-record largemouth bass and northern pike came from Worden Pond, and fishermen continue to entice lunkers to their landing nets.

This natural basin's maximum depth is 7 feet, with an average depth of only 4 feet. Extensive areas of bulrush grow in the shallows. In the cove west of Stony Point, a large seaplane hangar seems oddly alone at the pond's edge. From a sandy point just east of the hangar, you can reach a network of trails that crisscross Great Neck and extend along a dike built to maintain wildlife habitat in the swamp. Great Neck rises to a surprisingly high 182 feet.

On Great Neck in 1675, the Great Swamp Fight occurred—a battle in King Philip's ill-fated rebellion against the onslaught of European settlers. When the Pilgrims arrived in New England in 1620, American Indians befriended and kept them alive, teaching them how to plant corn and live off the New England environment. For several decades, peace reigned. But pressure built as more and more shiploads of settlers arrived in the New World, cleared land, built settlements, and through deeds and treaties pushed the American Indians onto smaller and smaller corners of remaining wilderness. Chief Massasoit of the Wampanoags had been a friend to settlers, but when he died in 1662, his son Metacom became chief and saw what was happening in a different light. Dubbed King Philip of Pokanoket by the colonists, Metacom convinced the Narragansetts and other tribes in the region to join in resisting the settlers.

In 1675 Metacom led his alliance in a series of offensives—known as King Philip's War—attacking and destroying settlements. As the first heavy snow of December fell on Great Neck, colonial soldiers from Connecticut joined those from the Massachusetts and Plymouth colonies and set out on a march inland from the burned-out garrison at Pettaquamscutt. They intended to attack a fortress somewhere in a vast swamp near Kingston. Their "enemy"—a band of about 1,000 Narragansetts, including women and children, plus King Philip's raiders—had gathered with their winter stores inside a freshly built fort. The devastating battle did not end King Philip's War, but it turned the tide.

Charles River

Either put in at the Route 2 access, or continue from the Chipuxet River down around the northern shore of Worden Pond from the seaplane hangar, rounding Case Point to reach the Charles River outlet. The Charles—along with the Wood, the major source of the Pawcatuck (Trips 66 and 67)—flows through a seemingly denser and more magical part of Great Swamp and twists even more tightly than the Chipuxet. Tall scarlet oak and red maple shade the river, while buttonbush, cinnamon fern, dogwood, swamp rose, swamp loosestrife, and arrowhead claim the shore. Dense canopies of grape, greenbrier, and other vines sweep down to the water's surface. You can almost imagine yourself in a tropical jungle here and expect to see howler monkeys and colorful macaws in the trees. In places, poison ivy drapes over fallen trees so thickly that you have a hard time avoiding brushing against it as you paddle underneath. If you are allergic to poison ivy, be wary and plan your attire appropriately; if you wash exposed skin with soap when you get home, you may not develop a rash. You may also have to carry your boat over or around an obstruction or two. Because of tight curves along the Charles, you will do much better in a shorter boat.

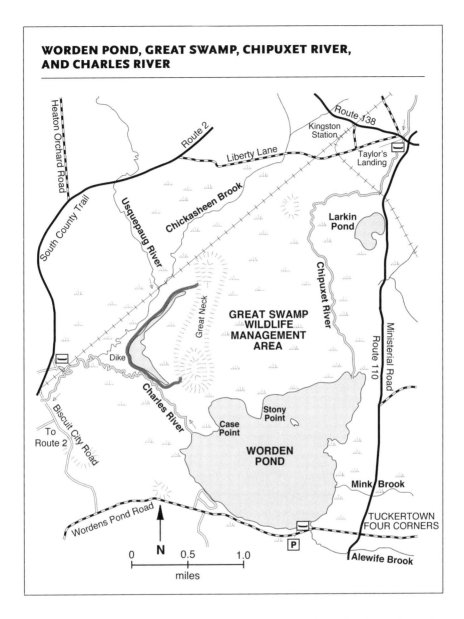

WORDEN POND, GREAT SWAMP, CHIPUXET RIVER, AND CHARLES RIVER

Heaton Orchard Road

Route 2

Route 138

Kingston Station

Liberty Lane

Taylor's Landing

South County Trail

Usquepaug River

Chickasheen Brook

Larkin Pond

Chipuxet River

Great Neck

GREAT SWAMP WILDLIFE MANAGEMENT AREA

Ministerial Road

Route 110

Dike

Charles River

Biscuit City Road

To Route 2

Stony Point

Case Point

WORDEN POND

Mink Brook

Wordens Pond Road

TUCKERTOWN FOUR CORNERS

0   N   0.5   1.0

P

Alewife Brook

miles

About a mile from Worden Pond, look for a built-up bank on the right and an obvious spot to pull up your boat by some concrete abutments. This dike creates the Great Swamp Waterfowl Impoundment, a 138-acre wetland providing nesting habitat for numerous waterfowl species. Climb the bank to the trail that extends along the dike and over to Great Neck. Bird-watching here is fantastic. On an early July trip, in a couple of hours we saw and heard perhaps 50 species of waterfowl, warblers, woodpeckers, flycatchers, thrushes, sparrows,

If you paddle any distance on the Chipuxet River, you will have to portage over beaver dams. This one is at the outlet of Thirty Acre Pond.

and other species. In a mid-October trip we were treated to the rare sight of a peregrine falcon and its nearly successful efforts to catch a teal.

You should see osprey here, diving for fish. Osprey nest atop the power line poles that cross the swamp. You can actually walk out into the swamp for quite a way on a plank boardwalk. Sections of boardwalk may have deteriorated, so be careful. While you might be tempted to carry your boat over the dike to explore the water on the east side, leave that area to the wildlife.

From the landing by the dike, the tightly twisting river continues west, passing under the power line and then joining with the Usquepaug River, entering from the northeast. You can explore this river for a way—it parallels the railroad tracks for about a mile then turns north, crossing under the railroad bridge. Continuing downstream at the rivers' confluence, you will reach the railroad tracks and the Route 2 access in about 0.75 mile. Paddle along the tracks for a short distance and watch for a fork to the right (look for a sign nailed to a tree indicating Boat Landing). Take this fork and paddle under the railroad tracks to the landing just ahead. If you miss the fork, you will soon reach the Biscuit City Road bridge followed by the Route 2 bridge. Very aromatic swamp azalea and swamp rose bloom in profusion in late June and early July along the section down to the Route 2 bridge.

63 | Tucker Pond

This small kettle pond harbors an impressive stand of rosebay rhododendron, the largest member of the heath family. Because the pond has no major inlet, water level varies with rainfall. This is a good place to paddle when the wind blows up big waves on nearby Worden Pond.

Location: South Kingstown, RI
Maps: *Connecticut/Rhode Island Atlas & Gazetteer*, Map 75: B15, 16; USGS Kingston
Area: 101 acres
Time: 2 hours
Habitat Type: wooded, natural kettle pond
Fish: largemouth bass, white and yellow perch, pickerel (see fish advisory, Appendix A)
Camping: Burlingame State Park; walk-in camping, Arcadia Management Area
Take Note: motors limited to 10 HP; limited development

GETTING THERE

From the junction of Routes 110 and 138 in West Kingston, go 3.8 miles (3.8 miles) south on Route 110, and turn left on Tuckertown Road. Go 0.5 mile (4.3 miles) to the access on the right (41° 24.564′ N, 73′ 32.945′ W).

From the junction of Routes 1 and 110, go north on Route 110, and turn right on Tuckertown Road. Go 0.5 mile to the access on the right.

WHAT YOU'LL SEE

Tucker Pond, just to the southeast of Worden Pond in southern Rhode Island, has perhaps the most dramatic stand of rosebay rhododendron (*Rhododendron maximum*) that we have seen north of the southern Appalachians. This largest member of the heath family—which includes mountain laurel, azalea, blueberry, cranberry, and leatherleaf—covers most of the shoreline. Although we haven't been here when these 15- to 20-foot-high rhododendrons bloom (typically late June or early July), they ought to be spectacular. On the pond's

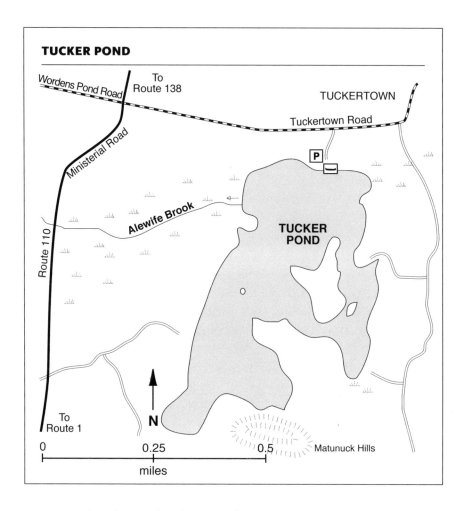

TUCKER POND

Wordens Pond Road

To Route 138

TUCKERTOWN

Tuckertown Road

Ministerial Road

Route 110

P

Alewife Brook

TUCKER POND

To Route 1

N

0   0.25   0.5   Matunuck Hills

miles

steeper south and east sides, they extend up quite high on the banks, with taller white oak, blackgum, and pitch pine extending above—as if emerging from a sea of green.

About a dozen houses appear around the pond but do not seem terribly imposing, and the 10 HP limit keeps boating activity to quiet fishing. The state-record white perch, a 2-pounder, was caught here in 1974. Because this natural kettle pond has no major inlet, the water level fluctuates with rainfall. In a dry year, the level can drop considerably. The last glacier, which receded about 12,000 years ago, created the hilly area that extends south from Tucker Pond for a few miles, known as the Charlestown recessional moraine or the Matunuck Hills. Tucker Pond and the collection of smaller kettle ponds to the south, formed from chunks of glacial ice, have shoreline ecosystems (some protected by The Nature Conservancy) that support a number of plant species quite rare in Rhode Island. Enjoy these plants from your boat.

A band of floating plants surrounds much of the perimeter, but most of the pond consists of open water. Where rhododendrons don't dominate the shoreline, highbush blueberry, sweetgale, sweet pepperbush, and red maple occur. Swamp loosestrife, pickerelweed, and bulrush populate the few marshy coves. Several islands rise from the pond, including a large one (with a house fairly well hidden near the peak).

64 | Ninigret Pond

Ninigret, Rhode Island's largest coastal pond, offers great opportunities for plant and wildlife viewing. Nineteen rare or endangered plant species inhabit the pond's shores and the Ninigret National Wildlife Refuge, and more than 250 bird species have been recorded here. We don't recommend this pond for novice paddlers because of tides, wind-driven waves, and boat traffic.

Location: Charlestown, RI
Maps: *Connecticut/Rhode Island Atlas & Gazetteer*, Map 74: E9, 10, F7, 8, 9, 10, 11, G7, 8; USGS Carolina, Quonochotaug
Area: 1,700 acres
Time: all day, shorter trips possible
Habitat Type: coastal tidal pond, shrubby marshlands, many islands and protected bays
Fish: bluefish, flounder (see fish advisory, Appendix A)
Information: tide charts, maineharbors.com; Ninigret National Wildlife Refuge, fws.gov/ninigret/
Camping: Burlingame State Park
Take Note: development; motors allowed; use caution due to boat traffic, wind, and tides; not recommended for novice paddlers; always wear your PFD

GETTING THERE
Charlestown (41° 22.881′ N, 71° 38.698′ W). From Route 1 northbound, take the Cross Mills/Charlestown Beach exit. From Route 1 southbound, make a

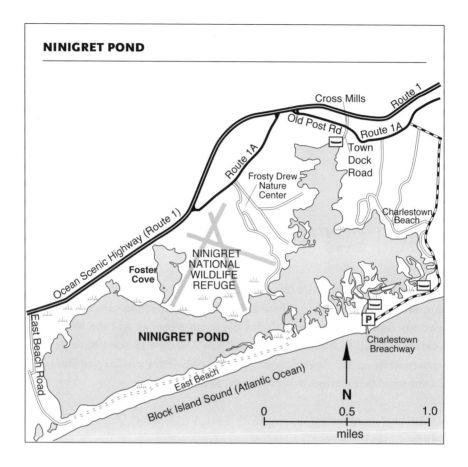

NINIGRET POND

Cross Mills
Route 1
Old Post Rd
Route 1A
Town
Dock
Road
Route 1A
Frosty Drew
Nature
Center
Charlestown
Beach
Ocean Scenic Highway (Route 1)
Foster
Cove
NINIGRET
NATIONAL
WILDLIFE
REFUGE
P
East Beach Road
NINIGRET POND
Charlestown
Breachway
East Beach
Block Island Sound (Atlantic Ocean)
N
0   0.5   1.0
miles

U-turn onto Route 1 north, just after the Route 2 exit, and turn right on Cross Mills. Go straight across Route 1A onto Town Dock Road. Access is at road's end, adjacent to Ocean House Marina. Jam your vehicle into the Japanese knotweed that lines the road's west side.

Charlestown Beach (41° 21.825′ N, 71° 37.598′ W). From the Cross Mills/ Charlestown Beach exit, turn left on Route 1A, following signs for the Breachway. Go 0.6 mile (0.6 mile), and turn right at the Breachway sign. Go 0.4 mile (1.0 mile), and turn right on Charlestown Beach Road. Go 1.3 miles (2.3 miles) to the access on the right, just after the causeway bridge.

WHAT YOU'LL SEE

Ninigret, Rhode Island's largest coastal pond, although quite developed in places, offers very enjoyable paddling and superb wildlife observation opportunities. Strong winds, tidal currents, and moderate motorboat traffic during summer weekends, however, can present hazards. Use caution, wear your PFD, and paddle the nearby Pawcatuck or Wood rivers when the wind howls. Novice paddlers should avoid Ninigret Pond.

Away from Charlestown's congestion, the western two-thirds of Ninigret Pond remain relatively wild, with much of it included in Ninigret National Wildlife Refuge. Most of this 868-acre refuge was once a U.S. Navy landing field, which explains the extensive paved areas. Hike around the old airfield to see how nature gradually reclaims miles of runway; more than 70 acres of pavement have been ripped up and carted away. More than 250 bird species have been recorded here, with prime birding during spring and fall migrations. But plants provide the real attraction for naturalists. More than half the total number of known plants of yellow fringed orchid (*Platanthera ciliaris*) in New England occur here, along with at least eighteen other rare or endangered plant species.

The northern and southern shores of Ninigret vary considerably. Northern shore vegetation consists primarily of shrubby grassland, along with bayberry, blueberry, beach plum, shadbush, wild cherry, dogwood, cedar, and seaside goldenrod—an ecosystem that provides excellent bird habitat, especially as a stopover for migrating warblers. The marshier tidal coves and inlets sport tall stands of *Phragmites*, with patches of *Spartina* occupying the lower, regularly flooded sections.

Along the pond's southern shore, next to the Ninigret Conservation Area barrier beach, salt marsh grasses—*Spartina patens* and *S. alterniflora*—dominate the vegetation. Carolina sealavender (*Limonium carolinianum*), a delicate plant with tiny lavender flowers resembling baby's breath, mixes with the *Spartina*. So much Carolina sealavender has been collected for dried-flower arrangements that in some areas of the Northeast it no longer adds its subtle lavender blush to the salt marsh. Enjoy the plant where it grows, and avoid the temptation to pick it.

The sand here appears almost white, and the water seems quite clean. You will see scallop shells washed up, patches of eelgrass flowing with tidal currents, and clumps of seaweed and sponge on rocks as you paddle the shallows. Anglers here catch lots of winter flounder, as well as bluefish in summer when they enter to feed on young flounder.

With the cleaning up of coastal waters after decades of dumping raw sewage and industrial wastes, commercial harvesting of soft-shell clams, quahogs, bay scallops, and oysters has ramped up once again. The huge oyster and other shellfish industry of centuries past, decimated by hurricanes and disease—diseases of both the shellfish and the humans who ate the tainted product—has risen to help fill our burgeoning population's insatiable demand for seafood. However, over the globe, we are already beginning to see the effects of global warming on the shellfish industry. With increasing amounts of carbon dioxide dissolved in the oceans, the water's acidity increases, which runs directly counter to the needs of shellfish larvae to develop their hard calcium carbonate shells in a low-acidity environment. And with warming waters, diseases that cause shellfish mortality and sickness in humans and that normally die back in winter may be present year round, further stressing shellfish production.

To enjoy crashing waves of the Atlantic, beach your boat and walk across the dunes to East Beach, accessible only by boat, foot, or four-wheel-drive vehicle. The wildlife refuge section of Ninigret's south shore remains closed to the public to protect nesting least terns and piping plovers—both threatened species in Rhode Island.

65 | Watchaug Pond and Poquiant Brook

Watchaug Pond is a recreation destination, with camping at Burlingame State Park, hiking on trails of the Kimball Wildlife Refuge, and paddling on the pond and its outflow stream as possibilities.

Location: Charlestown, RI
Maps: *Connecticut/Rhode Island Atlas & Gazetteer*, Map 74: D6, 7, 8, E6, 7, 8; USGS Carolina
Area/Length: Watchaug Pond, 573 acres; Poquiant Brook, 0.75 mile one way
Time: 4 hours
Habitat Type: large, open pond
Fish: rainbow and brown trout, largemouth and calico bass, yellow perch, pickerel, northern pike (see fish advisory, Appendix A)
Information: Kimball Wildlife Refuge, Audubon Society of Rhode Island, asri.org, 401-949-5454
Camping: Burlingame State Park
Take Note: motors and water-skiers; personal watercraft prohibited; limited development

GETTING THERE
From the junction of Routes 1 and 216, go 3.0 miles (3.0 miles) north on Route 1, and turn left, cross the median, and make a U-turn. Turn immediately right on Prosser Trail, following signs to Burlingame State Park. Go 0.8 mile (3.8

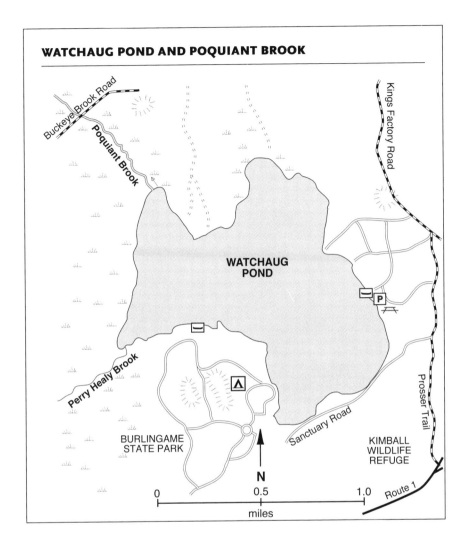

WATCHAUG POND AND POQUIANT BROOK

miles), passing the Kimball Wildlife Refuge entrance on the left, and turn left to the picnic area. Go 0.1 mile (3.9 miles), and turn left. Go 0.2 mile (4.1 miles) to the Barton C. Hurley Landing access on the right (41° 22.714′ N, 71° 40.787′ W).

WHAT YOU'LL SEE

Watchaug Pond, a large body of water located near Rhode Island's southern tip, sees heavy recreational use but can offer enjoyable paddling, particularly for a family camping at Burlingame State Park. For others, visit either early or late in the season to avoid the crowds.

While paddling on the pond for the first edition, we encountered several noisy personal watercraft, but the town of Charlestown banned them in

The best time to visit popular Watchaug Pond is in May or after Labor Day.

January 2002. Heavy use at the southeastern end near the public boat launch area, along with shoreline development on the pond's east side, may provide strong incentive to concentrate on the northern and western sections. The marshy western end feels much more remote and wild. As dusk approached, we watched an otter near the outlet at the northwestern tip. Even though you rarely see otters in southern New England, if you spend much time paddling around less developed lakes, ponds, and rivers around dawn or dusk, you should see this delightful mammal sooner or later.

You can get away from most Watchaug Pond activity by paddling down the outlet, Poquiant Brook, at the pond's northwestern tip. We followed this quiet, meandering brook for at least 0.5 mile through thick marsh. When the wind blows up whitecaps on Watchaug Pond, the brook offers a nice escape into a quiet, secluded area. Look for blueberry bushes, along with cedar, blackgum, and a wide assortment of marsh plants. Keep an eye out for the elusive wood duck here. The state-record calico bass, a 3-pounder, was caught in Watchaug Pond in 1976.

Kimball Wildlife Refuge, owned and managed by the Audubon Society of Rhode Island, abuts lands near the pond's southern end, with wonderful trails through oak and laurel woodland. With 755 campsites, Burlingame harbors one of the largest camping areas in New England. Nonetheless, the campground often fills to capacity during summer months.

66 | Pawcatuck River

The wide Pawcatuck River offers a great paddling opportunity along generally secluded wooded shores, with understory shrubs that bloom in profusion in spring. You will see osprey that nest here, along with myriad other bird species. Except for the Bradford put-in, access is difficult.

Location: Charlestown, Hopkinton, and Westerly, RI
Maps: *Connecticut/Rhode Island Atlas & Gazetteer*, Map 73: C24, Map 74: C1, 3, 4, D1, 2, 3; USGS Ashaway
Length: 8 miles one way
Time: all day, round-trip
Habitat Type: wide, undeveloped river, wooded shores
Fish: brook, rainbow and brown trout (see fish advisory, Appendix A)
Camping: Burlingame State Park
Take Note: motors allowed

GETTING THERE
Potter Hill (41° 24.829′ N, 71° 47.85′ W). From I-95, Exit 1 in Rhode Island, go 2.2 miles (2.2 miles) south on Route 3, and turn right on Hillside Avenue.

PAWCATUCK RIVER

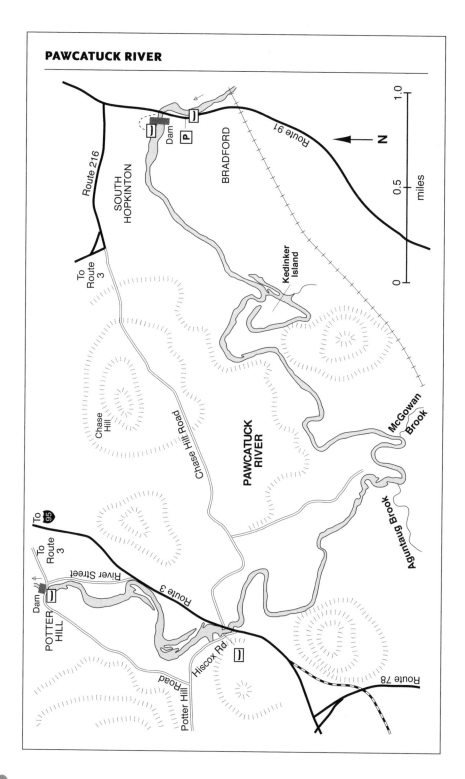

Go 0.2 mile (2.4 miles), and turn left on Laurel Street. Go 0.5 mile (2.9 miles), and turn right on Potter Hill Road. Launch at the Flora Whiteley Preserve, just across the bridge on the left. Finding a place to park can be quite difficult.

Hiscox Road (41° 23.966′ N, 71° 48.03′ W). It might be easier to park on Hiscox Road at the junction with Route 3, with parking for three vehicles. From I-95, Exit 1, go 3.7 miles south on Route 3, and turn right on Hiscox Road.

Bradford (41° 24.382′ N, 71° 44.888′ W). From Ashaway, go south on Route 216 until it joins Route 91. Continue south 0.4 mile to the access on the left, just after the bridge. This is the easiest access.

WHAT YOU'LL SEE

After the Wood River joins the Pawcatuck (also called the Charles above the Wood) just south of Alton Dam, the combined flow provides a broad, slow-flowing river between wooded shores. We paddled upstream from Potter Hill Dam, although with two cars you could paddle this one-way from Bradford (8 miles; the upstream put-in here), or from Alton Dam (13 miles) or Hope Valley (19.5 miles), both on the Wood River (Trip 67).

When we paddled here in July, we saw no other boats upstream of the Route 3 bridge. We loved the sculpted lateral branches of the blackgum trees (*Nyssa sylvatica*) that cluster along the shores in spots and look like splayed fingers; we wished that we could return in early fall when their leaves turn crimson. Occasional white pines would offer a dark, contrasting green to the fall foliage. Surprisingly, beaver have girdled a lot of the blackgums. We often see hemlocks

Lacy branches of blackgum, *Nyssa sylvatica*, extend out over the Pawcatuck River's banks.

girdled because, presumably, they have resinous bark unpalatable to beaver, but why would they want to kill off deciduous trees? Blackgum bark may also be resinous, given that the trees can withstand submersion for decades.

A number of active osprey nests, some on utility poles and some on artificial platforms, occur along this stretch of the Pawcatuck. We saw several osprey perched or fishing as we paddled along. We also saw and heard many other bird species, including great blue heron, green heron, wood duck, Canada goose, mute swan, cardinal, eastern wood-pewee, cedar waxwing, eastern towhee, chickadee, veery, tufted titmouse, catbird, and yellow warbler.

Lots of swamp rose, swamp loosestrife, swamp azalea, and dogwood form an understory beneath the mature canopy of red maple, ash, willow, gray birch, scarlet oak, beech, blackgum, and white pine. Occasional marshy areas occur along the normally wooded river course.

67 | Wood River and Alton Pond

This and the rivers of the Great Swamp are the two premier paddling destinations in Rhode Island. Expect to see large numbers of birds and other wildlife, along with diverse trees and shrubs. The river meanders through marshes on its way to join the Great Swamp's Charles River as the major tributaries of the Pawcatuck.

Location: Hopkinton and Richmond, RI
Maps: *Connecticut/Rhode Island Atlas & Gazetteer,* Map 70: J5, 6, K5, 6, L5, 6, Map 74: A5, 6; USGS Carolina
Length: 6.5 miles one way
Time: all day, shorter trips possible
Habitat Type: dammed-up meandering river, shrubby marshlands, many oxbows
Fish: brook, rainbow and brown trout; largemouth bass (see fish advisory, Appendix A)
Camping: Burlingame State Park; walk-in camping, Arcadia Management Area
Take Note: little development; no motors

WOOD RIVER AND ALTON POND

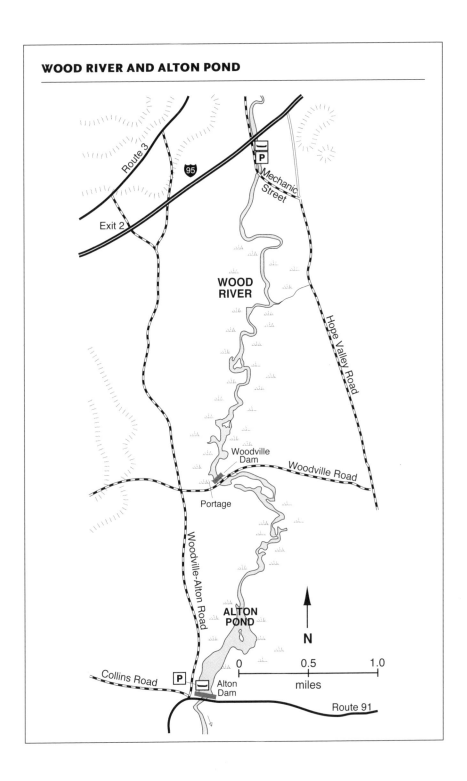

Route 3

95

Exit 2

Mechanic Street

P

WOOD RIVER

Hope Valley Road

Woodville Dam

Woodville Road

Portage

Woodville-Alton Road

ALTON POND

N

0   0.5   1.0
miles

Collins Road

P

Alton Dam

Route 91

GETTING THERE

Alton Dam (41° 26.284′ N, 71° 43.344′ W). From I-95, Exit 2 southbound, go 3.5 miles south on Woodville-Alton Road to the access on the left.

Hope Valley (41° 29.61′ N, 71° 42.96′ W). From the junction of Route 3 and Mechanic Street in Hope Valley, go 0.9 mile south on Mechanic Street to the access on the left, at the end of the guardrail just after the I-95 bridge.

WHAT YOU'LL SEE

The Wood River offers an outstanding paddling resource, certainly one of the most pristine in Rhode Island. The section included here, from Hope Valley to Alton Dam, can occupy you for anywhere from a few hours to a full day or two. We prefer putting in at Alton Dam and paddling upstream, although spring high water could preclude making it all the way to Woodville. With two cars, you could paddle downstream from the Hope Valley access to Alton Dam.

Paddling north from Alton Dam, after passing a few houses, the 39-acre pond narrows to a winding, deep channel, and you seem to leave most fishing activity behind. Along the wild Wood River, numerous oxbows, side channels, eddies, and hidden ponds harbor lots of wildlife. We saw several pairs of wood ducks, cormorants, green herons, mallards, kingfishers, and songbirds galore. Osprey wheeled overhead, diving occasionally for fish. Scattered shoreline piles of mussel shells bore evidence of successful raccoon or otter feasting. Paddling along quietly, you should see literally hundreds of painted turtles on a sunny day, basking on floating logs or on tussocks of grass that extend out into the water along the marshy shoreline.

Ancient blueberry bushes, blackgum, red maple, and white pine grow along the shore. Where the ground rises steeply from the water, dense, lush stands of mountain laurel bloom spectacularly in June. With the river flowing so slowly, we lost the main channel several times, finding ourselves on one of the oxbow ponds.

A couple of miles upstream, the channel forks. Paddling up the smaller left fork, you quickly come to an old farm, a long-abandoned mill building, and a dead end. The main channel curves right, where you soon reach the Woodville Road bridge over the river and a beautiful dam just beyond. Water was diverted here for the mill. Ruins of a much older stone mill building occur here. Take out on the right bank before the bridge, carry up and over the bridge, and put in on the left side.

Upstream from Woodville Dam, the stream meanders through more marshland, similar to that below the dam, except with less mountain laurel.

Eastern kingbirds appear often along the shores of New England's rivers and ponds. Note the dark head and back, white underbelly, and white-tipped tail.

Large patches of swamp rose make up for the lack of laurel, and arrowhead and pickerelweed line the shores. After about a mile, the marshland and streambed narrow to a shore lined with red maple, gray birch, oaks, ash, and blackgum. Painted turtles sun on the numerous snags and overhanging branches. We also enjoyed numerous iridescent green damselflies with black wings that landed on our boats. Two great horned owls eyed us warily from perches above.

Alton and Woodville, part of a string of old textile towns almost hidden along the Wood and Pawcatuck rivers in southern Rhode Island, formed the economic pillar of this area. Alton Pond formed behind the power-producing dam built by David L. Aldrich in 1860. His mill changed hands over the years but still produces textiles—elastic webbing rather than the cotton and wool of old. And, just like a hundred years ago, fishing remains the favorite activity on the quiet pond.

7 | EASTERN CONNECTICUT

The ten entries for Eastern Connecticut include mostly ponds and lakes, with a few interesting rivers thrown in. Five small ponds offer paddling among seas of aquatic vegetation. Stump Pond is a great place to observe waterfowl. You will see wood duck, great blue heron, and many more species. Ross Marsh— a quiet, out-of-the way pond—also contains a lot of waterfowl; look for muskrat and beaver in the evening.

Look for bryozoan colonies in Mono Pond if they have not been crowded out by invasive aquatic weeds. Also look for great blue heron, wood duck, and other marsh birds. We saw an otter family on Bishop Swamp, and you could also see muskrats and beaver. Canada goose and wood duck both nest there, and we watched crows mob a great horned owl. Bigelow Pond is the last of the shallow, weed-choked bodies of water in this section. It's part of Bigelow Hollow State Park; we watched an osprey fish on this tiny pond.

Standing in marked contrast to the five ponds mentioned above, Mashapaug Lake also lies within Bigelow Hollow State Park; you can see down at least 20 feet in the clear, oligotrophic waters. Few trips in this book can boast that kind of clarity. Popular Mansfield Hollow Lake offers many hours of varied paddling opportunities, including open lake, deep coves, islands, and several streams. Although motors are allowed, expect to see more canoes and kayaks. In the evening, expect to see beaver and muskrats in the inlet rivers.

Other entries in this section include small ponds with rivers that provide miles of paddling. West Thompson Lake is fun to paddle, and it's great to camp there and to hike the nearby trails. Then paddle up the Quinebaug River, enjoying the vine-draped shoreline, listening to birds calling from the canopy. After paddling the 41-acre Somersville Mill Pond, head up the narrow, meandering Scantic River, leading you through a bird-filled swampland. A very diverse set of aquatic and semi-aquatic plants line the shores, and in the upper reaches, branches and vines provide an ever-encroaching canopy.

Oneco Pond and the Moosup River start in Connecticut, with portions of the upstream river winding into Rhode Island. Marshy Eagleville Pond, at 80 acres, offers more nooks and crannies to paddle, and the Willimantic River offers hours more of exploration. Great blue and green herons patrol the shoreline, while song sparrow, cardinal, catbird, and common yellowthroat fill dense shrubs that line the shore. Look for Canada goose and wood duck, and for beaver and muskrat in the evening.

68 | Quaddick Reservoir and Stump Pond

Stump Pond is a great place to observe waterfowl amid a sea of aquatic plants. You will see wood duck, great blue heron, and many more species. Avoid this area when the speedway is running races.

Location: Thompson, CT
Maps: *Connecticut/Rhode Island Atlas & Gazetteer*, Map 57: E20, 21, F20, 21; USGS Thompson
Area: Quaddick Reservoir and Stump Pond, 467 acres
Time: 2 hours for Stump Pond
Habitat Type: marshy reservoir
Fish: largemouth and calico bass, yellow perch, pickerel, northern pike (see fish advisory, Appendix A)
Information: Thompson International Speedway race dates, thompsonspeedway.com
Camping: Mashamoquet Brook State Park, West Thompson Lake
Take Note: motors allowed; no development on northern section

QUADDICK RESERVOIR AND STUMP POND

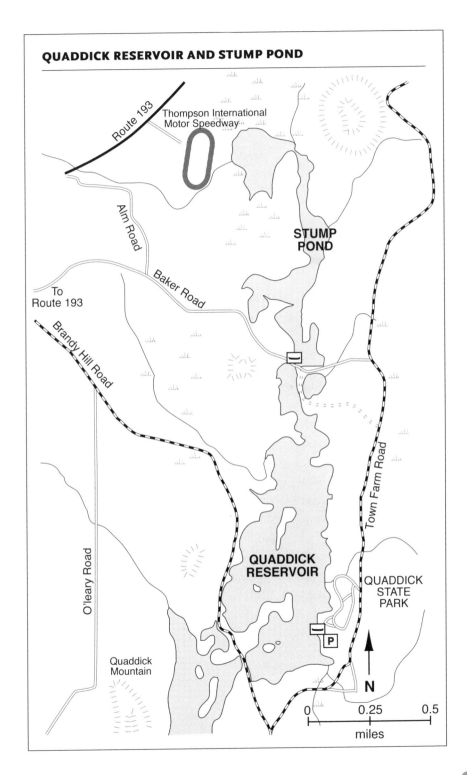

Route 193

Thompson International
Motor Speedway

Alm Road

Baker Road

To
Route 193

Brandy Hill Road

STUMP
POND

QUADDICK
RESERVOIR

Town Farm Road

QUADDICK
STATE
PARK

O'leary Road

P

Quaddick
Mountain

N

0   0.25   0.5
miles

GETTING THERE

From I-395, Exit 99 northbound, go 0.6 mile (0.6 mile) east on Route 200, and turn left on Route 193. Go 1.5 miles (2.1 miles), and turn right on Brandy Hill Road. Go 0.4 mile (2.5 miles), and bear left on Baker Road. Go 1.4 miles (3.9 miles) to the access by the bridge (41° 58.141′ N, 71° 19.015′ W).

WHAT YOU'LL SEE

Long, narrow Quaddick Reservoir nestles into the extreme northeastern corner of Connecticut, next to the Rhode Island and Massachusetts borders. Those seeking solitude should avoid the two southern sections, especially on sunny summer weekends, because they feature heavy development and teem with motorboats. The reservoir's northern section, described here—one of our favorite paddling spots in northeastern Connecticut—receives much less boat traffic because of abundant aquatic vegetation.

Floating waterlilies and submerged bladderworts, Carolina fanwort, and coontail clog the northern section's clear, shallow water. Water birds abound, especially mallard, black duck, wood duck, and great blue heron. The shallow coves and the far northern end—known as Stump Pond—provide the richest bird habitat. Thick woods of white pine and mixed deciduous trees surround the northern reservoir, along with sweet pepperbush, highbush blueberry, and sweetgale. Cattail, bulrush, and bur-reed embellish the shallow coves and inlets.

The only drawback to the northern section—besides the few motorboats that muscle their way in—is the noise that wafts in on a blue haze from Thompson International Speedway. The track backs right up to the Stump Pond marsh, filling it with race noises. To avoid the cacophony, check race dates on the speedway's website. Listening to your paddle dip methodically into water while watching wood ducks circle low over the marsh presents a stark contrast between your activity and that of several thousand auto racing buffs who congregate a few hundred yards away. Although a sad commentary that so many more people watch car races than go out to enjoy nature, we would rather have the marsh teem with birds than with paddlers or, worse, motorboats. We wonder what those wood ducks think about our species . . . .

When Thompson Speedway is not in use, a paddle on relatively wild and marshy Stump Pond should be quiet and relaxing.

69 | West Thompson Lake and Quinebaug River

This is a recreation destination, with camping, paddling, and hiking opportunities. The lake offers great paddling, free from development, but we prefer paddling up the river, enjoying the vine-draped shoreline, listening to birds calling from the canopy.

Location: Thompson, CT
Maps: *Connecticut/Rhode Island Atlas & Gazetteer*, Map 57: E14, 15, F15, 16, G15, 16; USGS Putnam
Area/Length: West Thompson Lake, 239 acres; Quinebaug River, 3 miles one way
Time: 5 hours
Habitat Type: reservoir; wide, shallow river
Fish: largemouth, smallmouth, and calico bass; yellow perch; pickerel; walleye; also trout in the river (see fish advisory, Appendix A)
Information: U.S. Army Corps of Engineers, West Thompson Lake, corpslakes.usace.army.mil/visitors/projects.cfm?Id=E619760
Camping: West Thompson Lake, Mashamoquet Brook State Park
Take Note: motors limited to 5 MPH; no development

GETTING THERE

From I-395, Exit 97 northbound, go 0.8 mile (0.8 mile) west on Route 44, and turn right on Route 12. Go 1.9 miles (2.7 miles) north, and turn left, following signs to West Thompson Lake. Go 0.3 mile (3.0 miles), and turn right on Reardon Road. Go 0.5 mile (3.5 miles), and turn left into the West Thompson Lake Recreation Area (41° 57.209′ N, 71° 53.983′ W).

WHAT YOU'LL SEE

This 200-plus-acre lake, managed by the U.S. Army Corps of Engineers, provides enjoyable paddling and camping opportunities. Indeed, only a few lakes in southern New England—most of them Corps of Engineers facilities—can boast no development along their shorelines. With a 5 MPH speed limit, you will encounter mostly canoes and kayaks.

The sandy, pebbly shore provides easy access around nearly the entire perimeter, where you can get out for a picnic or foray into the oak-hickory woods in the 2,200-acre recreational area surrounding the lake. The Corps

WEST THOMPSON LAKE AND QUINEBAUG RIVER

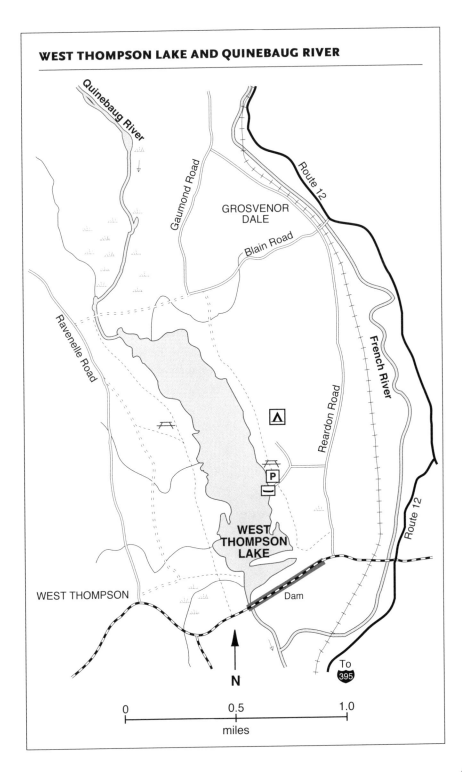

Quinebaug River

Gaumond Road

Route 12

GROSVENOR DALE

Blain Road

French River

Ravenelle Road

Reardon Road

P

WEST THOMPSON LAKE

Route 12

WEST THOMPSON

Dam

To 395

N

| 0 | 0.5 | 1.0 |

miles

maintains two picnic areas and a campground, which was less than half full on a mid-August Sunday. This lake used to suffer from expanses of muddy banks because of fluctuating water levels related to flood control, but since the early 1990s the Corps has raised the pool level, eliminating the band of exposed shoreline.

From the boat ramp on the eastern shore, paddle north and explore the inlets on the east shore and the small islands and rock outcroppings on the west shore. In one inlet that expands into a pickerelweed-choked pool about 125 feet across, we came across a very large snapping turtle hanging lazily near the surface, head pointed downward, searching for its next meal. Paddling north into the Quinebaug River, pretty quickly you pass under an old bridge on a 3.6-mile hiking trail that extends around the lake.

Wild grapevines drape over the wooded shoreline along the river, and a broad marsh opens up just above the footbridge, where we saw great blue and green herons, along with a pair of kingbirds chasing a sharp-shinned hawk. We saw a cuckoo feeding on tent caterpillars, and we spied another large snapping turtle, along with dozens of painted turtles out sunning on logs. Look carefully in the clear water, and you might also see the elusive underwater tire (*Goodyearis submergicus*); though many of them populate these waters, their bottom-dwelling habits frequently hide them from view. The farther upriver you paddle, the shallower it becomes, and the swifter the current; we paddled nearly 3 miles upstream before a riffle and very shallow water blocked our way.

70 | Mashapaug Lake and Bigelow Pond

Mashapaug Lake stands in contrast to most entries in this book, in that it is oligotrophic (meaning relatively nutrient-free waters). You can see down at least 20 feet in the clear water. Tiny Bigelow Pond, where we watched an osprey fish, stands in contrast as a shallow, marshy, nutrient-laden pond, more typical of most entries in this book.

Location: Union, CT
Maps: *Connecticut/Rhode Island Atlas & Gazetteer*, Map 56: B1, 2, 3, C1, 2, 3, D1, 2; USGS Wales, Westford
Area: Mashapaug Lake, 287 acres; Bigelow Pond, 26 acres
Time: 4 hours

MASHAPAUG LAKE AND BIGELOW POND

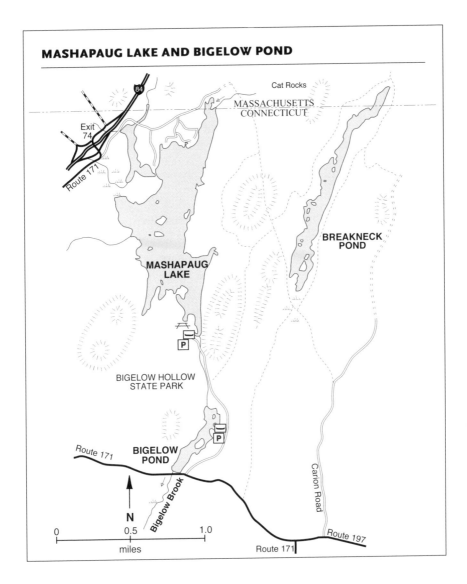

Habitat Type: oligotrophic natural lake, little aquatic vegetation

Fish: trout, largemouth and smallmouth bass, yellow perch, pickerel, walleye (see fish advisory, Appendix A)

Information: Bigelow Hollow State Park, Nipmuck State Forest, ct.gov/deep/cwp/view.asp?a=2716&q=325066; Bigelow Pond aquatic survey, ct.gov/caes/cwp/view.asp?a=2799&q=380212

Camping: Mashamoquet Brook State Park, West Thompson Lake

Take Note: some development and motors (10 MPH limit) on Mashapaug; no internal combustion motors or development on Bigelow

GETTING THERE

Bigelow Pond (41° 59.835' N, 72° 7.521' W). From I-84, Exit 74, go 3.6 miles (3.6 miles) east on Route 171, and turn left into Bigelow Hollow State Park. Go 0.3 mile (3.9 miles) to the access on the left.

Mashapaug Lake (42° 0.303' N, 72° 7.732' W). Go another 0.8 mile (4.7 miles) to the road's end. Just before the Mashapaug access, you pass the 1.2-mile trail to Breakneck Pond on the right.

WHAT YOU'LL SEE

Mashapaug Lake

This large, natural lake in northeastern Connecticut boasts deep coves, rocky shores, and beautiful surrounding hemlock and white pine woods. Bigelow Hollow State Park, with picnic tables on needle-carpeted ground overlooking the lake's blue water, hugs the southern shore. Trails along here wind among ancient stands of laurel, and the light filtering through the hemlock, pine, and oak canopy seems just right to support a wide array of wildflowers. Whether the hemlocks will withstand the hemlock woolly adelgid onslaught is an open question (see Trip 46). Most of the lake's eastern shore, with the land rising steeply from the water's edge, lies within 8,000-acre Nipmuck State Forest. In some areas, huge stone slabs extend down into the water.

While the south end of Mashapaug remains undeveloped except for the picnic area, some limited development fans out along the western and northern shores. Besides the development, road noise from I-84—just 0.5 mile away at the closest point—provides the only other reminder of civilization while you paddle this gorgeous place.

Few aquatic plants grow in these oligotrophic (low-nutrient) waters that boast 20-foot visibility. The state-record largemouth bass (12 pounds, 14 ounces) emerged from Mashapaug in 1961, and the state-record channel catfish (29 pounds, 6 ounces) was caught in Mashapaug in 2004.

Bigelow Pond

On a clear September day, we watched an osprey fish the clear water of Bigelow Pond. With only 26 acres, the pond takes little time to explore. It may be better just to picnic here and soak in the pond's scenic beauty.

In contrast with Mashapaug, this quite shallow pond abounds with floating vegetation and sphagnum moss-covered hillocks where tree stumps have long since rotted away. Look for sundews amid the sphagnum moss in these areas. In early October, we saw quite a few nodding ladies' tresses (*Spiranthes cernua*)—a small white orchid occasionally found in boggy areas. Along the shoreline, look for blueberry, sweet pepperbush, and laurel, along with hemlock and white pine growing farther from the water's edge. American white waterlily, yellow pond-lily, and watershield grow in the shallows. Beaver occur here at times, and you may see the occasional wood duck.

Breakneck Pond

In Nipmuck State Forest, a mile or so east of Mashapaug Lake, Breakneck Pond offers a wonderful paddling experience in a thick marshland. Intrepid explorers can reach this long, narrow pond only by hiking in—a very long carry with a boat.

71 | Somersville Mill Pond and Scantic River

The narrow, meandering Scantic River is a joy to paddle, leading you through a bird-filled swampland. A very diverse set of aquatic and semi-aquatic plants lines the shores, and in the upper reaches, branches and vines provide an ever-encroaching canopy.

Location: Somers, CT
Maps: *Connecticut/Rhode Island Atlas & Gazetteer*, Map 54: D5, 6, E4, 5; USGS Ellington
Area/Length: Somersville Mill Pond, 41 acres; Scantic River, 3 miles one way
Time: 3 hours
Habitat Type: shallow, marshy pond; narrow, winding river through swamp
Fish: trout, largemouth and calico bass, yellow perch, pickerel (see fish advisory, Appendix A)
Camping: Mashamoquet Brook State Park
Take Note: few motors, 6 MPH speed limit; development near dam

GETTING THERE

From I-91, Exit 47E, go east on Route 190 for 5.0 miles (5.0 miles), and turn right on Maple Street. Go 0.2 mile (5.2 miles) to the access on the left at the junction with School Street (41° 58.974′ N, 72° 29.224′ W).

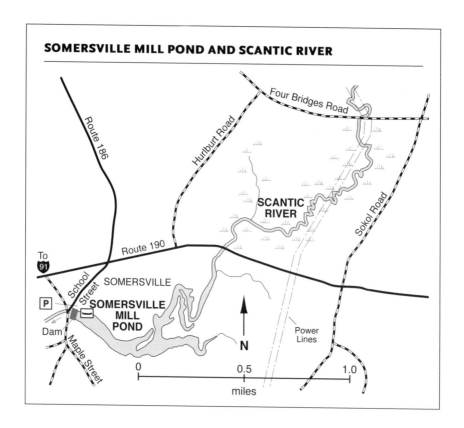

SOMERSVILLE MILL POND AND SCANTIC RIVER

WHAT YOU'LL SEE

Several small central Massachusetts brooks join to form the slowly meandering Scantic River as it drains extensive wooded marshlands. The section included here backs up behind a Somersville dam that, at the time of the second edition, was flanked by gorgeous old redbrick mills. Since then, those old mills have burned, leaving behind an unsightly heap of twisted steel and charred bricks.

Paddling out from the access, you quickly leave civilization behind. In the river's upper reaches, a golf driving range's net backs up to the riverbank, and twin high-voltage power lines appear overhead. Neither intrudes too much on the solitude.

Mist drifted off the water as we paddled out early one morning along the wooded shoreline. A kingfisher fled before us as cardinals, catbirds, song sparrows, and eastern towhees called from the dense undergrowth, and mourning doves sounded their plaintive coos overhead. We noted some big red oaks and very large swamp white oaks hanging out over the water. Shoreside shrubs, vines, and flowers stand out most, though, as you paddle up the picturesque Scantic River. Red-willow dogwood, alder, pickerelweed, arrowhead, willow,

The Scantic River meanders slowly through scenic marshlands.

buttonbush, purple loosestrife, cattail, pondweed, grapes, bur-reed, jewelweed, and American eelgrass line the shallow waterway's banks. We found lots of cardinal flower in bloom and many grapevines draped out over the water.

A beaver lodge just upstream from the Route 190 bridge had so many winter-forage branches surrounding the lodge that we almost couldn't get by. Check out the oxbows and side channels for birds; we saw or heard several species, including eastern phoebe, robin, chickadee, tufted titmouse, grackle, great blue heron, spotted sandpiper, crow, goldfinch, flicker, and red-bellied woodpecker.

Upstream, the channel narrows through tight-twisting turns with no perceptible current. Though plenty of water filled the main channel, we could not make it to Four Bridges Road because of overhanging grapevines and red-willow dogwoods. Maybe someone would be willing to prune back some of the more offending branches.

72 | Ross Marsh Pond

Ross Marsh is a quiet, out-of-the way pond, where you should find a lot of waterfowl, along with seas of aquatic vegetation. Look for muskrat and beaver in the evening.

Location: Killingly and Sterling, CT
Maps: *Connecticut/Rhode Island Atlas & Gazetteer*, Map 48: D10, E10; USGS East Killingly
Area: 55 acres
Time: 2 hours
Habitat Type: shallow, marshy pond
Fish: largemouth bass, pickerel (see fish advisory, Appendix A)
Camping: Mashamoquet Brook State Park
Take Note: no motors; no development; watch out for stumps

GETTING THERE

From the North. From I-395, Exit 91 southbound, go 3.5 miles (3.5 miles) east on Route 6, and turn right on Sawmill Hill Road. Go 1.7 miles (5.2 miles) to the access on the left, just over the bridge (41° 46.329′ N, 71° 47.757′ W).

From the South. From the Lodge Turnpike, go 1.6 miles (1.6 miles) south on Cucumber Hill Road, and turn right on South Killingly Road. Go 0.4 mile (2.0 miles), and turn right on Sawmill Hill Road. Go 0.2 mile (2.2 miles) to the access on the right, just before the bridge.

WHAT YOU'LL SEE

Ross Marsh, within Ross Marsh Wildlife Management Area, provides an outstanding paddling opportunity. Weaving our way north up the winding, open-water channel, we reveled in the solitude as mallards fed on abundant vegetation and hundreds of painted turtles slid off myriad stumps and logs into the water as we glided by. When we paddled here, beaver had dammed up the outlet, maintaining a slightly elevated water level. We startled a couple of fishing great blue herons and several flocks of wood ducks.

The diversity of aquatic vegetation and streamside shrubs and trees impressed us, especially the huge amount of eastern purple bladderwort in electric bloom. In most years, a few blooms appear here and there, but once or twice a decade, the lavender blooms erupt as though a brilliant carpet had

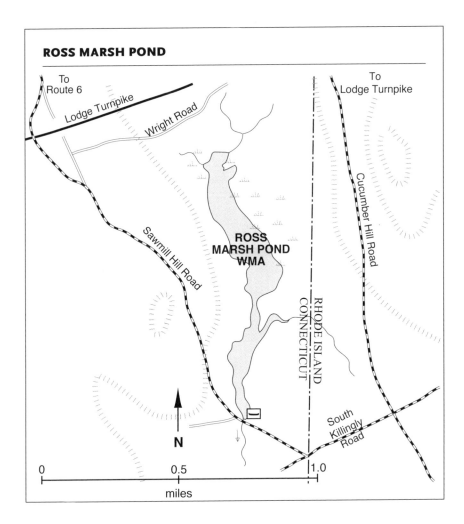

ROSS MARSH POND

To Route 6

Lodge Turnpike

Wright Road

To Lodge Turnpike

ROSS MARSH POND WMA

Sawmill Hill Road

Cucumber Hill Road

RHODE ISLAND
CONNECTICUT

South Killingly Road

N

0   0.5   1.0

miles

unfolded over the waterway. From late August through early September, we found dozens of ponds awash with color from *Utricularia purpurea* blooms. When we visited here in 2013, it was too early in the season to determine whether invasives, such as Eurasian or twoleaf watermilfoil, were crowding out the bladderwort.

On the pond's north end, among the buttonbush and bur-reed, *Phragmites* and cattails fight it out for dominance. You can paddle a couple of hundred yards up the narrow, winding inlet stream through a broad marsh, perhaps having to portage over a beaver dam. Dwarf red maple, streamside alder, and occasional swamp rose line the way. Watch out for stumps here and anywhere else in the pond outside the main channel.

CARNIVOROUS PLANTS
THE TABLE IS TURNED

Carnivorous plants thrive in New England's marshes, and their meat-eating adaptations make them one of nature's true wonders. Carnivory in plants apparently resulted from convergent evolution: the development of similar traits among unrelated species. Plant families on nearly every continent have some carnivorous species, with two common characteristics: they live in mineral-poor soils, supplementing soil nutrients with those from animals, and they use modified leaves to trap food.

Two capture strategies have evolved: active and passive. The Venus flytrap, which grows in sandy soils along the Carolina coast, uses an active capture strategy. A few other plants have adopted active strategies, including bladderworts (genus *Utricularia*), which form dense mats in shallow marshes. Bladderwort leaves consist of minute bladders that ingest and digest insect larvae and other organisms.

Passive capture strategies have taken two main paths. Pitcher plant— *Sarracenia purpurea*—collects rainwater in funnel-shaped leaves, and enzymes digest insects that fall into the leaves. Sundews (genus *Drosera*) form sticky pads that digest insects with enzymes.

Although each plant—bladderwort, pitcher plant, and sundew—captures prey in a different way, they all have the same reason for doing so: in nutrient-poor marshes, absorbing minerals from insects and other prey gives them a selective advantage over other plants. Tea-colored bog water, laden with organic acids from decaying vegetation, washes out minerals. Although carbon dioxide and water remain plentiful, nitrogen, phosphorus, potassium, and other important elements get leached out or bound up in underlying layers of sphagnum and peat.

Bladderwort. Bladderwort grows in shallow waters or in shoreline muck. Look for small yellow or purple snapdragon-like flowers, leading on short stalks to carnivorous underwater bladders that form dense, feathery mats, bearing hundreds of tiny (0.02 to 0.1 inch long), bulbous traps that form the plant's leaves. The bladders have two concave sides and a trapdoor. When a small organism bumps into the door's guard hairs, the bladder's sides pop out, and the door swings open, sucking in the hapless critter. This occurs in 0.002 seconds, followed by digestion by plant enzymes.

Mosquito larvae form the bulk of the bladderwort's diet, but the plant also ingests other larvae, rotifers, protozoa, and small crustaceans. With large prey, such as a tiny tadpole, the door closes around the organism, and the plant digests only part of it. The next time the hairs get triggered, the plant ingests more of the organism, eventually sucking it all in.

Several species of bladderworts grow in New England; two species have purple flowers, and as many as ten species have yellow flowers. We usually notice these plants when we see their snapdragon-like flowers protruding a few inches above the water's surface.

Pitcher Plant. The northern pitcher plant, *Sarracenia purpurea*, grows from British Columbia to Nova Scotia, southward through the Great Lakes region, and down the eastern coastal plain, crossing the Florida panhandle to the Mississippi River. Its pitcher-shaped leaves, initially green in spring, turn purple in fall and return to green next spring. Flowering occurs in June and July, and single reddish flowers, borne on stout stalks, tower a foot or more above the pitcher cluster.

The curved pitchers recline, allowing rain to fall into the open hood. Stiff, downward-pointing hairs in the plant's throat keep insects from climbing back out, and the narrow funnel leaves little room for airborne escape. The upper pitcher walls sport a waxy coating, making for slippery footing. A combination of plant and bacterial enzymes degrades the unlucky insects, and their nutrients pass easily through the unwaxed surface of the lower pitcher.

Insects drown in the modified pitcher plant leaves and are digested by plant and bacterial enzymes, providing essential plant nutrients.

The glistening sticky sundew leaves beckon insects to their doom.

Sundew. Sundew grows mainly in sphagnum bogs from Alaska to northern California, across the Canadian Rockies and plains, through the Great Lakes, north throughout Labrador, south to the Chesapeake Bay, and down through the Appalachians. The same plant grows in Europe, and four species occur in New England, including roundleaf sundew (*Drosera rotundifolia*), the most common species.

Sundew averages about 3 inches across and 1 inch high, with leaves modified into flattened oval pads, covered with red, stalked glands. Longer glands secrete a sticky fluid, while shorter glands secrete digestive enzymes. Attracted to nectarlike secretions, insects become trapped and then digested by plant enzymes. The usually white flowers hover well above the plant's leaves, borne on slender stalks. To find sundew, look for tiny glistening drops on their traps. Look carefully on sphagnum mats' reddish rosettes. You should also see several small insects in various stages of digestion.

73 | Moosup River and Oneco Pond

The Moosup River and Oneco Pond provide wonderful paddling just a few minutes from I-395 and close enough to Providence to escape for a morning or afternoon trip. Expect to see lots of painted turtles as well as the less common stinkpot turtle.

Location: Sterling, CT, and Coventry, RI
Maps: *Connecticut/Rhode Island Atlas & Gazetteer*, Map 48: J9, 10, 11; USGS Oneco
Length: 2 to 4 miles one way, depending on water level
Time: 2 to 4 hours round-trip
Habitat Type: shallow, meandering stream with wooded shores
Fish: trout (see fish advisory, Appendix A)
Camping: Hopeville Pond State Park, Pachaug State Forest (Green Falls and Mount Misery Campgrounds)
Take Note: private Riverbend Campground on Oneco Pond (http://riverbendcamp.com/)

GETTING THERE
From I-395, Exit 88, go 5.5 miles east on Route 14A to the access on the right, just over the bridge, at the Sterling Municipal Building (41° 41.566′ N, 71° 48.467′ W).

WHAT YOU'LL SEE
When we launched our boat on shallow, marshy Oneco Pond on an early-October afternoon, thick mats of Eurasian watermilfoil floated on the surface, and exposed mud flats greeted us. But as we paddled generally east into the Moosup River channel, our initial negative impression turned around completely.

The fairly wide river has a generally sandy bottom, although more rocks appear as you paddle upstream into Rhode Island. Many downed trees had fallen into the water some years earlier—judging from the decay—probably from a storm event, providing superb sunning locations for turtles, which you will see in profusion.

We saw probably more than a hundred painted turtles, but most skittered into the water long before we got too close. Another species found here, the

MOOSUP RIVER AND ONECO POND

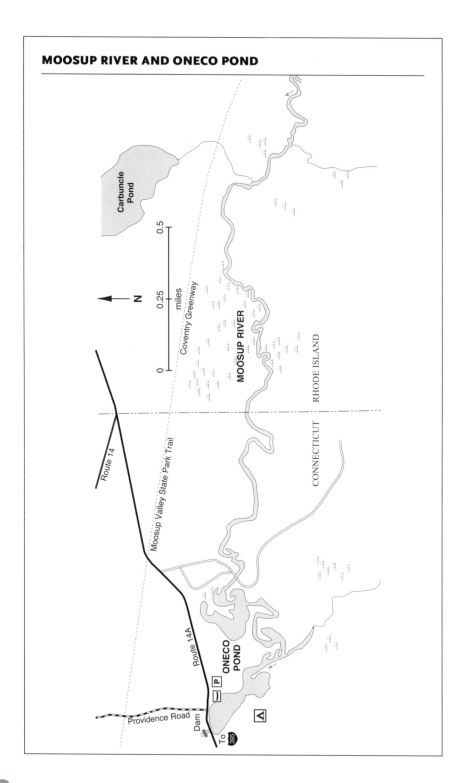

stinkpot or common musk turtle (*Sternotherus odoratus*), tolerates a much closer approach. We often paddled right up to this small turtle, which has a more steeply humped carapace than that of the painted turtle and is often coated with algae. Also note the more sharply pointed snout, which often points upward as the turtle basks on its chosen log. We have also found this somewhat more dexterous turtle fairly far up steeply pitched tree trunks, whereas the painted turtle almost always hovers close to the water.

We've never seen more stinkpot turtles than we saw here, counting seven in a 3-hour afternoon paddle. Although we didn't see any snapping turtles, which is not unusual, there should be lots of them as well.

Fortunately, we didn't see watermilfoil in the Moosup River. Shrubs along the banks include mountain laurel, winterberry, highbush blueberry, and sweet pepperbush. While white pine and red maple dominate the high ground, we also saw some blackgum, red and white oaks, American hornbeam or ironwood (*Carpinus caroliniana*), sassafras, alder, gray birch, and sugar maple.

In early October, the water level seemed to be down 8 to 12 inches—as evidenced by the undercut banks and high-and-dry eddies in the marshy ponds just east of Oneco Pond. It appeared that beavers had dug some deeper channels in these ponds, but we couldn't find clear evidence of that.

The low water hampered our paddling upstream. We didn't quite make it into Rhode Island but believe we could in the spring or during higher water levels. The current also flowed more quickly upstream, and in the spring, stronger current could be an issue in some places. After getting out a few times to ease our boat over downed logs or shallow gravel, we turned around and made our way back to the access.

From Oneco Pond, if you paddle under the Route 14A bridge (north), you'll get to a dam and waterworks that we suspect originally served a mill. Learning more about this installation would be an interesting research project.

Deciduous trees line the Moosup River's banks, lending spectacular colors in the fall.

74 | Mansfield Hollow Lake

Popular Mansfield Hollow offers many hours of varied paddling opportunities, including open lake, deep coves, islands, and several streams. Although motors are allowed, expect to see more canoes and kayaks. In the evening, expect to see beaver and muskrat in the inlet rivers.

Location: Mansfield and Windham, CT
Maps: *Connecticut/Rhode Island Atlas & Gazetteer*, Map 46: E10, 11, F11; USGS Spring Hill, Willimantic
Area: 500 acres
Time: all day
Habitat Type: wooded reservoir, deep coves, islands, and inlet rivers
Fish: trout, largemouth and calico bass, yellow perch, pickerel, northern pike (see fish advisory, Appendix A)
Information: Mansfield State Park, ct.gov/deep/cwp/view. asp?a=2716&q=325236

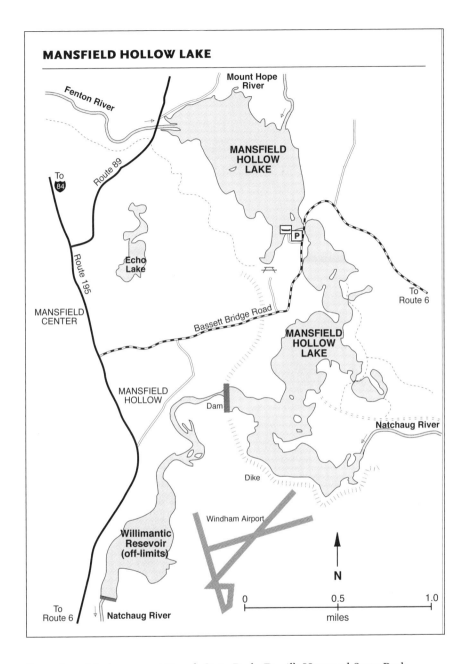

MANSFIELD HOLLOW LAKE

Mount Hope River

Fenton River

To 84

Route 89

MANSFIELD HOLLOW LAKE

Echo Lake

Route 195

MANSFIELD CENTER

P

To Route 6

Bassett Bridge Road

MANSFIELD HOLLOW LAKE

MANSFIELD HOLLOW

Dam

Natchaug River

Dike

Windham Airport

Willimantic Resevoir (off-limits)

N

0   0.5   1.0
miles

To Route 6

Natchaug River

Camping: Mashamoquet Brook State Park, Devil's Hopyard State Park

Take Note: recreational development only; motors limited to 8 MPH

GETTING THERE

From I-84, Exit 68, go south on Route 195, through Storrs, to Mansfield Center. Go 0.5 mile (0.5 mile) past the Route 89 junction, and turn left on Bassett Bridge Road. Go 1.4 miles (1.9 miles) to the access on the left (41° 46.099' N, 72° 10.53' W).

From the end of I-384, go east on Route 6, and turn left (north) on Route 195. Go 2.1 miles (2.1 miles), and turn right on Bassett Bridge Road. Go 1.4 miles (3.5 miles) to the access on the left.

WHAT YOU'LL SEE

Its large size, by southern New England standards, makes Mansfield Hollow Lake (or Naubesatuck Lake) a prime recreation destination, particularly for those who crave lots of exercise. Because of an 8 MPH speed limit, more hand-powered than motor-powered craft ply these waters. It would take at least a day to explore the entire shoreline, every island, and the reservoir's deep coves. You can also paddle up the three inlet rivers, adding greatly to your exploration time.

Bassett Bridge Road causeway divides the waterway roughly in half. The U.S. Army Corps of Engineers, in response to devastating flooding of Willimantic in 1936, created the lake in 1952 with a dam and dikes along the Natchaug River. Like many flood-control reservoirs, Mansfield Hollow's water level fluctuates, although the Corps tries to keep it bank-full in summer. Paddling here after Columbus Day, you may have to contend with an exposed gravelly shoreline.

The narrower southern section of Mansfield Hollow Lake, below Bassett Bridge Road, offers more coves and islands to explore. From the access, paddle through one of two large steel culverts into the northeast end of this lower section, where a hidden pond off to the east connects with the main lake by a small channel. This small pond feels very remote and quiet—especially on a windy day. You can carry into another, slightly larger pond farther to the southeast. As you paddle into the southern end, a massive dike looms over the lake like the Great Wall of China. The primary inlet into the lake, the Natchaug River, paddleable for a short distance upriver, flows in at the southeastern tip.

The northern, wider section of the lake, with fewer twisting coves to explore, has a somewhat more natural feel to it, particularly at the north end. Two inlets enter here: Mount Hope River, coming from the north, and Fenton River, coming from the northwest. A few hundred yards up Mount Hope River, a beaver lodge stands sentinel over the rapids and rocks that block your way. You can paddle under Route 89 and up the Fenton River much farther. We've gone about 0.5 mile up here and found the paddling very easy on the slow-moving, meandering channel. Beaver lodges occur along here as well, and numerous muskrats call the banks home; in the late afternoon, you should see both beaver and muskrats.

White pine and red oak dominate the lake's shoreline, along with white oak, shagbark hickory, pitch pine, red maple, gray birch, alder, aspen, elm, willow, and various shrubs, including sweetgale, buttonbush, blueberry, red-osier dogwood, wild grape, swamp azalea, swamp rose, swamp loosestrife, and winterberry. You will also see royal fern and the invasive purple loosestrife. Look for mussels on the sandy bottom and for the round, gelatinous balls of bryozoa colonies clinging to underwater logs. *Phragmites* (common reed) and other grasses populate the few small pockets of marsh. In early October, we saw osprey, red-tailed hawk, mallard, black duck, red-breasted merganser, and kingfisher species and quite a few eastern bluebirds in migration. The Connecticut state-record rainbow trout, 14 pounds, 10 ounces, was caught here in 1998.

75 | Eagleville Pond and Willimantic River

Marshy Eagleville Pond and the Willimantic River offer hours of exploration. Great blue and green herons patrol the shoreline, while song sparrow, cardinal, catbird, and common yellowthroat fill dense shrubs that line the shore. Look for Canada goose and wood duck, and for beaver and muskrat in the evening.

Location: Coventry and Mansfield, CT
Maps: *Connecticut/Rhode Island Atlas & Gazetteer*, Map 46: D3, 4, 5; USGS Coventry
Area/Length: Eagleville Pond, 80 acres; Willimantic River, 1.5 miles one way
Time: 3 hours round-trip
Habitat Type: shallow, marshy pond; vines and trees overhanging river
Fish: largemouth and smallmouth bass, yellow perch, pickerel (see fish advisory, Appendix A)
Information: Eagleville Pond aquatic survey, ct.gov/caes/cwp/view.asp?a=2799&q=513526

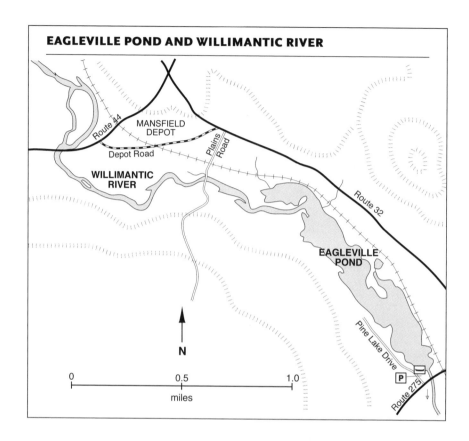

EAGLEVILLE POND AND WILLIMANTIC RIVER

MANSFIELD DEPOT

Route 44

Depot Road

Plains Road

WILLIMANTIC RIVER

Route 32

EAGLEVILLE POND

Pine Lake Drive

Route 275

N

0   0.5   1.0
miles

Camping: Mashamoquet Brook State Park, Devil's Hopyard State Park
Take Note: limited development; cartop access and shallow water limit motors, 8 MPH speed limit

GETTING THERE

From I-84, Exit 59, go east on I-384. When I-384 ends, go 7.7 miles (7.7 miles) east on Route 44, and turn right on Route 32. Go 1.8 miles (9.5 miles), and turn right on Route 275 (South Eagleville Road). Go 0.3 mile (9.8 miles) to the access on the right, just across the bridge (41° 47.062′ N, 72° 16.905′ W).

WHAT YOU'LL SEE

Eagleville Pond and the Willimantic River offer hours of wonderful paddling through labyrinthine channels around dozens of low, marshy islands and coves. Swamp loosestrife lines many of these channels, particularly at the pond's north end where the river enters. Carolina fanwort is the dominant underwater species. A railroad track parallels the pond's east shore, with a gravel pit beyond, and a few houses occur along the pond's southwest shore. Very little development impinges on most of the rest of this gorgeous habitat.

As we paddled up the pond, wood ducks rose from weed-choked coves, while red-winged blackbirds called from the streambanks. Skulking birds—song sparrows, cardinals, catbirds, and common yellowthroats—called from the dense undergrowth. Muskrats harvested pickerelweed along the shore, among the yellow pond-lily and watershield. Swamp azalea, jewelweed, joe-pye weed, and lots of alders lined the banks, along with great arbors of grapes overhanging the bankside shrubs. We spied a completely overgrown beaver lodge, noticeable only because of the large array of alders and other branches stuck butt-first into the mud for winter fodder.

Along the river, shagbark hickory, red maple, and basswood formed arching canopies in places, and the occasional gray birch, ash, willow, American hornbeam, black cherry, and black birch (twigs have a wintergreen odor when scratched) joined the ubiquitous red maple- and red oak-dominated shoreline. The first part of the river upstream from the pond has no discernible current, but shallow riffles that make paddling difficult start to occur well before the Route 44 bridge.

Paddling back downstream, a red-tailed hawk gave out its piercing cry from the treetops, while a green heron stalked the shoreline. Canada geese tried to look inconspicuous, and a great blue heron stood knee-deep among the lily pads. Amid all this wildlife and beautiful scenery, we hated to leave this wonderful place.

76 | Mono Pond

If the bryozoa have not been crowded out by invasive aquatic weeds, they offer a real treat when paddling Mono Pond's shores. Look for great blue heron, wood duck, and other marsh birds. Paddling can become difficult in the summer because of copious amounts of aquatic vegetation.

Location: Columbia, CT
Maps: *Connecticut/Rhode Island Atlas & Gazetteer*, Map 46: K3, L3; USGS Columbia

Area: 113 acres

Time: 2 hours

Habitat Type: shallow, marshy pond

Fish: largemouth bass, yellow perch, pickerel (see fish advisory, Appendix A)
Information: aquatic plant survey, ct.gov/caes/cwp/view asp?a=2799&q=522444

Camping: Devil's Hopyard State Park

Take Note: limited development; small size and aquatic vegetation limit motors, 8 MPH speed limit, no water-skiing

GETTING THERE

From the junction of Routes 6 and 66 just west of Willimantic, go 2.7 miles (2.7 miles) west on Route 66, and turn left on Pine Street. Go 1.0 mile (3.7 miles), and turn right on Hunt Road. Go 0.2 mile (3.9 miles) to the access on the left (41° 40.735′ N, 72° 18.639′ W).

WHAT YOU'LL SEE

When we paddled Mono Pond in 2002, it sported a new concrete boat ramp, a huge disappointment for this scenic pond. Though we could detect no Carolina fanwort or watermilfoil, boat trailers inevitably bring it in, infecting yet another pond with these invasive, nearly impossible-to-remove species. We fear that the underwater, gelatinous bryozoa colonies will disappear, as they appear to have done in nearby Holbrook Pond, smothered out by dense rafts of Carolina fanwort and watermilfoil. When we visited in 2013, it was too early in the season to see whether invasives had arrived; however, a 2012 plant survey revealed the presence of three invasives: twoleaf watermilfoil (*Myriophyllum heterophyllum*), Carolina fanwort, and Brazilian waterweed. Quoting from the survey, "*M. heterophyllum* was the most dominant plant in the lake."

Bryozoa had colonized many submerged logs in the pond's north end, and huge rafts of both a yellow-flowered and eastern purple bladderwort filled the water column at the south end. The bladderworts—whose underwater pods devour mosquito larvae—will become much reduced, if not eliminated, when the Carolina fanwort and milfoil take over.

But the bryozoa would be the real loss, because we see these colonies only rarely. They require pure water, and we assume that choking vegetation causes either stagnation, which compromises water quality or reduced ability for the cilia to sweep the water for the microscopic algae, protozoa, and diatoms that comprise their diet.

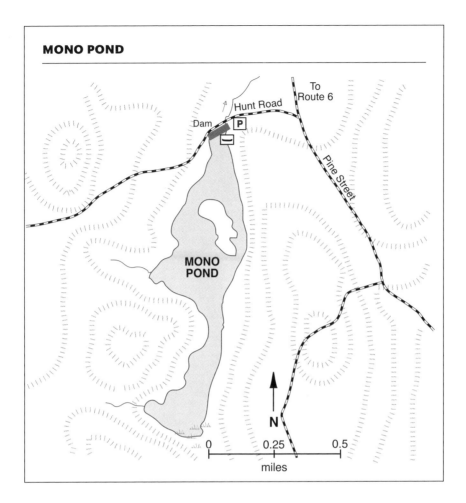

MONO POND

Hunt Road

To Route 6

Dam

P

Pine Street

MONO POND

N

0   0.25   0.5
miles

Thick stands of mostly deciduous trees cover the hillsides, hiding some limited development. Sweet pepperbush, highbush blueberry, swamp azalea, buttonbush, and swamp loosestrife line the banks, while seas of watershield and American white waterlily cover the water's surface on the south end. By August, paddling through this blanket of vegetation becomes difficult, but our foray into it gave us good looks at many wood ducks and an immature great blue heron as it stalked and ate sunfish along the shore.

A great blue heron takes a break from fishing.

77 | Bishop Swamp

Paddling is slow-going on this weed-choked pond. We saw an otter family here; you could see muskrat and beaver. Canada goose and wood duck both nest here. We watched crows mob a great horned owl.

Location: Andover, CT
Maps: *Connecticut/Rhode Island Atlas & Gazetteer*, Map 45: I22; USGS Marlborough
Area: 53 acres
Time: 2 hours
Habitat Type: shallow, marshy pond
Fish: largemouth and calico bass, pickerel (see fish advisory, Appendix A)
Camping: Devil's Hopyard State Park
Take Note: no development; no internal combustion motors

GETTING THERE
From I-84, Exit 59, go east on I-384. When I-384 ends, go 5.7 miles (5.7 miles) east on Route 6, and turn right on Route 316. Go 0.5 mile (6.2 miles), and turn right on Boston Hill Road. Go 1.4 miles (7.6 miles), and turn left on Jurovaty Road. Go 0.8 mile (8.4 miles) to the access on the right (41° 42.964′ N, 72° 23.358′ W).

WHAT YOU'LL SEE
Although beaver maintain channels through the abundant surface vegetation—mostly American white waterlily and watershield—you can't escape the even more abundant invasive watermilfoil and Carolina fanwort that fill the water column here. The abundant vegetation, of course, suited the Canada geese and wood ducks just fine, and amazingly it did not seem to affect the family of otters that cavorted on the pond's south end. Every time they surfaced, either to crunch loudly on fish or to cast a wary eye in our direction as we watched them through binoculars, aquatic vegetation clung to their heads and necks—a quite comical scene.

Though we did not see any beaver in the early morning, we did find several large, jewelweed-encrusted beaver lodges, a couple of them quite close together.

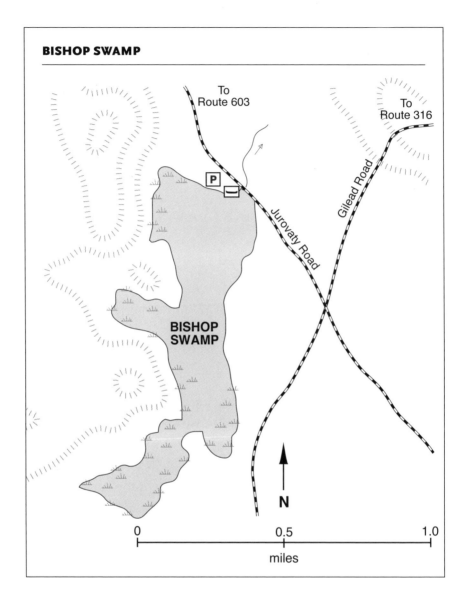

BISHOP SWAMP

To
Route 603

To
Route 316

Gilead Road

Jurovaty Road

P

BISHOP
SWAMP

N

0   0.5   1.0

miles

We wondered whether the otter had evicted the beaver from one of the lodges, causing them to construct another close by.

We saw a lot more in this wildlife paradise, a stone's throw away from Hartford. We watched crows mob a great horned owl on an island on the pond's south end. A couple of great blue herons stalked the shoreline, and dozens of tree swallows perched on limbs of dead trees standing in the water of the larger coves. Other birds foraged for food above the water or in the shoreside

A male green frog, *Rana clamitans*, eyes us warily from the lily pads.

foliage. We saw robins, goldfinches, mourning doves, red-bellied woodpeckers, kingbirds, red-winged blackbirds, and phoebes. Frogs hopped off the lily pads as we paddled along, trying to avoid the stumps and barely submerged logs.

This idyllic setting suffers, though, from alien invaders. Watermilfoil and Carolina fanwort (not a foreign invader but often introduced from elsewhere) crowd out the yellow- and purple-flowered bladderworts, and purple loosestrife crowds out the native swamp loosestrife, cattail, buttonbush, and joe-pye weed. Expect, also, to see fishermen here.

8 | SOUTHERN CONNECTICUT

The fifteen entries here include the Housatonic River estuary, embedded in the Charles E. Wheeler Wildlife Management Area, and also the Connecticut River's Great Island Estuary, along with four tributary streams. The coastal East River also has a small estuary. The other entries all consist of ponds and reservoirs.

The Housatonic River salt marsh is a birder's paradise, especially during shorebird migration in August, with more than 300 bird species observed here. The area is off-limits to motors until September 1, making for delightful paddling in the extensive channels that crisscross the marsh. Great Island Estuary also offers an extraordinary paddling opportunity. Birdlife abounds, which is why Roger Tory Peterson, the famed naturalist, chose to live in Old Lyme. The wildlife refuge now bears his name. East River provides a wonderful opportunity to explore an extensive *Spartina* salt marsh, or you can paddle upriver away from Long Island Sound. Look for fiddler crabs, herons and egrets, osprey, and northern harrier.

Lord Cove, just upriver from Great Island, offers one of the best places to watch osprey dive for fish. Look for herons and egrets, along with many shorebirds on the mud flats during spring and fall migrations. Labyrinthine waterways lace the marsh. Farther upstream, tiny Whalebone Creek penetrates an extensive, pristine freshwater marsh, filled with birds and wild rice. Adjacent Selden Creek offers great paddling and also camping on a gorgeous Connecticut River island. Across from the island, more marshlands beg to be explored.

Even farther upstream on the Connecticut, you can paddle several miles up the Salmon River, a great place for bird-watchers. Watch osprey dive for fish in the clear water, and look for songbirds in the tall trees on the shore and hillsides. Marshy coves harboring wild rice await exploration.

Several ponds populate the Pachaug State Forest area, including Hopeville Pond and the Pachaug River. Hopeville Pond is a recreation destination, with camping, paddling, swimming, and hiking available. Another section of the Pachaug River, along with Beachdale Pond, makes a great place to paddle up the river through a pristine swamp. Hiking and mountain biking trails course through the surrounding 23,000-acre Pachaug State Forest. Green Falls Pond, a recreation destination with camping, backpacking, hiking, biking, and paddling available, lies deep within the Pachaug State Forest. A mix of tall trees surrounds the pond and the shrub-lined shore. The woods has an open understory with loads of wildflowers in the spring.

Powers Lake boasts great tree diversity along its shores, including four oak species. We were fortunate to see a rare spotted turtle, along with a stinkpot turtle, painted turtles, and several northern water snakes. Nehantic State Forest borders one side of nearby Uncas Pond and offers an extensive network of hiking trails. Uncas Pond, with its clear water, is surrounded by a very diverse forest.

Babcock Pond lies within the 1,500-acre Babcock Pond Wildlife Management Area.. Best paddling is in the spring. Look for wood ducks and other waterfowl and muskrats. Nearby Moodus Reservoir is a popular lake with a fair amount of development and high-speed boating; best paddling is in early spring and in fall. For more solitude in summer, head to the deep southeast cove with its dense patches of watershield.

Undeveloped Pattaconk Reservoir sits amid Connecticut's second largest state forest and does not allow motors. Although a great place to paddle amid gorgeous hillsides, it also draws large crowds, particularly on weekends, for hiking, biking, swimming, and paddling. In contrast, nearby Messerschmidt Pond, surrounded by a wildlife management area, is a much quieter place to paddle. In our visits, we've seen painted and snapping turtles and listened to many birds calling from the woods.

78 | Hopeville Pond and Pachaug River

Hopeville Pond is a recreation destination, with camping, paddling, swimming, and hiking available. Besides paddling here, you can paddle upstream through Pachaug Pond into Glasgo Pond. Look for beaver in the evening. Expect to see great blue herons, ducks, geese, and turtles.

Location: Griswold, CT
Maps: *Connecticut/Rhode Island Atlas & Gazetteer*, Map 39: C13, 14, D14; USGS Jewett City
Area/Length: Hopeville Pond, 150 acres; Pachaug River, 3.6 miles one way
Time: 4 hours, all day to paddle into Glasgo Pond
Habitat Type: dammed-up meandering river
Fish: largemouth bass, yellow perch, walleye, pickerel, northern pike (see fish advisory, Appendix A)
Information: Hopeville Pond State Park, ct.gov/deep/cwp/view. asp?a=2716&q=325218
Camping: Hopeville Pond State Park, Pachaug State Forest (Green Falls and Mount Misery campgrounds)
Take Note: some development, state campground; motors limited to 8 MPH

GETTING THERE
From I-395, Exit 86, go 1.4 miles east on Route 201 to Hopeville Pond State Park on the right (41° 36.465′ N, 71° 55.583′ W).

WHAT YOU'LL SEE
Hopeville Pond, a widened 3-mile section of the Pachaug River, offers very pleasant, relaxing paddling. Its shores include Hopeville Pond State Park, the site of a former waterpower-driven woolen mill. The federal government purchased it in 1930, and the Civilian Conservation Corps (CCC) managed it until transferring it to the state in 1959. Today, the pond offers fine waterside family camping, hiking, swimming, and boating. The park adjoins Pauchaug State Forest, whose 14-mile Nehantic Trail meanders over low, hilly terrain, connecting the northeast side of Hopeville Pond with Green Falls Pond in Voluntown.

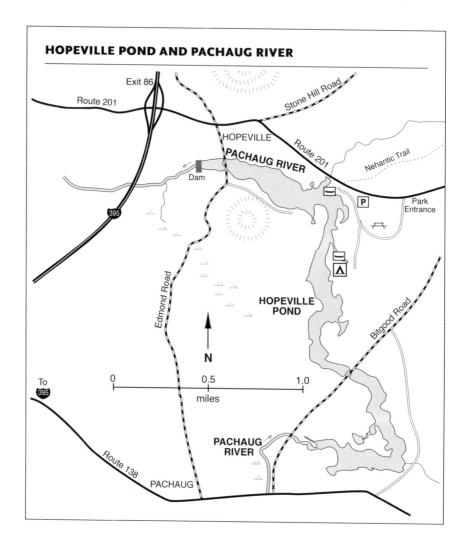

HOPEVILLE POND AND PACHAUG RIVER

Exit 86

Route 201

Stone Hill Road

HOPEVILLE

PACHAUG RIVER

Route 201

Nehantic Trail

Dam

395

P

Park Entrance

Edmond Road

Bitgood Road

HOPEVILLE POND

N

To 395

0   0.5   1.0

miles

PACHAUG RIVER

Route 138

PACHAUG

The pond winds through woodland, farmland, and areas with light cottage development between a dam at the north end close to I-395 and a section of river at the south end, connecting to other ponds farther upstream. To reach larger, more developed Pachaug Pond (831 acres) and much nicer Glasgo Pond (184 acres), continue upstream on the Pachaug River, carrying around the dam (Trip 79).

Like other bodies of water in this part of the state, Hopeville Pond's shallow water carries a deep, reddish brown color caused by natural tannins. You will see lots of painted turtles along here, as well as great blue herons, kingfishers, black ducks, mallards, and possibly wood ducks. Several male wood ducks in

We often see blue flag, *Iris versicolor*, growing along the banks of marshy ponds in New England.

full breeding plumage landed right in front of our boats near the south end of the pond where we had paused under cover of a tree. Upon seeing us, they immediately took to the air, emitting their high-pitched distress call. We also saw signs of beaver here and a lodge at the south end where the pond narrows to a river channel.

EASTERN PAINTED TURTLE
QUIETWATER COMPANION

You won't have to spend much time paddling before spotting your first painted turtle, but getting a really good look may prove a little more difficult. The eastern painted turtle, *Chrysemys picta*, the most visible of our turtle species, may not be the most common. That distinction may belong to the much larger snapping turtle, whose bottom-dwelling habit keeps it out of view most of the time. On marshy ponds you may see literally hundreds of painted turtles basking in the sun on stumps, partially submerged logs, rocks, and vegetation—but always within easy reach of underwater safety. The painted turtle remains alert to danger; if you paddle along noisily, it disappears from view long before you draw near.

The painted turtle's carapace—the smooth, gently arched top shell—reaches a length of 7 inches. The colorful, patterned carapace lends the species its name. Narrow lines of yellow separate the dark olive green scutes (interlocking plates evolutionarily adapted from vertebrae to form the shell), and a wider orange band defines the outer edge of the shell (a brownish deposit on the shell may obscure these colors). The head and neck sport distinctive yellow stripes, and dark blotches sometimes mark the yellow plastron (bottom shell).

The painted turtle, found throughout much of the United States, ranges farther north than any other turtle species. Of the four subspecies, two occur in southern New England. The much more common eastern painted turtle (*Chrysemys picta picta*) has carapace scutes that line up in rows across the back, while the midland painted turtle (*C.p. marginata*), found mostly in western parts of the region, has scutes that alternate instead of running straight across. You need to get a really close look to distinguish these subspecies.

Diet consists of both plant and animal material, and you may see them underwater, feeding on submerged vegetation and various crustaceans, tadpoles, snails, and insect larvae. Mostly you will see them basking, a habit attributed to having a body temperature that fluctuates with environmental temperature—emerging from cold water, they absorb solar radiation to raise their body temperature and, therefore, their metabolic rate, helping them grow faster. However, some evidence suggests that they also bask to dislodge attached leeches.

The painted turtle mates during spring or summer, usually from late April through mid-June. During courtship, one or more males swim around a stationary female. If she accepts his advances, she dives to the bottom where mating takes place. One to two months later, the female leaves the water to deposit a clutch of usually five to eleven eggs in a nest excavated on open, sloping sand or gravel banks, or even lawns not too far from water. She digs the shallow nest with her hind feet and deposits the soft-shell eggs. She may also build several false nests, probably to mislead skunk, raccoon, and other predators that dig up and consume about 90 percent of turtle nests. Incubation temperature determines hatchling gender: males emerge from cool nests (around 75 degrees Fahrenheit) and females from warmer ones (around 85 degrees Fahrenheit).

Amazingly, hatchling painted turtles can withstand freezing. In northern parts of their range, the young overwinter in their nests after hatching in fall. With the nest just a few inches deep, temperatures drop well below freezing. The hatchlings' muscle activity, breathing, heartbeat, and blood flow totally stop—yet they usually recover fully when the temperature rises.

While most biological functions stop, some minimal brain activity continues, and only about half of their body fluids actually freeze solid. Ice forms in the turtle's extremities and grows inward, but high concentrations of sugars in the blood work like antifreeze to keep the critical core fluids from solidifying, down to 25 degrees Fahrenheit. In years with sparse insulating snow cover, nest temperature drops below this point, and most hatchlings do not survive. While a few other reptiles and amphibians exhibit similar freezing adaptations, none is as well adapted as the painted turtle hatchling. After the first year, however, the painted turtle loses the ability to survive freezing.

The painted turtle hibernates at above-freezing temperatures in the pond's bottom mud—an area almost devoid of oxygen. Other turtle species also have the ability to hibernate underwater for periods of up to four months without coming up for air. During periods of very low activity, many turtles and frogs absorb oxygen and release carbon dioxide through specialized membranes. But painted turtles, and closely related sliders, survive in totally deoxygenated water for a period of several months. Indeed, these turtles have the greatest known tolerance for oxygen deprivation of any vertebrate in the animal kingdom, with an ability to survive in water totally devoid of oxygen for up to 150 days. Specialized biochemical adaptations make survival possible. The turtles store large reserves of the carbohydrate fuel glycogen, which breaks down to produce energy without using oxygen in a process called glycolysis. Because glycolysis produces lactic acid, another adaptation is required: the release of calcium and magnesium from the turtle's shell to buffer the acid.

And you thought you were looking at just an ordinary pond dweller! Instead, the painted turtle's veritable treasure trove of fascinating and unique biological adaptations enables it to survive the harsh conditions of New England and southern Canada. For more information on turtles, see David Carroll's *The Year of the Turtle: A Natural History* (see Appendix B), a naturalist's wonderful account of 40 years of turtle observation in New Hampshire.

79 | Pachaug River and Beachdale Pond

Look for osprey, mute swan, wood duck, and possibly otter. Paddle up the Pachaug River through a pristine swamp. Hiking and mountain biking trails course through the surrounding 23,000-acre Pachaug State Forest.

Location: Voluntown, CT

Maps: *Connecticut/Rhode Island Atlas & Gazetteer*, Map 39: D18, 19, E18; USGS Voluntown

Area/Length: Beachdale Pond, 46 acres; Pachaug River, 2.5 miles one way, could be shorter if vines block the river

Time: 4 hours round-trip

Habitat Type: dammed-up pond, narrow meandering river with dense overhanging shrubs, marshlands

Fish: trout, largemouth bass, yellow perch (see fish advisory, Appendix A) Information: Pachaug State Forest, ct.gov/deep/cwp/view. asp?a=2716&q=325068

Camping: Hopeville Pond State Park, Pachaug State Forest (Green Falls and Mount Misery campgrounds)

Take Note: campground but otherwise little development; aquatic vegetation limits motors, 8 MPH speed limit

GETTING THERE

From I-395, Exit 85, go 6.4 miles (6.4 miles) east on Route 138, and turn left on Route 49. Go 0.6 mile (7.0 miles) to the access on the right, just after crossing the bridge (41° 35.079′ N, 71° 51.309′ W).

WHAT YOU'LL SEE

Paddle downstream from the Pachaug River access to reach small, shallow Beachdale Pond with its extensive cover of marshy vegetation. Watch for painted turtles and frogs hiding amid the abundant arrowhead, pickerelweed, waterlilies, and grasses. Carolina fanwort, with white flowers and yellow stamens, bloomed when we paddled here in August. We watched an osprey fish, and a pair of mute swans paddled about with four cygnets. To the northwest, you can paddle up Mount Misery Brook, which winds through the marsh. We paddled upstream

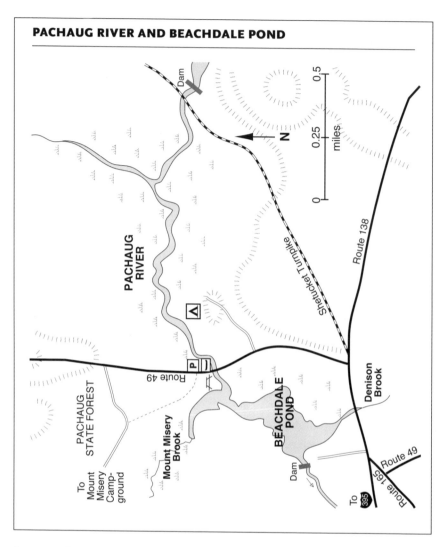

for a good 0.5 mile or so before an approaching thunderstorm convinced us to turn around.

Though the pond offers a nice diversion, the Pachaug River upstream from the access offers the real attraction. Once you clear Nature's Campsites, a private campground, you enter Pachaug–Great Meadow Swamp, winding your way upstream, dipping your paddle in the yellow-brown water of a pristine swamp on a gradually narrowing waterway. Red maple, grapevine, Virginia creeper, and ubiquitous poison ivy branches overhang the swamp. Eventually these branches block the way, unless some enterprising soul has hacked a path through them. Besides surprising an occasional wood duck brood, we saw many turtles out

Although graceful and elegant, mute swans (imports from Eurasia) drive away native species. Here adults paddle with nearly fully grown cygnets.

sunning themselves and reveled in the large patches of bright crimson cardinal flower growing along the banks.

Appropriately, Pachaug derives from a Narragansett word meaning "bend or turn in the river." Pequot, Narragansett, and Mohegan tribes inhabited this area prior to the arrival of Europeans. During the latter half of the seventeenth century, a combined force of colonists and Mohegans defeated the Narragansetts and Pequots, and in 1700, a 6-mile by 6-mile tract of land was granted to the Mohegan war veterans. Eventually the central portion of this tract became "Volunteer Town," incorporated as Voluntown in 1721.

Numerous hiking and mountain biking trails wend their way through various sections of the 23,000-acre Pachaug State Forest, the largest state forest in Connecticut. Nearby, a short loop trail traverses a wonderful Rhododendron Sanctuary—a quite unusual isolated stand of ancient rhododendron and white cedar. The Mount Misery camping area and Rhododendron Sanctuary are on the other side of Route 49 from the boat access.

80 | Green Falls Pond

Remote Green Falls Pond is a recreation destination offering camping, backpacking, hiking, biking, and paddling. A mix of tall trees surrounds the pond and the shrub-lined shore. The woods has an open understory with loads of wildflowers in the spring. Look for eastern purple bladderwort on the pond.

Location: Voluntown, CT
Maps: *Connecticut/Rhode Island Atlas & Gazetteer*, Map 39: G21, H21; USGS Voluntown
Area: 48 acres
Time: 2 hours
Habitat Type: wooded pond
Fish: trout, largemouth bass (see fish advisory, Appendix A)
Information: Pachaug State Forest, ct.gov/deep/cwp/view.asp?a=2716&q=325068; aquatic survey, ct.gov/caes/cwp/view.asp?a=2799&q=380986
Camping: Hopeville Pond State Park, Pachaug State Forest (Green Falls and Mount Misery campgrounds)
Take Note: no development; no internal combustion motors

GETTING THERE
From I-395, Exit 85, go 8.5 miles (8.5 miles) east on Route 138, and turn right at the sign for Green Falls Reservoir. Go 2.5 miles (11.0 miles) to the access, passing the picnic area on the right (41° 32.069′ N, 71° 48.645′ W).

WHAT YOU'LL SEE
Green Falls Pond, one of the most remote bodies of water in this guide, is a real treasure, ideal for a morning or afternoon of quiet paddling and a superb spot for family camping. Like Beachdale and Glasgo Ponds, Green Falls Pond lies within southeastern Connecticut's sprawling Pachaug State Forest—the largest tract of public land in southern New England. Well off the beaten path, the state forest generally attracts only hiking, paddling, or camping enthusiasts.

The beautiful woods surrounding Green Falls Pond—with a tall canopy of red, chestnut, and white oaks; sugar maple; yellow birch; hemlock; sassafras; and

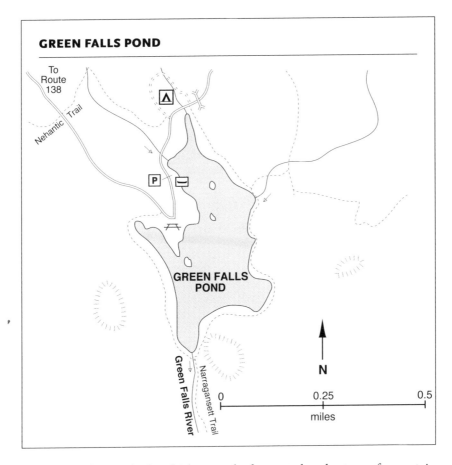

GREEN FALLS POND

To Route 138

Nehantic Trail

P

GREEN FALLS POND

N

Green Falls River

Narragansett Trail

0   0.25   0.5
miles

shagbark hickory—shade a fairly open, leaf-carpeted understory of mountain laurel, flowering dogwood, and a wide variety of spring wildflowers. Blueberry, mountain laurel, and other shrubs line the rocky shoreline, with plenty of places to pull out for a rest, walk in the woods, or picnic. Look for eastern purple bladderwort along the shore. A few islands dot the pond, and several trails weave through Pachaug State Forest, including Nehantic and Narragansett trails. From the pond's south end by the dam, you can walk downstream through a deep gorge, with majestic hemlock trees towering more than 100 feet overhead. Let's hope they can withstand the hemlock wooly adelgid onslaught (see Trip 46).

Pachaug State Forest permits backpacking, one of the few areas in Connecticut to do so, with special shelters and campsites available along trails for backpackers only (advance registration required).

81 | Powers Lake

Powers Lake boasts great tree diversity along its shores, including four oak species. Shrubs grow thickly along the shore, but you can get out on some protruding granite slabs. Expect to see lots of wildlife; we were fortunate to see a rare spotted turtle, along with a stinkpot turtle, painted turtles, and several northern water snakes.

Location: East Lyme, CT

Maps: *Connecticut/Rhode Island Atlas & Gazetteer*, Map 28: D6, 7; USGS Hamburg, Montville

Area: 144 acres

Time: 3 hours

Habitat Type: wooded pond

Fish: largemouth and calico bass, yellow perch, pickerel (see fish advisory, Appendix A)

Information: plant survey, ct.gov/caes/cwp/view.asp?a=2799&q=436854

Camping: Rocky Neck State Park, Hammonasset Beach State Park, Devil's Hopyard State Park, Hopeville Pond State Park

Take Note: limited development; motors limited to 8 MPH, no water skiing

GETTING THERE

From I-95, Exit 74 northbound, go 0.4 mile (0.4 mile) north on Route 161, and turn left on Route 1 (Post Road). Go 0.6 mile (1.0 mile), and turn right on Upper Pattagansett Road. Go 2.7 miles (3.7 miles), and turn right on Whistletown Road. Go 0.6 mile (4.3 miles), and turn right on the access road (41° 23.601′ N, 72° 15.409′ W).

WHAT YOU'LL SEE

Except for the state-owned boat access, Yale University owns the entire surrounding area (some 2,000 acres) here. Yale students, faculty, and associated groups use the recreation area at the lake's southwest end for retreats, picnics, and outdoor recreation. The paddling is great, the woodland flora varied, and the wildlife abundant. A surprising diversity of deciduous trees grows along the shoreline: four different species of oaks (red, white, scarlet, and chestnut), American chestnut, sassafras, yellow birch, red maple, tulip tree, hickory, blackgum, beech, and Atlantic white cedar. Mountain laurel, blueberry, alder,

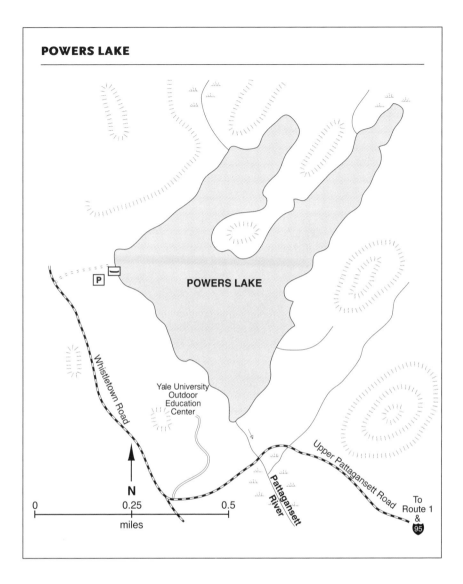

POWERS LAKE

POWERS LAKE

P

Whistletown Road

Yale University
Outdoor
Education
Center

N

Upper Pattagansett Road

Pattagansett
River

To
Route 1
&
95

0	0.25	0.5

miles

and other shrubs form thick stands along the shore, making landing difficult, but some protruding granite slabs provide access to shore for a picnic lunch or a break from paddling.

Two long fingers of this horseshoe-shaped lake make it seem larger than 144 acres. The longer finger frames a beautiful marshy area, though various water-lilies pretty well block access to the northernmost section by midsummer. In this part of the lake, look for tiny, delicate sundews on hummocks of grass and sphagnum moss. You should find two different species of this unusual plant—round-leaved sundew, *Drosera rotundifolia*, and spatulate-leaved sundew,

D. intermedia—that gains sustenance from insects caught by sticky hairs on its leaves. Look, also, for the four species of carnivorous bladderwort that inhabit the pond.

Most exciting, however, was the reptile life around the lake. We saw a number of northern water snakes, lots of painted turtles, a stinkpot turtle, and a quite rare spotted turtle (*Clemmys guttata*).

While close to major population centers, Powers Lake remains undeveloped. Vegetation covers the surface of the northeastern end.

82 | Uncas Pond

The Nehantic State Forest borders one side of Uncas Pond and offers an extensive network of hiking trails. Uncas Pond, with its clear water, is surrounded by a very diverse forest. With no motors allowed, the pond is usually pretty quiet.

Location: Lyme, CT
Maps: *Connecticut/Rhode Island Atlas & Gazetteer*, Map 28: E2, 3;
USGS Hamburg, Old Lyme
Area: 69 acres
Time: 2 hours
Habitat Type: small, elongated, wooded pond, (see fish advisory, Appendix A)
Fish: trout, largemouth bass, yellow perch, pickerel
Information: Nehantic State Forest, ct.gov/deep/cwp/view.
asp?a=2716&q=325064; aquatic plant survey, ct.gov/caes/cwp/view.
asp?a=2799&q=376298
Camping: Rocky Neck State Park, Hammonasset Beach State Park, Devil's
Hopyard State Park, Hopeville Pond State Park
Take Note: limited development; no motors

GETTING THERE
From I-95, Exit 70, go 3.7 miles (3.7 miles) north on Route 156, and turn right on Keeny Road at the access sign for Nehantic State Forest. Go 1.2 miles (4.9 miles), and stay right at the fork (left goes to the picnic area). Go 0.3 mile (5.2 miles) to the access (41° 22.371′ N, 72° 19.334′ W). An alternate access is at the picnic area.

WHAT YOU'LL SEE
Located in Nehantic State Forest, Uncas Pond offers a wonderful paddling experience. Though small and with some development on the southwest shore, the forested hillsides, clear water, and absence of motors beckon paddlers. The pond bears the name of Chief Uncas of the Pequot Nation. Uncas, which means "fox," recalls different images, depending upon your viewpoint. James Fenimore Cooper's *The Last of the Mohicans* transplanted this chief into the forests of upper New York. To his Native rivals—the Niantic and Narragansett—and even to his adopted Pequot, his name conjured up a circling forager who would

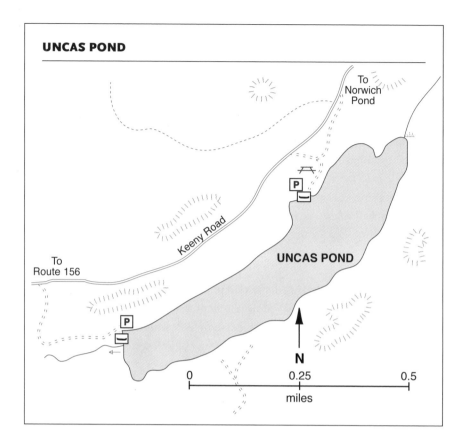

UNCAS POND

To Norwich Pond

To Route 156

Keeny Road

UNCAS POND

N

0   0.25   0.5

miles

strike when opportunity came, and indeed he did. The son of Mohegan Chief Owenoco, Uncas joined the more powerful Pequot after marrying a daughter of their Chief Sassacus, but rebelled several times against his father-in-law's rule. Banished to the Narragansett, he later subdued them. Uncas sided in each fight with English settlers and in their successful war against King Philip's coalition in 1675. A monument to Uncas in nearby Norwich honors this friendship.

Uncas Pond's environs sport a tremendous diversity of trees and shrubs, almost all deciduous, including white, red, and scarlet oaks; blackgum; red and sugar maples; beech; gray and yellow birches; sassafras; tulip tree; American chestnut (sprouts from blight-killed trees); a few hemlock; alder; mountain laurel; and swamp azalea. Around most of the pond, the land rises steeply from the water's edge. Laurel, in particular, grows densely along the shore. In some areas you can't even see the actual shoreline, much less get out and walk along the bank. A narrow band of aquatic vegetation—pickerelweed, American white waterlily, watershield, pondweed, and yellow pond-lily—protects the shoreline. At the northeast end, floating vegetation grows thicker in a small marshy area.

Uncas Pond nestles into the hills of Nehantic State Forest and offers a very pleasant morning or afternoon of paddling—without motors.

We also found pipewort (*Eriocaulon aquaticum*), with its buttonlike flower heads, poking up out of the shallow water. Look for freshwater mussels along the sandy bottom.

Nehantic State Forest offers an extensive trail network and a nice picnic area near the pond's north end. From the access, a trail extends along the north side of the pond through a beautiful area of huge boulders, thick carpets of ferns, huge mountain laurel, and feathery flowering dogwoods.

83 | Babcock Pond

Babcock Pond lies wholly within the 1,500-acre Babcock Pond WMA. Best paddling is in the spring because mats of aquatic vegetation take over the surface in summer. Look for wood duck and other waterfowl, and muskrat.

Location: Colchester, CT
Maps: *Connecticut/Rhode Island Atlas & Gazetteer*, Map 36: G9, 10; USGS Moodus
Area: 147 acres

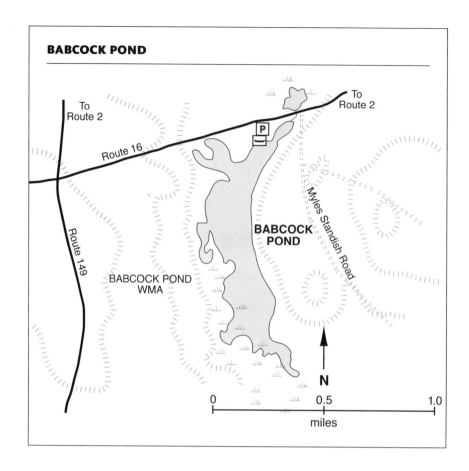

BABCOCK POND

Time: 3 hours

Habitat Type: shallow, marshy pond

Fish: largemouth bass, yellow perch, pickerel (see fish advisory, Appendix A)

Information: Babcock Pond WMA map, ct.gov/deep/lib/deep/wildlife/pdf_files/maps/maps_hunting_area/map17a.pdf

Camping: Devil's Hopyard State Park

Take Note: no development; cartop access and shallow, weedy pond limit motors; 8 MPH speed limit

GETTING THERE

From Route 2, Exit 16, go 3.3 miles (3.3 miles) south on Route 149, and turn left on Route 16. Go 1.0 mile (4.3 miles) to the access on the right (41° 22.371′ N, 72° 19.334′ W).

A muskrat, unconcerned by our presence, munches on vegetation.

From Route 2, Exit 18, go 3.3 miles west on Route 16 to the access on the left.

WHAT YOU'LL SEE

Babcock Pond, although small, offers superb marshland paddling. This shallow pond, lying within the 1,500-acre Babcock Pond Wildlife Management Area, sports huge, unbroken rafts of American white waterlily, along with other abundant aquatic vegetation, including pickerelweed, watershield, yellow pond-lily, and at least two species of bladderwort—yellow- and purple-flowered. Because of the aquatic vegetation, paddling here can present a challenge, especially late in the season, and works best with the goal of a leisurely visit to study the plants.

If other paddlers have not beaten you to the water, expect to see wood duck, a few other waterfowl, and the occasional muskrat. The undeveloped wooded shoreline consists primarily of deciduous trees, with red maple seeming to be most abundant, along with a shrubby understory.

If you paddle under Route 16 onto the small pond north of the road on sunny days, expect to see lots of painted turtles sunning themselves in a pond literally ringed with swamp loosestrife. We spent quite some time trying to photograph pollinators on the loosestrife's purple axillary flowers.

84 | Moodus Reservoir

Moodus is a popular reservoir with a fair amount of development and high-speed boating. Best paddling is in early spring and in fall. For more solitude in summer, head to the deep southeast cove with its dense patches of watershield. Expect to see wood ducks, other waterfowl, and green and great blue herons.

Location: East Haddam, CT
Maps: *Connecticut/Rhode Island Atlas & Gazetteer*, Map 36: I8, 9, 10, J9, 10; USGS Deep River, Moodus
Area: 486 acres
Time: 5 hours
Habitat Type: shallow, marshy pond with deep coves
Fish: largemouth and calico bass, yellow perch, pickerel (see fish advisory, Appendix A)
Information: aquatic survey, ct.gov/caes/cwp/view.asp?a=2799&q=520074
Camping: Devil's Hopyard State Park
Take Note: highly developed on the western half; motors allowed, 35 MPH speed limit

GETTING THERE

Launching Area Road Access (41° 30.248′ N, 72° 24.528′ W). From Route 9, Exit 7, go 4.9 miles (4.9 miles) east on Route 82, and turn left on Route 151. Go 1.2 miles (6.1 miles), and turn right on East Haddam–Colchester Turnpike. Go 2.6 miles (8.7 miles), and turn right on Launching Area Road. Go 0.2 mile (8.9 miles) to the access.

From Route 2, Exit 18, go 4.3 miles (4.3 miles) west on Route 16, and turn left on Route 149. Go 1.7 miles (6.0 miles), and go straight on Eli Chapman Road as Route 149 veers right. Go 0.4 mile (6.4 miles), and turn left on Mott Lane. Go 0.8 mile (7.2 miles), and turn right on East Haddam–Colchester Turnpike. Go 0.6 mile (7.8 miles), and turn left on Launching Area Road. Go 0.2 mile (8.0 miles) to the access.

From Route 2, Exit 16, go 3.3 miles south on Route 149 to the junction with Route 16, and continue as above.

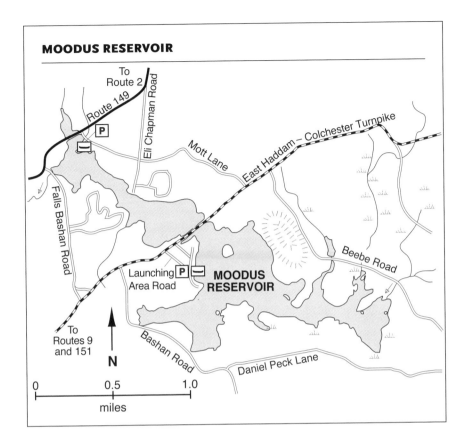

MOODUS RESERVOIR

To Route 2

Route 149

Eli Chapman Road

P

Mott Lane

East Haddam – Colchester Turnpike

Falls Bashan Road

Launching Area Road

P

MOODUS RESERVOIR

Beebe Road

To Routes 9 and 151

Bashan Road

Daniel Peck Lane

N

0   0.5   1.0
miles

WHAT YOU'LL SEE

Moodus comes from the Pequot word *machimoodus*, meaning "land of bad noises." The area's loud booms have mystified residents for hundreds or even thousands of years. A deep fault line may cause these booms, which a resident says sound like sonic booms and which generally cannot be felt—only heard. Geologists attribute them to "micro earthquakes." These tremors should have no impact on your paddling (although neither the authors nor AMC can guarantee that a huge chasm won't suddenly open up—emptying the reservoir and swallowing you and your boat).

The reservoir provides excellent paddling, particularly on a calm spring day when the shorelines come alive with nesting songbirds and spectacular wood ducks try to hide in the marshy coves. You could easily spend a day on this shallow reservoir, exploring the many long, sinewy coves and watching for painted turtles amid the floating pond vegetation. We recommend that you paddle early or late in the day and avoid busy summer weekends; we

Tree swallows nest in standing dead trees on the shallow, marshy east end of Moodus Reservoir.

paddled here early on a Sunday in July and found plenty of solitude. As boating popularity grows, best paddling would be early spring and fall.

Don't bother exploring the reservoir's smaller section, northwest of the East Haddam–Colchester Turnpike causeway; detractions include a much more developed shoreline, more water-skiers, and bigger boats than southeast of the causeway. The development that does occur on the larger, southeastern section clusters near the access.

In the marshy coves keep an eye out for wood ducks, green herons, great blue herons, and painted turtles. You may also see hundreds of tree swallows, which inhabit the standing dead trees in the eastern end of the reservoir and feed on flying insects above the water's surface. In the twenty years since this book's first edition, most of those trees have fallen, leaving fewer nesting cavities for swallows. Typical trees surround the reservoir: red, scarlet, and white oaks; sassafras; yellow and gray birches; red maple; beech; and a few white pine. Along the shores, look for mountain laurel, highbush blueberry, and large patches of swamp azalea, with long, sticky white flowers that bloom in late June.

When we paddled here in July, huge rafts of watershield, with its relatively inconspicuous red flower and gelatinous underwater sheath, filled the deeper coves, particularly in the southeast, covering the surface so densely that we could see no water. In more open areas, the small, white Carolina fanwort flowers and a yellow-flowered bladderwort put on a nice display.

85 | Salmon River

This is a great place for bird-watchers, with high numbers and high diversity of bird species. Watch osprey dive for fish in the clear water, and look for songbirds in the tall trees on the shore and hillsides. Marshy coves harboring wild rice await exploration.

Location: East Haddam and Haddam, CT
Maps: *Connecticut/Rhode Island Atlas & Gazetteer*, Map 36: J4, 5, K5; USGS Deep River, Moodus
Length: 4 miles one way
Time: 4 hours round-trip
Habitat Type: shallow, marshy, tidal Connecticut River estuary
Fish: trout (see fish advisory, Appendix A)
Information: Machimoodus State Park, ct.gov/deep/cwp/view. asp?a=2716&q=478996&deepNav_GID=1650; Goodspeed Opera House, goodspeed.org
Camping: Devil's Hopyard State Park
Take Note: some development upstream; motors in lower stretches

GETTING THERE

From Route 9, Exit 7, go 3.5 miles (3.5 miles) east on Route 82, and turn left on Route 149. Go 1.0 mile (4.5 miles) to the marked access on the left (41° 28.03′ N, 72° 28.083′ W). Along the way, you will pass the Goodspeed Opera House.

From Route 2, Exit 18, go 4.3 miles (4.3 miles) west on Route 16, and turn left on Route 149. Go 7.2 miles (11.5 miles) to the access on the right.

From Route 2, Exit 16, go 10.5 miles south on Route 149 to the access on the right.

WHAT YOU'LL SEE

The Salmon River, popular with canoers and kayakers (we encountered several dozen on a Sunday in July), provides outstanding bird-watching opportunities. A red-tailed hawk soared far overhead as we watched a pair of ospreys hover above the clear water, looking for a meal. Later, we watched an osprey feed on a silvery fish. We paddled through an unconcerned pod of 46 mute swans—an invasive species that competes with native birds—and listened to the songs of many streamside and woodland bird species: red-winged blackbird, grackle,

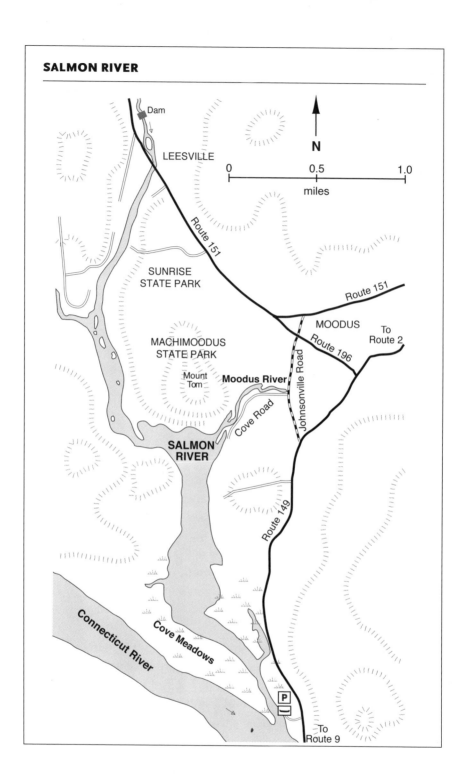

SALMON RIVER

Dam

LEESVILLE

N

0   0.5   1.0
miles

Route 151

SUNRISE
STATE PARK

Route 151

MOODUS

To
Route 2

MACHIMOODUS
STATE PARK

Route 196

Johnsonville Road

Mount
Tom

Moodus River

Cove Road

**SALMON
RIVER**

Route 149

Connecticut River

Cove Meadows

P

To
Route 9

common yellowthroat, yellow warbler, white-throated sparrow, goldfinch, ovenbird, tufted titmouse, robin, catbird, veery, phoebe, great crested flycatcher, brown thrasher, kingfisher, and tree and barn swallows.

Machimoodus State Park, crisscrossed with hiking trails, and Sunrise State Park (under development) protect the river's west side. The marshy lower section near the access, including the cove immediately on the right, has a much different feel from that of the wooded sections upstream near Leesville Dam and its fish ladder. Look for gorgeous patches of swamp rose, particularly in the cove on the right, which also sports vigorous patches of wild rice. Upstream, some gorgeous stands of hemlock grace the hillsides; mountain laurel and other shrubs fill the shoreline in places, backed up on hillsides clad in a rich diversity of woodland tree species. Although some development occurs upstream, including a small resort that's being converted into Sunrise State Park, the shallow water limits motorboat access. We found it well worth the paddle up to Leesville Dam.

If you arrive here from Route 9, you will pass the historic Goodspeed Opera House, built in 1876, which hosted national premieres of musicals such as *Annie* and *Man of La Mancha*. It continues to put on renowned musical theater.

86 | Selden Creek and Whalebone Creek

Whalebone Creek offers paddling in an extensive, pristine freshwater marsh filled with birds and wild rice. Selden Creek offers great paddling and also camping on a gorgeous Connecticut River island. Across from the island, more marshlands beg to be explored. Novice paddlers should avoid this area.

Location: Lyme, CT
Maps: *Connecticut/Rhode Island Atlas & Gazetteer*, Map 27: B20, 21, C20, 21, D20, 21, 22; USGS Deep River
Length: Selden Creek, 2.7 miles one way; Whalebone Creek, 1 mile one way
Time: all day
Habitat Type: Connecticut River estuaries, marshlands, protected coves
Fish: largemouth, smallmouth, and calico bass; yellow and white perch; walleye; northern pike (see fish advisory, Appendix A)

Information: Selden Neck State Park, ct.gov/deep/cwp/view.
asp?A=2716&Q=435364; The Nature Conservancy, nature.org; tide charts,
maineharbors.com

Camping: Rocky Neck State Park, Hammonasset Beach State Park, primitive
camping on Selden Neck

Take Note: no development; motors allowed, 6 MPH speed limit on Selden
Creek; use extreme caution off Selden Neck cliffs—novice paddlers should
avoid this area, wear your PFD

GETTING THERE

From Route 9, Exit 6, go 2.7 miles east on Route 148, cross the Connecticut
River on the Chester–Hadlyme Ferry, and park immediately on the left. If the
ferry is not operating, go north on Route 154, cross over the Connecticut on
Route 82, go south to Route 148, and go right to the parking area and access at
the ferry (41° 25.231′ N, 72° 25.702′ W).

From I-95, Exit 70, go 8.4 miles (8.4 miles) north on Route 156, and turn
left on Route 82. Go 3.2 miles (11.6 miles) to the junction with Route 148.
Go straight onto Route 148, and go 1.6 miles to the access at the ferry.

WHAT YOU'LL SEE

Whalebone Creek

Just downriver from the access, the inlet to Whalebone Creek provides entry to
one of the most pristine tidal freshwater marshes in Connecticut. The Nature
Conservancy protects a portion of this important wetland.

How can it be tidal and freshwater at the same time? The incoming tidal
rush raises Connecticut River water levels as far north as Hartford, but strong
river currents keep salt water from coming much more than about 10 miles
upstream. Just to the south of Whalebone Creek, fresh and salt water mix
to create brackish water conditions; not until Great Island do salt marsh
ecosystems dominate.

Two signal lights guard the entrance to Whalebone Creek. Entering, you
pass a tall, granite cliff on the left, festooned with wild grape and other vines—
a preferred habitat for the hard-to-see white-eyed vireo. In the early morning
light we watched a raccoon scurry up the rock face, peering down with obvious
annoyance. Heavily wooded hillsides occur on the left, but marsh dominates the
right, dotted here and there with trees and shrubs adapted to the ever-changing
water level.

Farther in, wild rice (*Zizania aquatica*), which reaches 10 feet or more in
height, dominates the marsh. Its round, jointed, hollow stems grow up to an

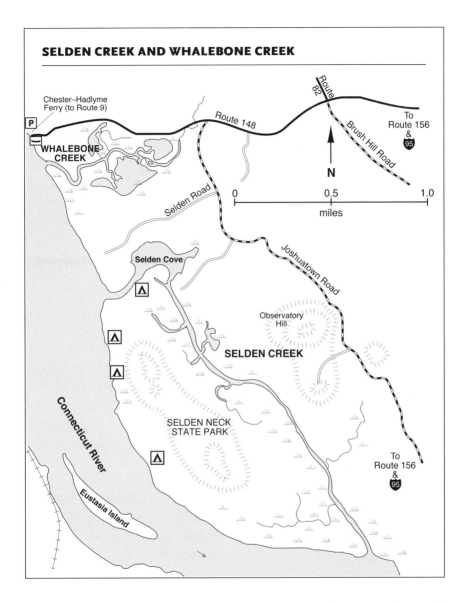

SELDEN CREEK AND WHALEBONE CREEK

Chester–Hadlyme Ferry (to Route 9)

P

Route 148

Route 82

To Route 156 & 95

Brush Hill Road

WHALEBONE CREEK

Selden Road

N

0   0.5   1.0

miles

Joshuatown Road

Selden Cove

Observatory Hill

SELDEN CREEK

Connecticut River

SELDEN NECK STATE PARK

To Route 156 & 95

Eustasia Island

inch in diameter at the base. Long, wide leaves up to 4 feet long and as much as 2 inches wide emanate from the stalk, whose top bears flowers and seeds in a form called panicles. Paddling here in late summer, you get a feel for how American Indians in Minnesota harvest grain from a closely related species (*Z. palustris*). Carefully bend over one of the tall stems and shake it to release the sheathed seeds. In the thick wild rice marshes of Minnesota, American Indians literally fill their canoes as they harvest the grain.

Along with wild rice, look for bulrush, buttonbush, cattail, pickerelweed,

Snowy egrets are a common sight in the lower Connecticut River. We watched this one fish for several minutes before it took flight.

blue iris, and a host of other marsh plants. Birdlife abounds. Even in early autumn, the place seemed alive with red-winged blackbirds, marsh wrens, swallows, kingfishers, black ducks, wood ducks, great blue herons, Canada geese, and mute swans. At high tide—the preferred time to paddle here—you can explore quite far into Whalebone Creek, with winding channels and pools of open water.

Selden Creek

About 0.75 mile south of the access, Selden Creek extends left around a tall, 607-acre hilly island, Selden Neck State Park. It returns to the Connecticut nearly 3 miles south, forming one of southern New England's true paddling and camping gems. The Nature Conservancy protects the creek's opposite shore, containing wonderful marshlands. A 6 MPH speed limit on Selden Creek keeps down motorboat traffic, but we would avoid busy summer weekends.

Paddling in one of the small side creeks accessible at high tide, we watched schools of small, silvery alewives or herring skip along the water's surface, using their strong tails in an apparently defensive response to our disturbance. In some cases, a fish overthrust and flopped back and forth, getting nowhere, but most seemed to skip along for a foot or two at a time.

When you get to the southern access onto the Connecticut River, we strongly recommend that you turn around and paddle back up Selden Creek. Wakes reflecting off the outer Selden Neck cliffs cause huge waves that can swamp an open boat. As you paddle downriver from the ferry and any other time you paddle the river, we strongly recommend wearing your PFD. Novice paddlers should avoid this area.

The state permits primitive camping on Selden Neck. Of the four campsites, you reach one from Selden Creek, the others from the Connecticut River. Our favorite remains Quarry Knob—the farthest south—where you camp on a knoll overlooking the river and have easy access to the 226-foot rocky peak of Selden Neck. You may stay for one night after registering and paying a fee. Book your site early.

While in the area, you might want to take a side trip to Gillette Castle, a fascinating stone mansion built between 1914 and 1919 by the eccentric stage actor William Gillette, who became famous for his portrayal of Sherlock Holmes. The state purchased the property in 1943 to become Gillette Castle State Park.

87 | Lord Cove

Lord Cove offers one of the best places to watch osprey dive for fish. We've seen osprey here every summer trip. Also look for herons and egrets, which appear here in numbers, along with many shorebirds on the mud flats during spring and fall migrations. Try to avoid getting lost in the maze of waterways.

Location: Lyme and Old Lyme, CT
Maps: *Connecticut/Rhode Island Atlas & Gazetteer*, Map 27: F23, 24, G23, 24, Map 28: G1, H1; USGS Old Lyme
Area: 351 acres, 5-mile maze of waterways
Time: 5 hours
Habitat Type: Connecticut River estuary, brackish marshland, many islands and protected coves
Fish: striped bass (see fish advisory, Appendix A)
Information: The Nature Conservancy, nature.org; tide charts, maineharbors.com
Camping: Rocky Neck State Park, Hammonasset Beach State Park
Take Note: little development; shallow water limits motors

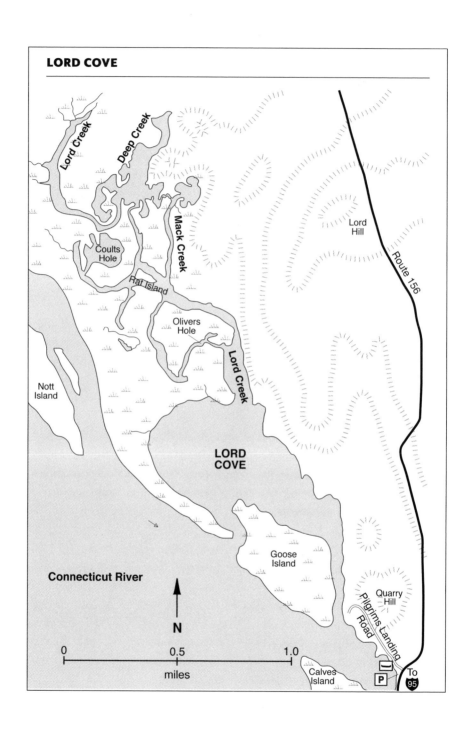

LORD COVE

Lord Creek

Deep Creek

Mack Creek

Lord Hill

Route 156

Coults Hole

Rat Island

Olivers Hole

Lord Creek

Nott Island

LORD COVE

Connecticut River

N

Goose Island

Quarry Hill

Pilgrims Landing Road

0   0.5   1.0
miles

Calves Island

P

To 95

Osprey are common in Lord Cove. We watched one dive and catch a large, silvery fish.

GETTING THERE

From I-95, Exit 70, go 0.7 mile north on Route 156 to the access on Pilgrims Landing Road on the left, a few feet in (41° 19.782′ N, 72° 20.428′ W). Parking for about six vehicles. If parking is full, leave someone with the boats at the landing, park at the Exit 70 commuter lot, and hoof it back to the access.

WHAT YOU'LL SEE

Lord Cove offers splendid paddling through a 5-mile maze of waterways, particularly during shorebird and waterfowl migrations. The Nature Conservancy, Old Lyme Land Trust, and Connecticut Department of Energy and Environmental Protection protect the cove from development and have instituted a program to remove invasive *Phragmites*.

Brackish marshes dotted with low, grassy islands take at least half a day to explore fully. Though you won't see as many shorebirds, we recommend paddling here around high tide to avoid exposed mud flats. To access more northern reaches, you have to paddle over a large, shallow, open-water expanse. When winds from the south whip up whitecaps, paddle nearby Powers Lake (Trip 81) or Uncas Pond (Trip 82).

We saw ducks and laughing gulls, along with many snowy egrets on Lord Cove. Look for marsh wren nests in—and muskrats harvesting—narrow-leaved cattails. You can paddle way back into the marsh, twisting and turning among the many islands. We sat still and watched an osprey hover over the marsh, eventually diving talons-first on a fish, submerging completely beneath the surface. Popping up, it beat its wings furiously, first against the water's surface, then against the sky, straining to gain altitude with a heavy-bodied, silvery fish, fully as long as the osprey, clutched in its talons. We watched the two sail out of sight, gulls in hot pursuit, hoping to make it drop its prized possession.

88 | Great Island Estuary and Roger Tory Peterson Wildlife Area

The Great Island Estuary offers an extraordinary paddling opportunity, and that's reflected in the large kayak groups that paddle here on weekends. Escape the crowds by paddling into the estuary's side channels. Birdlife abounds, which is why Roger Tory Peterson, the famed naturalist, chose to live in Old Lyme for a while. The wildlife refuge now bears his name.

Location: Old Lyme, CT
Maps: *Connecticut/Rhode Island Atlas & Gazetteer*, Map 28: G2, H1, 2, I1, 2, 3, J1, 2, 3, K1, 2, 3; USGS Old Lyme
Area/Length: wildlife area, 588 acres; Lieutenant River, 3.5 miles one way; Blackhall River, 3.0 miles one way
Time: all day, shorter trips possible
Habitat Type: shallow saltwater estuary, grassy marshlands, many islands and protected bays
Fish: striped bass, bluefish (see fish advisory, Appendix A)
Information: map of Roger Tory Peterson Wildlife Area, ct.gov/deep/lib/deep/wildlife/pdf_files/maps/maps_hunting_area/map194a.pdf; tide charts, maineharbors.com
Camping: Rocky Neck State Park, Hammonasset Beach State Park
Take Note: little development; no motors allowed in wildlife area

GETTING THERE
Lieutenant River (41° 18.851′ N, 72° 20.238′ W). From I-95 northbound, Exit 70, go 0.4 mile south on Route 156 to the access on the right, just before the bridge. From I-95 southbound, Exit 70, go 0.7 mile (0.7 mile) west on Route 1, and turn left on Route 156 south. Go 0.5 mile (1.2 miles) to the access on the right.

GREAT ISLAND ESTUARY AND ROGER TORY PETERSON WILDLIFE AREA

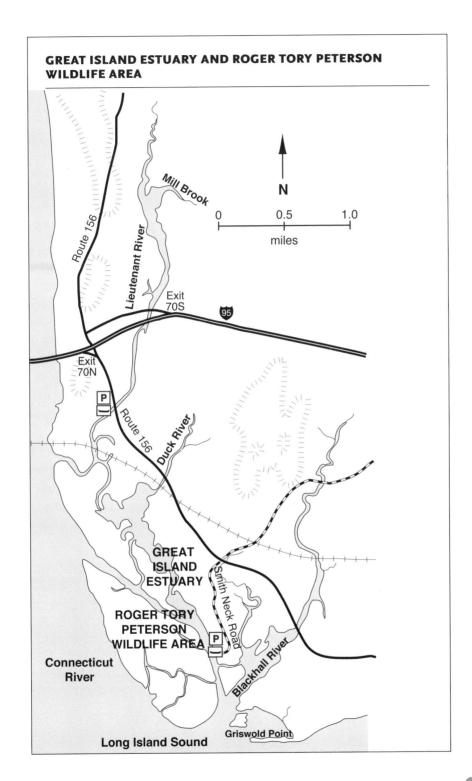

N

0   0.5   1.0
miles

Mill Brook

Route 156

Lieutenant River

Exit 70S

95

Exit 70N

P

Route 156

Duck River

GREAT
ISLAND
ESTUARY

ROGER TORY
PETERSON
WILDLIFE AREA

P

Smith Neck Road

Connecticut
River

Blackhall River

Long Island Sound

Griswold Point

Smith Neck (41° 17.243′ N, 72° 19.438′ W). Go 1.4 miles (1.4 miles) south on Route 156 from the Lieutenant River access, and turn right on Smith Neck Road. Go 0.8 mile (2.2 miles) to the access at road's end.

WHAT YOU'LL SEE

This shallow saltwater estuary draws large groups of sea kayakers on summer weekends. Paddling here on a Sunday in late August, we saw more kayaks than we have seen anywhere else in the Northeast. You can get away from the crowds, however, by paddling into the twisting channels of Roger Tory Peterson Wildlife Area. Note that the Griswold Point sandspit washed away in a storm and no longer offers a protected place to paddle. Threatened piping plovers and least terns still nest on area sand dunes.

On one trip, with fall shorebird migration in full swing, we saw hundreds of sandpipers and plovers, including least and semipalmated sandpipers, black-bellied and semipalmated plovers, and greater and lesser yellowlegs. Soras (a type of rail), and saltmarsh sharp-tailed and seaside sparrows, skulked in the dense stands of *Spartina* and *Phragmites*. We also noted a large number of mute swans.

Scientists discovered osprey eggshell thinning caused by DDT here in the 1960s, which resulted in a lawsuit that ultimately led to the banning of DDT. Having exhibited a remarkable recovery, twenty or more osprey pairs now nest in the refuge, and we watched them hover and dive for fish.

The Blackhall, a beautiful marshy river, provides wonderful paddling. Red, scarlet, and white oaks line the banks, along with sassafras, blackgum, cedar, blueberry, and the occasional mountain laurel. *Phragmites*, which gives way to narrow-leaved cattails upstream, creeps out from the shore. Look for marsh wren nests in the cattails. We saw green herons, snowy and great egrets, osprey, and cormorants here.

Up on the Lieutenant River, we watched barn swallows snatch insects on the wing, while listening to numerous catbirds and cardinals call from the dense shoreline vegetation. Kingfishers fled before us up the river, while flocks of ducks took wing or fled into high grass. A fish ladder installed on a tributary, Mill Brook, provides spawning access for alewives to a series of small ponds and, someday, with another ladder, to Rogers Lake.

SALT MARSH
WHERE RIVER AND SEA MEET

The salt marsh ecosystem enjoys tremendous biological productivity yet stresses its inhabitants—plants especially—so severely with constant change that few species can survive. Incoming tides flood the marsh, saturating the peaty soil. As tides recede, the exposed surface may actually dry out on a hot, breezy day, but changing salinity, even more than fluctuating water level, determines what can survive.

As seawater surges into the marsh, salinity increases, reaching a peak at high tide. As the tide drops, so does the salinity, reaching a minimum at low tide when incoming fresh water from inlet streams dilutes the seawater. Salinity conditions often vary markedly in different portions of a salt marsh—from nearly pure fresh water at one end to salinity nearly matching that of the ocean at the other. The volume of fresh water flowing into the marsh, the tidal differential along that section of coastline, and the size and configuration of the connection to the sea each control salinity.

Such salinity conditions allow just two species of grass—*Spartina alterniflora* (smooth cordgrass) and *S. patens* (saltmeadow cordgrass)—to dominate this ecosystem. The *Spartinas* comprise a rare natural monoculture for as far as the eye can see in the largest salt marshes. The instability inherent in monocultures has apparently not affected the *Spartina* marshes, which have exhibited little evidence of disease or significant die-off over many thousands of years.

Spartina alterniflora occupies the lower ground, where twice-daily flooding inundates it with salt water. In ideal conditions *S. alterniflora* reaches 10 feet in height, though more commonly it reaches less than half that. *S. patens*, which grows to 2 feet, dominates the high marsh—the firmer land flooded only irregularly, at spring tides and during storms. Generations of coastal New England farmers harvested this species as feed for their livestock (an acre of salt marsh produces twice as much hay as the best dry-land hayfields). You can recognize *S. patens* by the broad "cowlicks" that form on the marsh as swaths of the grass get matted down. A lower, flexible stem section defends against wave forces and strong current.

Glasswort (*Salicornia depressa*), a succulent species able to withstand salt marsh rigors, grows upright with swollen, jointed stems. Its name may derive from its one-time use in making glass (the ash is very high in sodium carbonate, an ingredient in older glass-making processes). Amid the *S. patens* you may also see the delicate flowers of Carolina sealavender (*Limonium carolinianum*), a plant long collected for dried flower arrangements. Pressure from collectors has reduced Carolina sealavender abundance considerably; please enjoy it from your boat. Look for other specialists here—seaside goldenrod with thick fleshy leaves, sea aster, sea plantain, and sea purslane among them.

Complex mechanisms allow plants to adapt to high and constantly changing salinity levels. Organisms maintain a fairly precise balance of fluid and dissolved substances in their cells. When concentrations of dissolved compounds vary across cell membranes, water tends to flow from the less concentrated to the more concentrated to equalize the "osmotic gradient." Water in plant cells that is more dilute than seawater—the case with most plants—flows out through the cell membrane, drying and killing the plant cells. This drying is why most plants cannot survive in the salt marsh. *Spartina* can survive through a complex series of evolutionary adaptations, of which *Life and Death of the Saltmarsh* (see Appendix B) contains an excellent discussion.

In the less saline areas, you may see wild rice and other less salt-tolerant species. On tidal rivers, seawater can only penetrate upriver a short distance before fresh water dilutes it to such an extent that freshwater plants and animals can survive. Paddling up these rivers, you can watch the progression of species—and species diversity. On a large-volume river such as the Connecticut, salt water cannot penetrate far upstream. The tidal rush, however, slows the river's flow and raises the water level for many miles upstream without increasing its salinity.

Most animals, unlike plants, can move about to counter changing water levels. Most mollusks and invertebrates either bury themselves deep in the muck or swim in the current, like the fish that live or spawn here. Mussels and barnacles attach tightly to rocks, pilings, or other solid objects and so cannot move about. To survive the twice-daily drying at low tide, these mollusks close up tightly. Some salt marsh fish can regulate their osmotic balance with changing salinity. Some lower invertebrates actually bloat up in lower-salinity water, then shrink as salinity increases.

The fiddler crab (named for the large claw-size difference) has several adaptations to salt marsh life. Like all crabs, it has gills, but it also has a primitive lung, enabling it to breathe air as long as it keeps the lung moist. It also can

Along with the more common *Spartina alterniflora* and *S. patens*, you may also see the more dramatic *S. cynosuroides*, or big cordgrass, along tidal rivers.

survive without oxygen for long periods when it tunnels down into oxygen-deficient mud. The fiddler crab also maintains constant osmotic equilibrium in diluted seawater and in water more concentrated than seawater, as found in briny tidal ponds where water has evaporated.

The rich, salt marsh birdlife needs to adapt less to the environment. At low tide, dozens of wading birds feed on insect larvae and crustaceans in exposed mud flats. Clapper rails and marsh wrens nest amid the *Spartina*. Harriers weave back and forth low over the marsh in search of mice, and ospreys scan the deeper water for fish. Snowy and great egrets and little green and great blue herons patrol the marsh for small fish and other prey. During spring and fall migrations, many waterfowl species stop over in salt marshes before winging southward. Early morning paddlers may see raccoons and an occasional river otter.

Insects also play an important role in the salt marsh, and efforts to control them—chiefly mosquitoes—have caused some of the most significant human impact on this ecosystem. In the 1930s, the Civilian Conservation Corps drained vast areas of salt marsh. Evidence of this only modestly successful effort to eliminate standing water can still be seen clearly today. After 50 years, you can still paddle a short way into some of these long, straight, mosquito-control ditches at high tide.

Many commercially important fish and shellfish species depend on the salt marsh ecosystem. A full two-thirds of the eastern U.S. commercial fish and shellfish catch—including oysters, scallops, clams, blue crabs, shrimp, bluefish, flounder, and striped bass—depend on the salt marsh for at least some phase of their life cycle.

Sustaining nutrients, borne on incoming rivers and streams, support this productivity. Inflowing fresh water spreads out and deposits its sediment, rich with minerals and nutrients. Unfortunately, this same water carries pollutants as well. All too often we see signs warning of polluted water off-limits to shellfishing. But the salt marsh also plays a vitally important role in breaking down many of these pollutants. Like a giant sewage treatment plant, it purifies water and extracts toxins, making the organisms toxic in the process. The long-lasting pesticide DDT, used from the late 1940s until the early 1970s, concentrated in salt marsh organisms from crustaceans and fish up the food chain to ospreys, bald eagles, and other predators. By the time of DDT's banning, the osprey and bald eagle had almost vanished from New England's salt marshes.

Hundreds of thousands of acres of coastal salt marsh, though vitally important to us economically and biologically, have been lost to development during the past hundred years. The relatively small remnants of these once vast stretches are still threatened by development and pollution. Feeling the tidal current under a boat while watching *Spartina* wave in the breeze and an osprey fish overhead helps us appreciate the importance of these resources.

Those of us who value the salt marsh's unique beauty and who understand this ecosystem's fragile nature must guarantee that additional salt marsh acreage will not be lost to development and pollution. Learn about the salt marsh environments in your area, and talk to local planning officials to find out how you can help protect these wonderful places.

89 | Pattaconk Reservoir

Undeveloped Pattaconk Reservoir sits amid Connecticut's second largest state forest and does not allow motors. Although a great place to paddle amid gorgeous hillsides, it also draws large crowds, particularly on weekends, for hiking, biking, swimming, and paddling.

Location: Chester, CT
Maps: *Connecticut/Rhode Island Atlas & Gazetteer*, Map 27: C14; USGS Haddam
Area: 56 acres
Time: 2 hours
Habitat Type: shallow, marshy pond
Fish: brown trout, largemouth bass, pickerel (see fish advisory, Appendix A)
Information: Cockaponset State Forest, ct.gov/deep/cwp/view. asp?a=2716&q=325056
Camping: Rocky Neck State Park, Hammonasset Beach State Park
Take Note: no development; no motors

GETTING THERE

From Route 9, Exit 6, go 1.5 miles (1.5 miles) west on Route 148, and turn right on Cedar Lake Road. Go 1.6 miles (3.1 miles), and turn left into the Pattaconk Lake State Recreation Area. Go 0.3 mile (3.4 miles) to the large parking area (41° 24.534′ N, 72° 31.525′ W). Carry your boat about 75 yards down to the water.

WHAT YOU'LL SEE

Pattaconk Reservoir in south-central Connecticut is hidden away in Cockaponset State Forest, the state's second largest state forest. A small but stunning undeveloped body of water in an area known more for tidal river paddling, Pattaconk offers a refreshing alternative with a real mountain pond feel to it. If you visit here in summer, you will see dozens of people paddling, swimming, hiking, and off-road bicycling. If you prefer more solitude, paddle similar, but larger, Messerschmidt Pond (Trip 90) nearby.

Deciduous trees dominate the surrounding woods, including four different

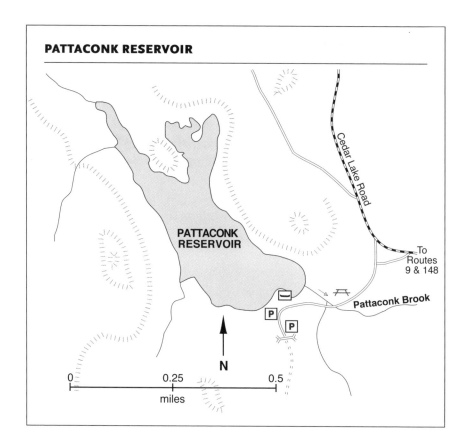

PATTACONK RESERVOIR

PATTACONK RESERVOIR

Cedar Lake Road

To Routes 9 & 148

Pattaconk Brook

N

0   0.25   0.5

miles

oak species (red, white, chestnut, and scarlet), three birch species (gray, black, and yellow), red maple, sassafras, beech, shagbark hickory, blackgum, American chestnut, and tulip tree. Mountain laurel, highbush blueberry, and sweet pepperbush grow densely along the shore, overhanging the water in many places, making the shoreline mostly inaccessible. Where you can get onto the shore, the open woods beyond offer great hiking.

Some vegetation floats on the water (American white waterlily, pondweed, watershield, yellow pond-lily). When we paddled here in 1992, very little vegetation appeared underwater. When we returned ten years later, an infestation of watermilfoil had begun to fill the void, literally. The clean water with sandy bottom supports freshwater mussels and patches of what we think are small, nodding white orchids in the shallows. Occasional boulders dot the shoreline of this beautiful pond.

90 | Messerschmidt Pond

Quiet Messerschmidt Pond, surrounded by a wildlife management area, is a great place to paddle. In our visits, we've seen painted and snapping turtles and listened to many birds calling from the woods. We found large patches of relatively rare little floatingheart here.

Location: Deep River and Westbrook, CT
Maps: *Connecticut/Rhode Island Atlas & Gazetteer*, Map 27: G16; USGS Essex
Area: 73 acres
Time: 2 hours
Habitat Type: shallow, marshy pond
Fish: largemouth bass, yellow perch, pickerel (see fish advisory, Appendix A)
Information: aquatic plant survey, ct.gov/caes/cwp/view.asp?a=2799&q=381496
Camping: Rocky Neck State Park, Hammonasset Beach State Park
Take Note: no development; no motors

GETTING THERE
From Route 9, Exit 5, go 3.6 miles (3.6 miles) west on Route 80, and turn left on Route 145 (Stevenstown Road). Go 1.3 miles (4.9 miles) to the access on the left (41° 20.424′ N, 72° 29.578′ W).

From I-95, Exit 64, go 3.0 miles north on Route 145 to the access on the right.

WHAT YOU'LL SEE
Although small, Messerschmidt Pond offers an opportunity for a wonderful morning of paddling. Lying wholly within Messerschmidt Wildlife Management Area, the pond's low earthen dam at the south end and a couple of groves of Norway spruce provide the only evidence of human presence. Paddling the entire shoreline takes much more time than the pond's acreage would suggest because of undulating deep coves, peninsulas, and a couple of very large wooded islands.

Shrubs line the shore, leading to hillsides covered with deciduous trees, many of them oaks. A large patch of buttonbush, its fluffy ball-like flowers festooned with bees in mid-July, cover the backside of one island, while stands

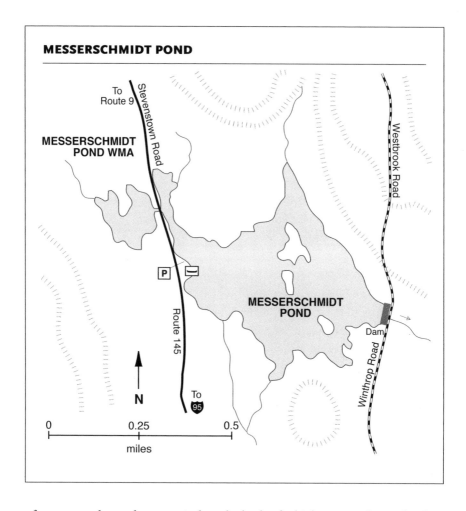

MESSERSCHMIDT POND

To Route 9

Stevenstown Road

MESSERSCHMIDT POND WMA

Westbrook Road

P

Route 145

MESSERSCHMIDT POND

Dam

Winthrop Road

N

To 95

| 0 | 0.25 | 0.5 |

miles

of swamp azalea and mountain laurel—both of which put on showy displays in June—dominate stretches of shoreline.

Though American white waterlily and watershield rule the surface, a yellow-flowered bladderwort and Carolina fanwort fill much of the underwater volume. Carolina fanwort is now crowding out the five species of bladderwort found in this pond. Surprisingly, we also found some fairly large patches of little floatingheart (*Nymphoides cordata*), an uncommon aquatic plant, in bloom in mid-July.

As we paddled into the northern cove, eastern kingbirds chased a red-tailed hawk, while catbirds, cardinals, and hermit thrushes called from the undergrowth. We had a very relaxing paddle here, away from the motorboats and development that characterize most bodies of water in the area.

91 | East River

The East River offers a wonderful opportunity to explore an extensive *Spartina* salt marsh, or you can paddle upriver away from Long Island Sound. Look for fiddler crabs, herons and egrets, osprey, northern harrier, and many other bird species.

Location: Guilford and Madison, CT
Maps: *Connecticut/Rhode Island Atlas & Gazetteer*, Map 26: I5, 6, J6, 7, K6, 7; USGS Guilford
Length: 6 miles one way
Time: 5 hours round-trip, more if you explore side streams
Habitat Type: salt marsh estuary and tidal river
Fish: trout, striped bass (see fish advisory, Appendix A)
Information: tide charts, maineharbors.com ; Guilford Salt Marsh Scantuary, guilford.audubon.org
Camping: Hammonasset Beach State Park
Take Note: limited development with areas protected by the Connecticut Audubon Society; motors allowed; plan your paddle around wind and tides

GETTING THERE

From I-95, Exit 59, go 1.6 miles (1.6 miles) east on Route 1, and turn right on Neck Road. Bear right after a few hundred yards, and go 2.1 miles (3.7 miles) to the access on the right; follow boat launch signs (41° 16.166′ N, 72° 39.42′ W).

You can also launch from the northeast parking lot off Route 1 where it crosses the river (41° 17.149′ N, 72° 38.811′ W).

WHAT YOU'LL SEE

The East River—the boundary between Guilford and Madison—provides superb tidal salt marsh paddling. From the access on Grass Island, the river extends about 6 miles inland in a fairly wide, gently winding channel, with lots of small tributary streams to explore. Near the boat launch, the Neck River bears off to the right but heads into a more populated area. You could easily spend a full day exploring this area, observing the many changes caused by rising and falling tides.

At high tide you can look out over the broad expanses of *Spartina* (salt

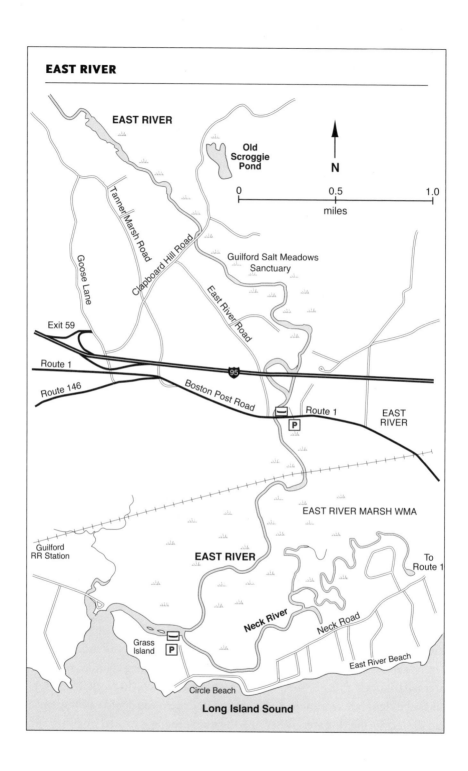

EAST RIVER

EAST RIVER

Old Scroggie Pond

N

0   0.5   1.0
miles

Tanner Marsh Road

Clapboard Hill Road

Goose Lane

East River Road

Guilford Salt Meadows Sanctuary

Exit 59

Route 1

Route 146

95

Boston Post Road

Route 1

P

EAST RIVER

EAST RIVER MARSH WMA

Guilford RR Station

EAST RIVER

To Route 1

Neck River

Neck Road

Grass Island

P

East River Beach

Circle Beach

Long Island Sound

marsh cordgrasses). As the tide falls, the horizon disappears behind high sod banks clad with mussels and alive with fiddler crabs and other generally hidden salt marsh creatures. Look for herons and egrets hunting small crabs and fish in the network of water-filled drainage ditches that extend through the marsh.

In the 1930s and 1940s, drainage ditches were dug throughout coastal salt marshes in an effort to eliminate mosquito-breeding stagnant water pools. Although only marginally successful, the effort put hundreds of people to work during the Great Depression. At high tide, you can squeeze your boat into some of these long, straight ditches, getting away from the main tidal river current and permitting close examination of salt marsh flora and fauna.

You pass under a number of bridges, including one for Amtrak on the heavily traveled Northeast Corridor, about 1.5 miles upstream. A quarter mile

Spartina alterniflora dominates the banks of the East River. Look for cedars and oaks on higher ground.

past that, you can stop at the Route 1 bridge to visit one of the stores along the highway—on an incoming tide, make sure to tie your boat securely. The I-95 bridge follows just after the Route 1 bridge, and highway noise here can detract somewhat from this wonderful stretch of river, but it gradually fades as you paddle upriver.

A short distance north of I-95, the Connecticut Audubon Society protects land known as the Guilford Salt Meadows Sanctuary on both sides of the river. At high tide you can explore numerous small inlet streams teeming with birdlife, including osprey, northern harrier, heron, and egret. Red and white oaks, sassafras, sumac, cedar, flowering dogwood, and a few blackgum trees grow along the high ground. Watch out for poison ivy and Lyme disease-carrying deer ticks if you decide to explore on foot.

By timing your visit, you can paddle upriver from the access on an incoming tide, enjoy paddling around the salt marsh at high tide, then paddle back after the tide turns. Several miles up East River, high tide occurs quite a bit later than at the coast, which is about twenty minutes before Bridgeport. The wind, however, may cause more difficulty than the modest current. Visit in early morning or early evening to avoid the typical afternoon wind.

92 | Charles E. Wheeler Wildlife Management Area, Housatonic River Estuary

This salt marsh is a birder's paradise, especially during shorebird migration in August. More than 300 bird species have been observed here. The area is off-limits to motors until September 1, making for delightful paddling in the extensive channels that crisscross the marsh. Paddle here near high tide.

Location: Milford, CT
Maps: *Connecticut/Rhode Island Atlas & Gazetteer*, Map 21: C15, D14, 15, E14, 15; USGS Milford
Area: Wildlife management area, 812 acres
Time: 4 hours or more
Habitat Type: Housatonic River estuary, brackish marshland, many protected waterways
Fish: striped bass, bluefish (see fish advisory, Appendix A)

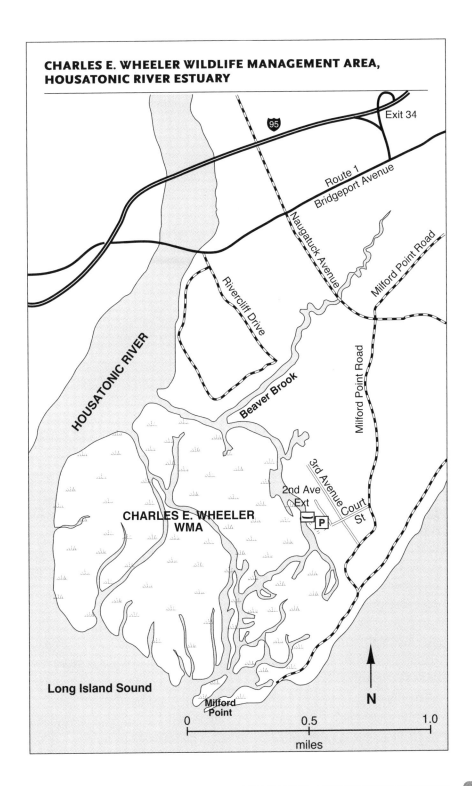

CHARLES E. WHEELER WILDLIFE MANAGEMENT AREA, HOUSATONIC RIVER ESTUARY

Exit 34

95

Route 1
Bridgeport Avenue

Naugatuck Avenue

Milford Point Road

Rivercliff Drive

HOUSATONIC RIVER

Beaver Brook

Milford Point Road

3rd Avenue

2nd Ave
Ext

Court

St

CHARLES E. WHEELER
WMA

P

Long Island Sound

Milford
Point

N

0   0.5   1.0

miles

Information: Connecticut Audubon Coastal Center at Milford Point, ctaudubon.org/coastal-center-at-milford-point, 203-878-7440; Charles E. Wheeler WMA, lisrc.uconn.edu/coastalaccess/site.asp?siteid=515&maptool=3; tide charts, maineharbors.com

Camping: Kettletown State Park, Hammonasset Beach State Park

Take Note: little development; motors limited to after September 1; in the river and on Long Island Sound, winds, tides, and wakes can be dangerous, wear your PFD; best to paddle close to high tide

GETTING THERE

From I-95, Exit 34, turn right (west) on Route 1, go 0.5 mile (0.5 mile), and turn left on Naugatuck Avenue. Go 0.6 mile (1.1 miles), and turn right on Milford Point Road. Go 0.8 mile (1.9 miles), and turn right on Court Street. Go 0.2 mile (2.1 miles) and continue straight onto the access road (41° 16.166′ N, 72° 39.42′ W).

WHAT YOU'LL SEE

The Charles E. Wheeler Wildlife Management Area's protected waters harbor a wide array of interesting bird species. A number of long, wide passageways, each with several side channels, penetrate the heart of the marsh, which extends a little over a mile in both the north–south and east–west directions. If you can, paddle here in August during peak shorebird migration. Until September 1, the access is limited to cartop boats, and the marsh remains off-limits to motorized boats. From September 1 through February, the gate is opened for trailered boats for waterfowl hunting.

As we explored the *Spartina*-lined waterways, we saw many bird species, including herring, great black-backed and ring-billed gulls; double-crested cormorant; great blue heron; snowy and common egrets; semipalmated and piping plovers; short-billed dowitcher; lesser and greater yellowlegs; unidentified peeps (probably semipalmated sandpiper and possibly others); black duck; mute swan; Canada goose; cardinal; kingfisher; osprey; red-winged blackbird; and swamp, song, and saltmarsh sharp-tailed sparrows. Two rather tame clapper rails—normally very elusive—stepped out into plain view as we lingered nearby, begging to be photographed. Look also for yellow-crowned night-heron, glossy ibis, willet, and marsh wren, all of which breed here. The Connecticut Audubon Society has a webcam on an osprey nest here in the spring; check its website.

Note that paddling is best with a few hours of high tide. At other times, some side channels become difficult, if not impossible, to paddle.

9 | WESTERN CONNECTICUT

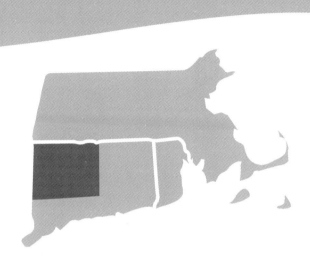

Western Connecticut includes long sections of six rivers: the Housatonic, Farmington, Pequabuck, Mattabesset, Coginchaug, and Bantam. It also includes seven ponds and lakes. The Housatonic River, flowing lazily down from the Massachusetts border, is justifiably very popular for canoeing and kayaking. Tree species diversity along the river is high, with lots of basswood and silver maple lining the banks. You can paddle the Farmington River in summer when other rivers get scratchy. Despite its proximity to large population centers, it remains relatively wild. You should see plenty of wildlife here and lots of tree species. The Pequabuck rarely gets paddled, but it is a challenge to paddle and great for honing paddling skills.

The Mattabesset and Coginchaug rivers end at Cromwell Meadows, a wetland of global significance, teeming with wildlife. We watched muskrats, deer, and many bird species amid the acres and acres of wild rice, feathery golden tips swaying in the light breeze. The Bantam River represents one of the preeminent paddling resources in western Connecticut. Flowing through a 4,000-acre nature preserve protected by the White Memorial Foundation, it's a great place to see wildlife. You should see osprey, beaver, deer, and possibly bald eagle.

Wood Creek Pond exudes a northern wilderness feel, especially on the north end where the red spruce Holleran Swamp begins. Look for nesting Canada goose and other waterfowl species here. West Branch Reservoir impounds a section of the West Branch Farmington River, just below much larger Colebrook Lake. Scenic, tree-clad hillsides flow upward from the water's edge. We can't decide if we prefer paddling Lake Winchester in the spring with abundant mountain laurel in bloom or in late summer when the highbush blueberries ripen. At either time, we love this lake's varied shoreline, rocky coves, gorgeous hillsides, and abundant spring wildflowers. You should see beaver in the evening and birdlife everywhere.

A popular recreation destination, Lake McDonough's long, narrow profile, with exceptionally clear water, nestles among gorgeous wooded hillsides. It's a great place to cruise down a waterway unimpeded, getting lots of exercise.

93 | Housatonic River

This slow moving section of the Housatonic River is popular, especially on summer weekends. The biological diversity—both on the banks and at nearby Bartholomew's Cobble—is remarkable. This area does have a significant amount of PCB contamination.

Location: Canaan, North Canaan, Salisbury, CT, and Sheffield, MA
Maps: *Connecticut/Rhode Island Atlas & Gazetteer*, Map 49: B24, C24, D23, 24, E23, 24, F23, Map 50: A1; *Massachusetts Atlas & Gazetteer,* Map 44: L5; USGS Ashley Falls, South Canaan
Length: 11.5 miles one way
Time: all day, shorter trips possible
Habitat Type: broad, tree-lined river
Fish: the river holds 45 species of fish but cannot be eaten from this portion of the river because of PCB contamination (see fish advisory, Appendix A)
Information: Bartholomew's Cobble: The Trustees of Reservations, thetrustees.org, 978-921-1944
Camping: Housatonic Meadows State Park, Macedonia Brook State Park
Take Note: little development; few motors; lots of canoes and kayaks on summer weekends

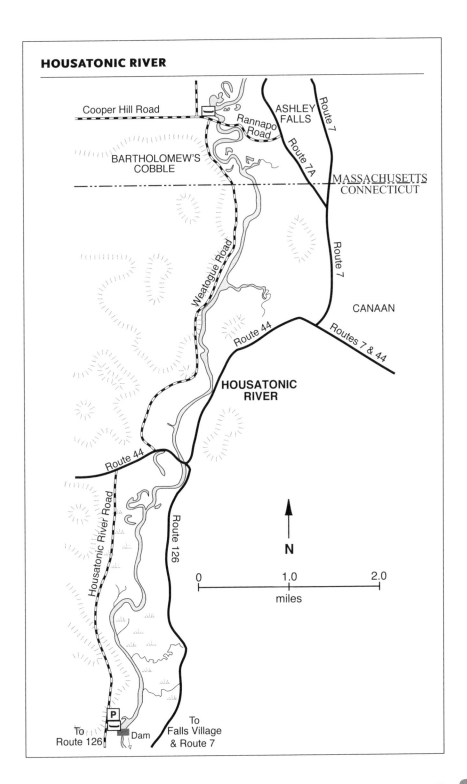

HOUSATONIC RIVER

Cooper Hill Road

ASHLEY FALLS

Route 7

Rannapo Road

Route 7A

BARTHOLOMEW'S COBBLE

MASSACHUSETTS
CONNECTICUT

Weatogue Road

Route 7

CANAAN

Route 44

Routes 7 & 44

HOUSATONIC RIVER

Route 44

Housatonic River Road

Route 126

N

0   1.0   2.0
miles

P

To
Route 126

Dam

To
Falls Village
& Route 7

GETTING THERE

Falls Village, CT (41° 57.83′ N, 73° 22.313′ W). From Canaan, go south on Route 7, and turn right on Route 126 (Main Street). Go 0.3 mile (0.3 mile), and fork right on Brewster Road/Route 126. Go 0.3 mile (0.6 mile), and go left at the T. Take an immediate right on Water Street, go 0.5 mile (1.1 miles), and just after crossing the iron bridge, turn right on Housatonic River Road. Go 0.5 mile (1.6 miles) to the access on the right at the dam.

Ashley Falls, MA (42° 3.53′ N, 73° 20.952′ W). From Ashley Falls at the junction of Route 7A and Rannapo Road, go 0.8 mile west on Rannapo Road to the access at the bridge. From the north, when Routes 7 and 7A split, go 0.6 mile (0.6 mile) south on Route 7A, and turn right on Rannapo Road. Go 1.6 miles (2.2 miles) to the access on the left, just before the bridge.

Bartholomew's Cobble (42° 3.449′ N, 73° 21.054′ W). From the Ashley Falls access, go 0.1 mile west on Rannapo Road, and turn left on Weatogue Road.

WHAT YOU'LL SEE

When we paddled here on an August weekend, dozens of canoes floated by us as we traveled upstream through the lazy current. If you crave solitude, stay away from this section of the Housatonic River on summer weekends. Little development marks the river's shores, but for one short section of a little more than a mile, busy Route 44 parallels the river.

Though we did not see large amounts of wildlife because of boat traffic, tree-species diversity along the river impressed us; we quit identifying species after fifteen. Basswood and silver maple appeared in profusion. This section of the Housatonic Valley harbors hundreds of rare native plants, drawing scores of naturalists. The northern section of the Housatonic River included here, just over the border in Massachusetts, flows along Bartholomew's Cobble, arguably the most important plant preserve in the Northeast.

Because of PCB contamination, no one should eat the fish from this section of the river. We would also limit children's contact with the water here. See the Housatonic River entry for Massachusetts (Trip 48) for more information

Bartholomew's Cobble

The 329 acres of Bartholomew's Cobble—a National Natural Landmark—harbor an extraordinary number of rare plant species. Several trails wind through the woods along the Housatonic River and up over limestone and marble outcroppings. Because you must stay on trails, binoculars may be advantageous if you'll be scanning the cliffs for rare ferns.

Maidenhair spleenwort, *Asplenium trichomanes*, is one of the many species of fern that grow at Bartholomew's Cobble.

More than 50 species of ferns and fern allies grow here, along with 800 plant species from nearly a hundred families. You will need a plant guide, available at the visitor center, if you hope to distinguish purple-stemmed cliffbrake from maidenhair spleenwort. You can download a trail map from the website. For anyone with strong interests in plants, Bartholomew's Cobble represents an unparalleled northeastern resource.

94 | Wood Creek Pond

Although you can see a few houses from its shores, Wood Creek Pond exudes a northern wilderness feel, especially on the north end where the red spruce Holleran Swamp begins. Look for nesting Canada goose and other waterfowl species here. Surface vegetation can make paddling slow, especially in summer.

Location: Norfolk, CT
Maps: *Connecticut/Rhode Island Atlas & Gazetteer*, Map 50: A10, B10; USGS South Sandisfield

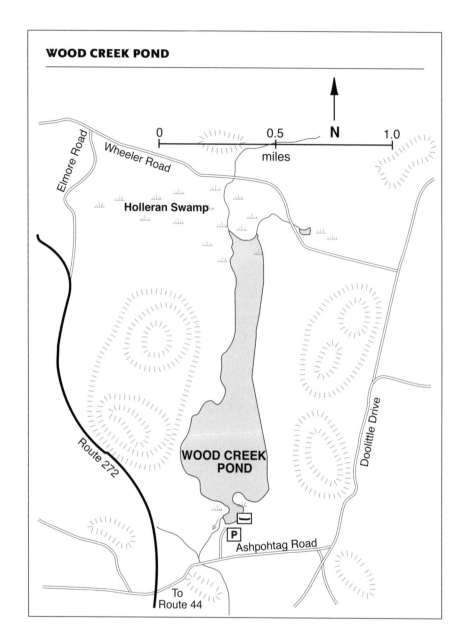

WOOD CREEK POND

Area: 151 acres

Time: 3 hours

Habitat Type: shallow, marshy pond

Fish: largemouth bass, yellow perch, pickerel (see fish advisory, Appendix A)

Camping: American Legion State Forest

Take Note: no development; vegetation and shallowness limit motors

Very shallow and thick with vegetation, Wood Creek Pond provides hours of exploration and discovery for the quietwater paddler.

GETTING THERE

From Route 44 in Norfolk, go 1.4 miles (1.4 miles) north on Route 272, and turn right on Ashpohtag Road at the Wood Creek Pond launch sign. Go 0.4 mile (1.8 miles) to the access road on the left (42° 1.101′ N, 73° 11.599′ W).

WHAT YOU'LL SEE

Located in an out-of-the-way setting near Connecticut's northwest tip, Wood Creek Pond offers a very pleasant morning or afternoon of paddling in a shallow, marshy, heavily vegetated pond about a mile long. Near the south end, you may see nesting Canada geese. As you approach, if the geese have young, notice the adults' defensive posturing, ruffling their neck feathers to look more forbidding to would-be aggressors.

As you paddle north, hillsides rise steeply from the shore, heavily wooded with mountain laurel, red maple, and other deciduous trees interspersed with hemlock and white pine. The pond's surface vegetation of American white waterlily, watershield, pondweed, and yellow pond-lily can get quite thick; coontail and a yellow-flowered bladderwort hang in large masses beneath the surface. Take a few minutes to look at the yellow pond-lily flowers. The waxy yellow "petals" are actually sepals; the smaller true petals look more like stamens. A wide pistil with yellow cap and reddish sides covers the middle of the flower.

The shallow north end, adjacent to the important red spruce Holleran Swamp, can be almost impenetrable, with thick soupy muck a few inches beneath the surface, made up of decades-old, partially decomposed vegetation on its way to becoming peat. Methane, hydrogen sulfide, and other gases bubble out with the distinctive odor of anaerobic digestion. Wend your way carefully around stumps and submerged logs camouflaged by the soupy water.

Look for the shallow, bowl-shaped depressions that pumpkinseed sunfish make for depositing eggs in the sandy bottom. The aggressive male stands guard over the eggs until they hatch, fanning them with his tail, and then defending the young until they're large enough to survive on their own. The males show such perseverance that you can hover right over them, watching them from inches away.

---

95 | West Branch Reservoir

Undeveloped West Branch Reservoir nestles among scenic hillsides, with nearby mountains visible in the surrounding state forests. Its deep, cool waters harbor a trout fishery. Bald eagles nest in the area, and you have a good chance of seeing them here.

Location: Colebrook and Hartland, CT
Maps: *Connecticut/Rhode Island Atlas & Gazetteer*, Map 51: C19, 20, D20; USGS Tolland Center, Winsted
Area: 201 acres
Time: 3 hours
Habitat Type: deep, forested, mountain reservoir
Fish: brown and rainbow trout, smallmouth bass, yellow perch (see fish advisory, Appendix A)
Camping: American Legion State Forest
Take Note: no development; cartop access only

GETTING THERE
From Route 20 northbound in Riverton, turn left on Robertsville Road where Route 20 makes a right turn. Go 1.2 miles (1.2 miles), and turn right on End Hill

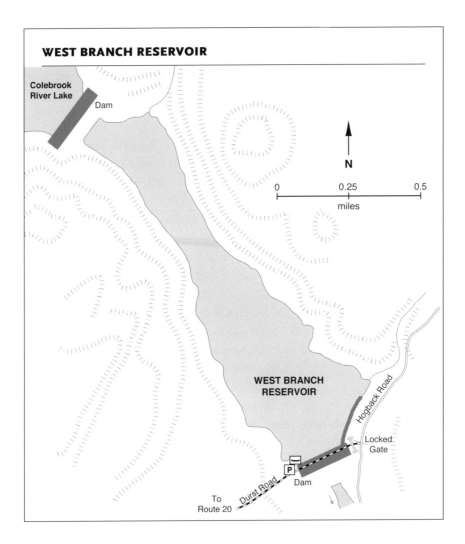

WEST BRANCH RESERVOIR

Colebrook
River Lake

Dam

N

0   0.25   0.5

miles

WEST BRANCH
RESERVOIR

Hogsback Road

Locked
Gate

Dam

P

To
Route 20

Durst Road

Road. Go 0.7 mile (1.9 miles), and turn right on Durst Road. Go 0.8 mile (2.7 miles) to the access on the left just before the dam (41° 59.332′ N, 73° 1.351′ W).

WHAT YOU'LL SEE

West Branch Reservoir, also called Hogsback Reservoir, offers a different environment from most trips in this book. Its location in a scenic, deep mountain valley surrounded by northern deciduous forest, coupled with its 90-foot depth, distinguishes it from the many shallow, marshy ponds and streams you'll find throughout this book. The reservoir's cool depths support a cold-water fishery, mainly trout, but fishermen catch smallmouth bass here as well.

The Metropolitan District of Hartford owns 6,000 acres surrounding West

Branch Reservoir and enormous Colebrook River Lake, whose dam hovers over the reservoir's north end. Currently used for flood control by the U.S. Army Corps of Engineers, these two bodies of water could eventually supply water to a growing population. Fortunately, the scenic hillsides and nearby mountains, some in the Algonquin and Tunxis state forests, will remain protected for generations to come.

Occasional white pine and eastern hemlock infiltrate the predominately deciduous forest. Look for red oak; sugar and red maple; black, yellow, and white birch; ash; shagbark and pignut hickory; and black cherry on the steep hillsides.

When we paddle in this out-of-the-way area, we often couple it with a trip to nearby Upper Spectacle Pond (Trip 52) or West Branch Farmington River (Trip 51), both in Massachusetts and both offering a contrasting marshy paddling experience. No matter where you paddle in this area, keep your eye out for soaring majestic bald eagles that nest near Colebrook River Lake; their nest is the first in this area in 100 years. In our travels to Colebrook and West Branch reservoirs and other nearby bodies of water over the last fifteen years, we've seen them on most trips, including high above Upper Spectacle Pond.

The surrounding forest harbors the usual woodland bird species—we especially enjoy listening to thrushes calling from the understory in the evening—and you should see an occasional great blue heron patrolling the shoreline. We've also seen Canada geese here, and if you're lucky, you could see a flock of wild turkeys.

---

96 | Lake Winchester

We can't decide if we prefer paddling this wonderful place in the spring with abundant mountain laurel in bloom or in late summer when the highbush blueberries ripen. At either time, we love paddling Lake Winchester because of the varied shoreline, rocky coves, gorgeous hillsides, and abundant spring wildflowers. You should see beaver in the evening and birdlife everywhere.

Location: Winchester, CT
Maps: *Connecticut/Rhode Island Atlas & Gazetteer*, Map 50: H12, I12; USGS Norfolk

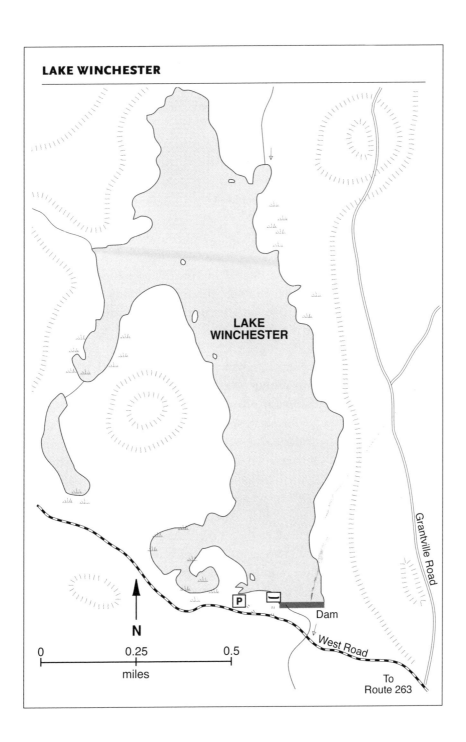

LAKE WINCHESTER

LAKE
WINCHESTER

Grantville Road

P

Dam

N

0   0.25   0.5

miles

West Road

To
Route 263

Area: 246 acres

Time: 3 hours

Habitat Type: shallow reservoir, shrubby marshlands, protected bays

Fish: largemouth and calico bass, yellow perch, pickerel, northern pike (see fish advisory, Appendix A)

Information: aquatic plant survey, ct.gov/caes/cwp/view.asp?a=2799&q=436654

Camping: American Legion State Forest

Take Note: no development; motors limited to 8 MPH; watch out for submerged rocks and tree stumps

GETTING THERE

From the northern terminus of Route 8 in Winsted, go 1.4 miles (1.4 miles) west on Route 44, and turn left on Route 263. Go 4.5 miles (5.9 miles), and as Route 263 curves left, go straight on West Road at the Winchester Lake sign. Go 0.6 mile (6.5 miles) to the access on the right (41° 54.466′ N, 3° 9.121′ W).

WHAT YOU'LL SEE

Lake Winchester's beautiful setting, coupled with little development, makes it one of our favorite destinations in northwestern Connecticut. You could easily spend half a day exploring this small, shallow lake's highly varied shoreline and rocky coves. We prefer paddling here in spring when the abundant mountain laurel blooms, and in summer when the highbush blueberries ripen. Also look for pink lady's slipper, trillium, Solomon's seal, and other spring wildflowers. By midsummer, American eelgrass, watershield, and waterlilies begin to cover the surface in shallower areas. In August, look for the purple blooms of the abundant eastern purple bladderwort (*Utricularia purpurea*). Amazingly, an aquatic survey in 2007 found no invasive species.

Paddling here in the evening, expect to see beaver swimming about, especially in the coves. The clean water supports freshwater mussels and good fishing. We also enjoyed the abundant birdlife in the lake's more hidden reaches. Look for red maple, beech, red oak, and black and gray birches among the large pines and hemlocks along the shore. As you paddle along, watch out for rocks lurking just below the water's surface, along with old stumps from trees cut off at ice level after the reservoir's formation.

97 | Lake McDonough

Lake McDonough is a popular recreation destination. This long, narrow body of water with exceptionally clear water nestles among gorgeous wooded hillsides. This is a great place for a picnic and for swimming. It lacks the marshy areas loaded with plants that characterize other entries in this book, but lack of plants also means that you can cruise down the waterway unimpeded, getting lots of exercise.

Location: Barkhamsted, CT
Maps: *Connecticut/Rhode Island Atlas & Gazetteer*, Map 51: I23, 24, J24, K24; USGS New Hartford
Area: 391 acres
Time: 5 hours
Habitat Type: forested oligotrophic reservoir
Fish: trout, largemouth and smallmouth bass, yellow perch (see fish advisory, Appendix A)
Information: for updated fees, 860-379-3036/0916; open third Saturday in April through Labor Day
Camping: American Legion State Forest
Take Note: development limited to park facilities; 10 MPH speed limit, northwest arm off-limits to motors; $6 parking fee and $5 launch fee in 2013

GETTING THERE

From Route 8 northbound in Winsted, go 3.1 miles (3.1 miles) east on Route 44, and turn left on Route 318. Go 2.9 miles (6.0 miles), and turn right on Route 219, just after crossing Barkhamsted Reservoir's Saville Dam. Go 0.5 mile (6.5 miles) to the Lake McDonough Recreation Area on the right (41° 54.302′ N, 72° 57.411′ W).

From I-91, Exit 40, go 12.7 miles (12.7 miles) west on Route 20, and turn left on Route 219. Go 6.9 miles (19.6 miles) to the access on the right, just past the junction with Route 318.

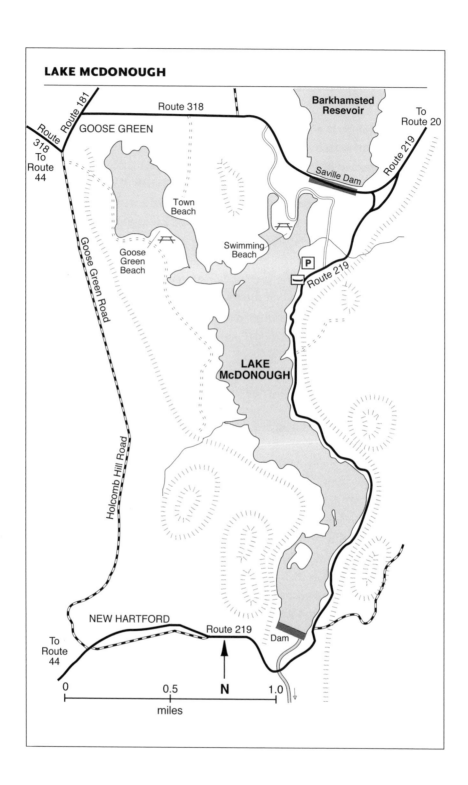

LAKE MCDONOUGH

Route 181

Route 318

GOOSE GREEN

Route 318
To Route 44

Barkhamsted Resevoir

To Route 20

Route 219

Saville Dam

Goose Green Road

Town Beach

Swimming Beach

Goose Green Beach

P

Route 219

Holcomb Hill Road

LAKE McDONOUGH

NEW HARTFORD

Route 219

Dam

To Route 44

0   0.5   **N**   1.0

miles

WHAT YOU'LL SEE

Lake McDonough lies just to the south of enormous Barkhamsted Reservoir, which supplies drinking water to the Hartford area. The Hartford Metropolitan District maintains both reservoirs, although Lake McDonough does not supply drinking water. Even though you have to pay to get in and to launch a boat, anglers and recreational boaters flock to the exceptionally clear waters of this beautiful place on sunny summer weekends. You can get a real workout here, paddling on open water along gorgeous forested hillsides.

Make sure to paddle the northwest arm, the nicest section because of a ban on motors and greater distance from Route 219, which extends along the lake's north–south axis. Grassy shores, clear water, and a generally sandy bottom characterize this section. Surprisingly, we could find no floating vegetation anywhere on the lake; the metropolitan district may lower the water level each fall, which would discourage vegetation from getting established. With so little natural vegetation, the lake seems somewhat sterile. We saw no turtles and only a few birds—including a family of Canada geese. The one beaver lodge appeared old and long abandoned. On warm days, you should be able to find northern water snakes.

The larger portion of the lake extending to the south sports a few attractive islands that provide great picnic spots. We found the west shore—with its many coves and small inlets—a lot more interesting than the east shore, along which Route 219 passes.

---

98 | Farmington River and Pequabuck River

You can paddle the Farmington in summer when other rivers get scratchy. Despite its proximity to large population centers, it remains relatively wild. You should see plenty of wildlife here and lots of tree species. The challenging Pequabuck rarely gets paddled, but it's a great site for honing paddling skills. We recommend shorter boats.

Location: Avon, Farmington, and Simsbury, CT
Maps: *Connecticut/Rhode Island Atlas & Gazetteer*, Map 43: A21, B20, 21, C20, D20, E20, F20, G20, H19, 20, I19; USGS Avon, New Britain
Length: Farmington River, 11 miles one way; Pequabuck River, 2 miles one way

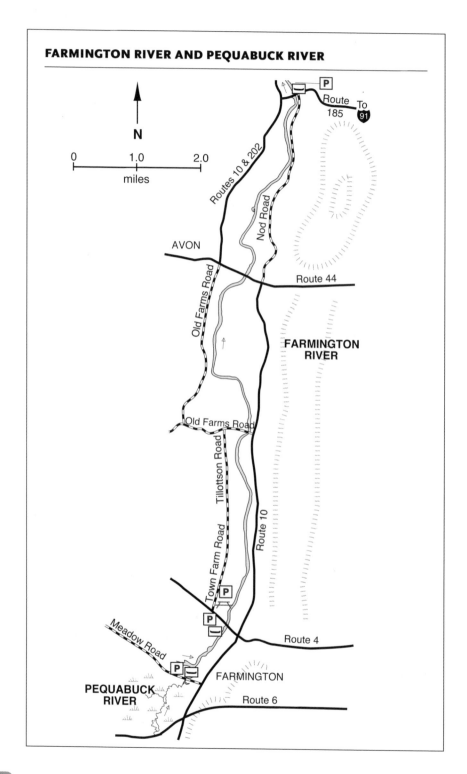

FARMINGTON RIVER AND PEQUABUCK RIVER

N

0   1.0   2.0

miles

Routes 10 & 202

Nod Road

Route 185

To 91

AVON

Old Farms Road

Route 44

FARMINGTON RIVER

Old Farms Road

Tillottson Road

Town Farm Road

Route 10

Route 4

Meadow Road

FARMINGTON

PEQUABUCK RIVER

Route 6

Time: Farmington River, all day round-trip; Pequabuck River, 2 hours round-trip

Habitat Type: slow-flowing, tree-lined river

Fish: trout (see fish advisory, Appendix A)

Camping: American Legion State Forest, Black Rock State Park

Take Note: little development; few motors because of shallow water; watch out for poison ivy near the Farmington River downstream parking area and boat launch; challenging paddling on the Pequabuck

GETTING THERE

Farmington River, Downstream Access (41° 50.875′ N, 7° 48.414′ W). From I-91, Exit 36, go 6.2 miles (6.2 miles) west on Route 178, and turn right on Route 185. Go 2.5 miles (8.7 miles) to the access on the right, at the stoplight just before the bridge. Note the huge sycamore in the parking area.

Farmington River, Upstream Access (41° 43.705′ N, 72° 49.776′ W). From the junction of Routes 4 and 10 in Farmington, go 0.2 mile west on Route 4, and turn left into the access, immediately after crossing the bridge.

Pequabuck River (41° 43.032′ N, 72° 50.464′ W). From the junction of Routes 4 and 10 in Farmington, go 1.0 mile (1.0 mile) south on Route 10, and turn right on Meadow Road. Go 0.3 mile (1.3 miles) to the access on the right, just over the bridge.

WHAT YOU'LL SEE

Farmington River

We would save the Farmington River for those summer months when other rivers get too scratchy for enjoyable paddling. In the middle of a dry summer, our boats floated in plenty of water. Even at low water levels, however, the Farmington does flow along. Paddling here in spring or other times of high water would have to be a one-way trip. If you want to do a round-trip, we recommend paddling upstream to start and letting the current help you back to the put-in.

On our way up the river from the Route 185 access, we encountered a few minor riffles. By staying near shore in faster water, we had no problem getting by. Because of the current, it took us twice as much time to go upstream, compared with the same distance downstream. Along the way we met a few rowing crews and many groups of canoes. You may hear firearms from the Connecticut State Police Training Area about a mile upstream from the access, and you may see a golf cart or two cross over the river on a narrow bridge, but otherwise the Farmington River flows through surprisingly undeveloped land,

A red-breasted merganser prepares to dive for fish on the Farmington River.

given its close proximity to large population centers.

We watched a family of red-breasted mergansers dive for fish and saw black ducks, kingfishers, spotted sandpipers, many treetop species, and a pair of red-tailed hawks soar overhead. We noticed substantial diversity of deciduous tree species, including silver maple, basswood, ash, hickory, red and white oaks, catalpa, elm, sycamore, and paper birch. Shiny leaves of lushly growing poison ivy appeared everywhere. Watch for poison ivy surrounding the boat launch and, indeed, around the entire parking area.

The huge sycamore, *Platanus occidentalis*, at the Route 185 access, named for Gifford Pinchot, is the largest tree in Connecticut. It could be 300 years old and claims the distinction of being either the largest or second largest American sycamore. It stands 104 feet tall, with a 28-foot circumference and an average canopy diameter of 147 feet—truly a magnificent tree!

Pequabuck River

The Pequabuck flows into the Farmington River just downstream from the access on Meadow Road. Paddling the Pequabuck upstream into the current as the river twists and turns through Shade Swamp can provide quite a challenge. We recommend paddling here in shorter boats. The insides of turns consist of shallow water over sand, so you have to make wide turns. In doing so, however, the onrushing current pushes your boat's front end into the bank that curves back toward you. Overhanging branches make paddling even more difficult.

So why paddle here?

Because of the wildness within a stone's throw of metropolitan Connecticut, because of the swamp's beauty, because of the challenge, because of the opportunity to hone your paddling skills, or because of the lack of other paddlers, we loved paddling here for the nearly two hours it took to go up to Route 6 and back. We saw evidence of beaver activity and lots of painted turtles, along with cedar waxwings, goldfinches, yellow-rumped and yellow warblers, and several other species.

99 | Mattabesset River, Coginchaug River, and Cromwell Meadows State Wildlife Area

Cromwell Meadows is a wetland of global significance, teeming with wildlife. We watched muskrats, deer, and many bird species amid the acres and acres of wild rice, feathery golden tips swaying in the light breeze.

Location: Cromwell and Middletown, CT

Maps: *Connecticut/Rhode Island Atlas & Gazetteer*, Map 35: D17, 18, E17, 18; USGS Middletown

Length: Mattabesset River, 5 miles one way; Coginchaug River, 2 miles one way

Time: 6 hours round-trip, shorter trips possible

Habitat Type: river through extensive marshland, many bays and side channels

Fish: trout, largemouth and smallmouth bass, pickerel, northern pike (see fish advisory, Appendix A)

Information: Mattabesset River Watershed Association, mrwa-ct.org ; Mattabesset River Canoe/Kayak Trail, conservect.org/ctrivercoastal/PDFs/MattabessetCanoe.pdf

Take Note: no development; motors allowed; because of wind, waves, and wakes on the Connecticut River, wear your PFD; novice paddlers should avoid the Connecticut River

GETTING THERE

Connecticut River Access (41° 33.546′ N, 72° 38.63′ W). From downtown Middletown, go south on Main Street, and turn left on Union Street at the

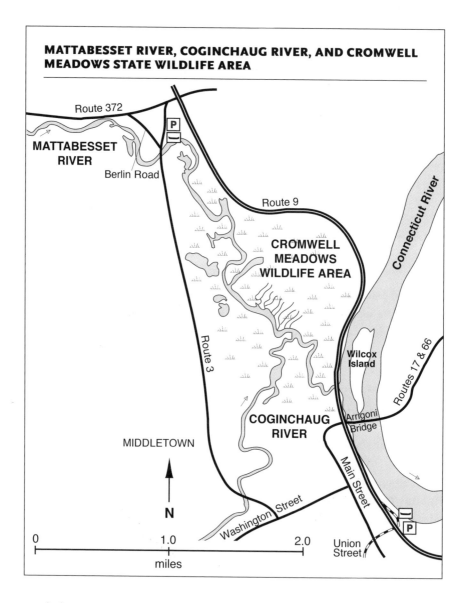

MATTABESSET RIVER, COGINCHAUG RIVER, AND CROMWELL MEADOWS STATE WILDLIFE AREA

Route 372

MATTABESSET RIVER

Berlin Road

Route 9

CROMWELL MEADOWS WILDLIFE AREA

Route 3

Connecticut River

Wilcox Island

Routes 17 & 66

COGINCHAUG RIVER

Arrigoni Bridge

MIDDLETOWN

N

Main Street

Washington Street

0   1.0   2.0   Union Street

miles

stoplight. Go 0.1 mile, pass under Route 9, veer left for 100 feet, and turn right into the Harbor Park parking area.

Mattabesset River Access (41° 35.985′ N, 72° 40.574′ W). From downtown Middletown, go north on Route 3. When Berlin Road goes left, continue on Route 3 for 100 yards, and turn right into the gravel parking lot.

WHAT YOU'LL SEE

Though some road noise emanates from numerous four-lane divided highways that ring Middletown, the Cromwell Meadows State Wildlife Area still represents an extraordinary paddling resource, all the more so because of its metropolitan location. Huge numbers of nesting and migrating waterfowl congregate here, and nowhere else in our exploration of Connecticut have we seen so much wild rice (*Zizania aquatica*).

If you paddle north from the Connecticut River Harbor Park access, nominally upstream—the tidal surge travels this far upriver—you may have to paddle against the current in either direction. The current presents little problem, however, compared with motorboat wakes and wind-driven waves that pile up over a couple of miles of open water. Because the Connecticut bends and bows, the winds cause less havoc here than on straighter stretches of river. Under windy conditions, we strongly recommend that you wear your PFD, or better yet, paddle elsewhere. Novice paddlers should avoid the Connecticut River.

You could also use the Mattabesset River access off Route 3, but that gets pretty muddy at low tide. According to the Mattabesset River Watershed Association, the incoming tide at the Mattabesset's mouth lags the incoming tide at the Saybrook Jetty at the Connecticut River mouth by 2 hours and 45 minutes. The Route 3 access gets the incoming tide 45 minutes later, for a total incoming tide lag of 3 and a half hours. This might be helpful in trying to avoid the mud.

On a late August afternoon, the first time we paddled under the Route 9 bridge and into the Mattabesset River, a big surprise unfolded before us: the vast, wild, Cromwell marshlands, full of wood ducks, kingfishers, and cardinals. The area teems with wildlife and interesting plants. Chimney swifts and barn swallows darted over the water's surface, while spotted sandpipers and great blue herons stalked the shores. The rich, golden tops of wild rice, backlit in the setting sun, swayed in the light breeze. Deer came down for an evening drink, and muskrats swam by, towing grasses destined for winter stores. We sat just watching, reluctant to leave this enchanted place. We and the waterfowl will return to watch the spring unfold.

100 | Bantam River, Bantam Lake, and Little Pond

The Bantam River represents one of the preeminent paddling resources in western Connecticut. Flowing through a 4,000-acre nature preserve protected by the White Memorial Foundation, it's a great place to see wildlife. You will see osprey and should see beaver in the evening. Deer come to the water to drink, and many bird species occur along the shore and in the woods. You might see bald eagles here as well.

Location: Litchfield and Morris, CT
Maps: *Connecticut/Rhode Island Atlas & Gazetteer,* Map 41: G21, 22, H21, 22, I20, 21, J20; USGS Litchfield
Area/Length: Bantam Lake, 933 acres; Bantam River, 2 miles one way
Time: 3 hours for entire river, through Little Pond, round-trip
Habitat Type: large natural lake; meandering river, shrubby marshlands
Fish: largemouth, smallmouth, and calico bass; yellow and white perch; northern pike (see fish advisory, Appendix A)
Information: White Memorial Foundation, whitememorialcc.org, 860-567-0857
Camping: White Memorial Foundation, Black Rock State Park
Take Note: development and motors on lake; no development or internal combustion motors on river

GETTING THERE

From Litchfield, at the junction of Routes 63 north and 202, go 2.1 miles (2.1 miles) west on Route 202, and turn left on Bissell Road. Go 0.7 mile (2.8 miles), veer right on Whites Wood Road, and go 0.1 mile (2.9 miles) to the access on the right, just over the bridge (41° 43.509′ N, 73° 12.334′ W).

WHAT YOU'LL SEE

At 933 acres—the largest natural body of water in Connecticut—Bantam Lake draws many motorboaters, especially on weekends. We much prefer the lake's north end and the motor-free Bantam River inlet that flows through a marshland owned by the White Memorial Foundation. Though you will not paddle alone on Bantam River, especially on weekends, it offers one of the premier paddling destinations in western Connecticut.

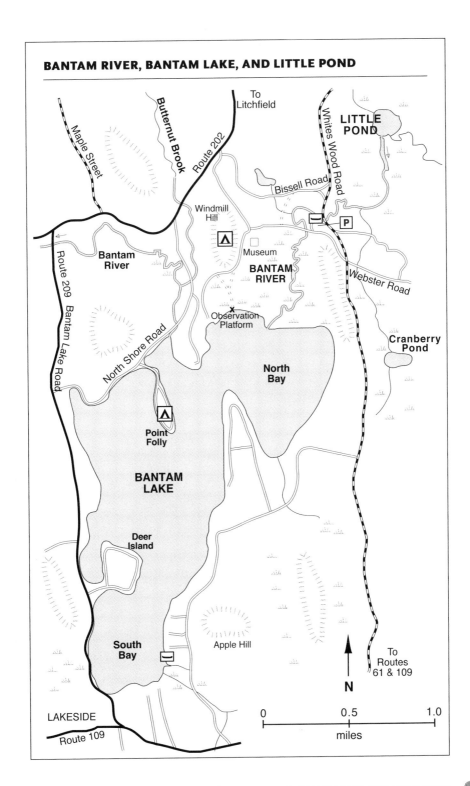

BANTAM RIVER, BANTAM LAKE, AND LITTLE POND

To
Litchfield

LITTLE
POND

Butternut Brook

Maple Street

Route 202

Whites Wood Road

Bissell Road

Windmill
Hill

P

Bantam
River

Museum

BANTAM
RIVER

Webster Road

Route 209

Bantam Lake Road

North Shore Road

Observation
Platform

Cranberry
Pond

North
Bay

Point
Folly

BANTAM
LAKE

Deer
Island

Apple Hill

South
Bay

N

To
Routes
61 & 109

LAKESIDE

Route 109

0   0.5   1.0
miles

The White Memorial Foundation, founded in 1913, protects one of southern New England's finest wildlife sanctuaries. The 4,000-acre tract includes upland hardwood forests, fields, marshlands, and open water. The foundation manages some land for forest production or wildlife habitat but leaves some untouched for research on natural succession. More than 35 miles of trails crisscross the area, including 1,700 feet of elevated boardwalk around Little Pond. The foundation stocks many natural history publications on the area at the White Memorial Conservation Center.

On the winding Bantam River you can expect to see osprey, kingfisher, great blue heron, and many other bird species. Look for beaver near dusk; each time we paddled here, we had to portage over small beaver dams. We watched many basking painted turtles splash into the water as we cruised by. The barely noticeable current does not impede upstream paddling as this wonderful river passes through a sparse red maple swamp, the shores festooned with alder, willow, viburnum, dogwood, buttonbush, winterberry, cattail, bulrush, bur-reed, pickerelweed, and grasses galore.

Few places in Connecticut boast as much bird diversity as found here, with nearly 250 recorded species (115 nesting here). Highlights for us included an osprey perched in a dead tree over the river, feeding on a fish clutched in its talons, and a normally secretive swamp sparrow, with its bright rufous cap and prominent white throat patch, hopping around in plain view.

Paddling around to the right as you enter North Bay from the river, note the old concrete piers left over from a railroad spur used to cart away blocks of ice sawn from the frozen lake. Some of the piers now hold a bird observation platform. Farther down the lake, Point Folly houses a White Memorial Foundation campground, complete with another bird observation platform.

Appendix A: Fish Advisories

The key below includes only the gamefish listed in this book's entries. For other fish, shellfish, and crustacean species, see the web pages below.

MASSACHUSETTS

See webapps.ehs.state.ma.us/dph_fishadvisory/default.aspx for updates.
Also see mass.gov/eohhs/gov/departments/dph/programs/environmental-health/exposure-topics/fish-wildlife/fish/a-guide-to-eating-fish-safely-in-massachusetts.html.

Water Body	Towns or Areas	Fish Advisory*	Hazard
All bodies of water not listed below		P2 (BF, SB)	PCBs
Coast	Coast and coastal rivers	P2 (BF, SB)	PCBs
Ashland Reservoir	Ashland	P1 (all species), P5	Mercury
Buckley Dunton Lake	Becket	P1 (LMB), P3 (LMB)	Mercury
Charles River	Dover, Medfield, Millis, Natick, Norfolk, Sherborn	P1 (all species), P5	Mercury, Chlordane, DDT
Concord River	Bedford, Billerica, Carlisle, Concord	P1 (all species), P2 (LMB), P4	Mercury
Lake Denison	Winchendon	P1 (LMB), P3 (LMB)	Mercury
East Brimfield Lake, Holland Pond, Long Pond, Quinebaug River	Brimfield, Holland, Sturbridge	P1 (all species), P5	Mercury
Housatonic River	All towns, Dalton through Sheffield	P9	PCBs

*See Fish Advisory and Fish Species keys later in this appendix.

Water Body	Towns or Areas	Fish Advisory*	Hazard
Ipswich River	Hamilton, Ipswich, Topsfield, Wenham	P1 (all species), P5	Mercury
Millers River downstream from Otter River; Otter River	Templeton, Winchendon	P1 (all species), P2 (BT), P4	PCBs
Nashua River, Pepperell Pond	Groton, Pepperell	P1 (all species), P2 (LMB), P4	Mercury
Neponset River	Canton, Dedham, Milton, Norwood	P1 (all species), P4	PCBs, DDT
New Bedford Reservoir	Acushnet	P1 (all species), P3 (LMB)	Mercury, DDT
Lake Nippenicket	Bridgewater	P1 (LMB), P3 (LMB), P4	Mercury
Parker River	Newbury	P1 (BF), P3 (BF)	PCBs
Plainfield Pond	Plainfield	P1 (LMB), P3 (LMB)	Mercury
Quaboag Pond	Brookfield, East Brookfield	P1 (all species), P2 (LMB), P4	Mercury
Lake Rohunta	Athol, New Salem, Orange	P1 (all species), P5	Mercury
Sudbury River	Concord, Lincoln, Sudbury, Wayland	P9	Mercury
Walden Pond	Concord	P1 (LMB, SMB), P3 (LMB, SMB)	Mercury
Whitehall Reservoir	Hopkinton	P1 (all species), P4	

CONNECTICUT

See ct.gov/dph/cwp/view.asp?a=3140&Q=387460 for updates.

Water Body	Towns or Areas	Fish Advisory*	Hazard
All bodies of water not listed below		P1A, P8	Mercury
Housatonic River	Above Lake Lillinonah	P2 (T, NP), P1 (LMB, SMB, WP), P7 (LMB, SMB, WP), P6 (YP)	PCBs
Housatonic River	Lakes Lillinonah, Zoar, Housatonic	P2 (T, NP), P6 (LMB, SMB, WP, YP)	PCBs
Lake McDonough	Barkhamsted	P1 (LMB, SMB, CP), P6 (LMB, SMB, CP)	Mercury
Long Island Sound	Coast and coastal rivers	P2 (BF, SB)	PCBs

RHODE ISLAND

See www.health.ri.gov/healthrisks/poisoning/mercury/about/fish/

Water Body	Towns or Areas	Fish Advisory*	Hazard
All bodies of water not listed below		P1A, P8	Mercury
Coast	Coast and coastal rivers	P2 (BF, SB)	PCBs
All bodies of water		P1B, P2 (CP, LMB, NP, SMB, WP, YP), P6 (CB)	Mercury

Fish Advisory Key

P1
(all species)
Children under 12, pregnant women, women who might become pregnant, and nursing, mothers should not eat any fish from these waters

P1
(listed species)
Children under 12, pregnant women, women who might become pregnant, and nursing, mothers should not eat the listed fish from these waters

P1A
(all species)
Children under 12, pregnant women, women who might become pregnant, and nursing, mothers may eat one meal per month of all fish; no limit on trout under 15 inches

P1B
(all species)
Children under 12, pregnant women, women who might become pregnant, and nursing, mothers should not eat any fish from these waters; no limit on trout under 15 inches

P2
(listed species)
No one should consume the listed fish from these waters

P3
(listed species)
Limit consumption of listed fish from these waters to two meals per month

P4
Limit consumption of non-affected fish from these waters to two meals per month

P5
Limit consumption of all fish from these waters to two meals per month

P6
(listed species)
Limit consumption of listed fish from these waters to one meal per month

P7
(listed species)
Limit consumption of listed fish from these waters to one meal per two months

P8
Limit consumption of all fish from these waters to one meal per week; no limit on trout under 15 inches

P9
No one should consume any fish from these waters

Fish Species Key

BF Bluefish

BT Brown trout

CB Calico bass (black crappie)

CP Chain pickerel

LMB Largemouth bass

NP Northern pike

SMB Smallmouth bass

SB Striped bass

T All trout

WP White perch

YP Yellow perch

Appendix B: Further Reading

AMC River Guide: Massachusetts, Connecticut, Rhode Island, 4th ed. Boston: Appalachian Mountain Club Books, 2006.

Brame, Rich, and David Cole. *Soft Paths: How to Enjoy the Wilderness Without Harming It*, 4th ed. Mechanicsburg, Pa.: Stackpole Books, 2011.

Burk, John. *Massachusetts Trail Guide*, 9th ed. Boston: Appalachian Mountain Club Books, 2009.

Burk, John, and Michael Tougias. *AMC's Best Day Hikes near Boston*, 2nd ed. Boston: Appalachian Mountain Club Books, 2011.

Carroll, David. *The Year of the Turtle: A Natural History*. New York: St. Martin's Press, 1996.

Cole, Jim. *Paddling Connecticut and Rhode Island: Southern New England's Best Paddling Routes*. Guilford, Conn.: Falcon, 2009.

Connecticut and Rhode Island Atlas & Gazetteer, 4th ed. Yarmouth, Maine: DeLorme, 2007.

Connecticut River Joint Commission. Connecticut River maps. crjc.org/boating/boating1.htm.

Connecticut River Watershed Council. *The Connecticut River Boating Guide: Source to Sea*, 3rd ed. Guilford, Connecticut: Falcon, 2007.

Evans, Lisa. *Sea Kayaking Coastal Massachusetts*. Boston: Appalachian Mountain Club Books, 2000.

Hutchinson, Derek. *Basic Book of Sea Kayaking*, 2nd ed. Guilford, Conn.: Falcon, 2007.

Jacobs, Robert, and Eileen O'Donnell. *A Fisheries Guide to Lakes and Ponds of Connecticut*, 2nd ed. Hartford, Conn.: Connecticut Department of Energy and Environmental Protection, 2002.

Jacobson, Cliff. *Canoeing and Camping: Beyond the Basics*, 3rd ed. Guilford, Conn.: Falcon, 2007.

Laubach, Rene. *AMC's Best Day Hikes in the Berkshires*. Boston: Appalachian Mountain Club Books, 2009.

Laubach, Rene, and Charles Smith. *AMC's Best Day Hikes in Connecticut*, 2nd ed. Boston: Appalachian Mountain Club Books, 2013.

Leave No Trace information and materials, Leave No Trace Center for Outdoor Ethics, lnt.org.

Lessels, Bruce, and Karen Blom. *Paddling with Kids: AMC Essential Guide for Fun and Safe Paddling*. Boston: Appalachian Mountain Club Books, 2002.

Massachusetts Atlas & Gazetteer, 4th ed. Yarmouth, Maine: DeLorme, 2009.

McAdow, Ron. *The Charles River: Exploring Nature and History on Foot and by Canoe*. Bliss Publishing, 1999.

McAdow, Ron. *The Concord, Sudbury and Assabet Rivers*. Bliss Publishing, 1990.

O'Connor, Michael. *Discover Cape Cod*. Boston: Appalachian Mountain Club Books, 2009.

Older, Julia, and Steve Sherman. *Nature Walks along the Seacoast*. Boston: Appalachian Mountain Club Books, 2003.

Roberts, Harry, and Steve Salins. *Basic Essentials Canoe Paddling*, 3rd ed. Guilford, Conn.: Falcon, 2006.

Seidman, David. *The Essential Sea Kayaker*, 2nd ed. Camden, Maine: Ragged Mountain Press, 2001.

Sinai, Lee. *Discover Martha's Vineyard*. Boston: Appalachian Mountain Club Books, 2009.

Smith, Charles, and Susan Smith. *Discover the Berkshires of Massachusetts*. Boston: Appalachian Mountain Club Books, 2003.

Spring, Sue. *Appalachian Trail Guide to Massachusetts–Connecticut*, 12th ed. Harpers Ferry, WV: Appalachian Trail Conservancy. 2010.

Teal, John, and Mildred Teal. *Life and Death of the Salt Marsh*. New York: Ballantine Books, 1976.

Tougias, Michael, and Rene Laubach. *Nature Walks in Central and Western Massachusetts*, 2nd ed. Boston: Appalachian Mountain Club Books, 2000.

List of Waterways

About the Authors

John Hayes, a former professor of biochemistry and environmental science at Marlboro College in Vermont, is now Director of Sustainability at Pacific University in Oregon. Besides exploring the lakes and rivers of his new home in the Northwest, he has paddled Minnesota's Boundary Waters Canoe Area, Georgia's Okefenokee Swamp, and Florida's Everglades, as well as throughout the Northeast. Hayes has written for *National Geographic Traveler* and has edited numerous solar energy conference proceedings. He was book review editor of the *Passive Solar Journal* and served as vice chair of the American Solar Energy Society. He has led natural history field trips to Central America, Mexico, Southwest deserts, Rockies, Everglades, Borneo, and Africa. He and Alex Wilson are co-authors of paddling guides to all New England states and New York.

Alex Wilson is the founder of BuildingGreen, a company that has been publishing information on environmentally responsible design and construction since 1985. He is a widely published author, focusing primarily on building technology, energy, and the environment. Besides the Quiet Water series, he has authored or co-authored *Your Green Home* (Mother Earth News, 2006), *The Consumer Guide to Home Energy Savings*, 10th edition (ACEEE, 2012), and *Green Development: Integrating Ecology and Real Estate* (Wiley, 1998). Prior to starting BuildingGreen, he worked for a solar organization in New Mexico and was executive director of the Northeast Sustainable Energy Association. He was the first recipient of the NESEA Lifetime Achievement Award in 1993, and received the U.S. Green Building Council's Leadership Award for Education in 2008 and the Hanley Award for Vision and Leadership in Sustainable Housing in 2010. He lives with his wife in southern Vermont.

About the AMC in Southern New England

The Boston, Southeastern Massachusetts, Worcester, Berkshire, Connecticut, and Narragansett chapters of AMC represent more than 42,000 of the organization's total 150,000 members. They organize outdoor activities for a wide variety of ages, skill levels, and interests and contribute to important stewardship and conservation efforts. To view a list of AMC activities in southern New England and other parts of the Northeast, visit trips.outdoors.org.

AMC Books Updates

AMC Books strives to keep our guidebooks as up-to-date as possible to help you plan safe and enjoyable adventures. If after publishing a book we learn that trails have been relocated or route or contact information has changed, we will post the updated information online. Before you hit the trail, check for updates at outdoors.org/bookupdates.

While hiking, biking, or paddling, if you notice discrepancies with the trip description or map, or if you find any other errors in the book, please let us know by submitting them to amcbookupdates@outdoors.org or in writing to Books Editor, c/o AMC, 5 Joy Street, Boston, MA 02108. We will verify all submissions and post key updates each month. AMC Books is dedicated to being a recognized leader in outdoor publishing. Thank you for your participation.

AMC BOOKS & MAPS

EXPLORE THE POSSIBILITIES

Appalachian Mountain Club

Founded in 1876, AMC is the nation's oldest outdoor recreation and conservation organization. AMC promotes the protection, enjoyment, and understanding of the mountains, forests, waters, and trails of the Northeast outdoors.

People

We are more than 150,000 members, advocates, and supporters, including 12 local chapters, more than 16,000 volunteers, and over 450 full-time and seasonal staff. Our chapters reach from Maine to Washington, D.C.

Outdoor Adventure and Fun

We offer more than 8,000 trips each year, from local chapter activities to adventure travel worldwide, for every ability level and outdoor interest—from hiking and climbing to paddling, snowshoeing, and skiing.

Great Places to Stay

We host more than 150,000 guests each year at our AMC lodges, huts, camps, shelters, and campgrounds. Each AMC destination is a model for environmental education and stewardship.

Opportunities for Learning

We teach people skills to safely enjoy the outdoors and to care for the natural world around us through programs for children, teens, and adults, as well as outdoor leadership training.

Caring for Trails

We maintain more than 1,800 miles of trails throughout the Northeast, including nearly 350 miles of the Appalachian Trail in five states.

Protecting Wild Places

We advocate for land and riverway conservation, monitor air quality, research climate change, and work to protect alpine and forest ecosystems throughout the Northern Forest and Mid-Atlantic Highlands regions.

Engaging the Public

We seek to educate and inform our own members and an additional 2 million people annually through the media, AMC Books, our website, our White Mountain visitor centers, and AMC destinations.

Join Us!

Members meet other like-minded people and support our mission while enjoying great AMC programs, our award-winning *AMC Outdoors* magazine, and special discounts. Visit outdoors.org or call 800-372-1758 for more information.

APPALACHIAN MOUNTAIN CLUB
Recreation • Education • Conservation
outdoors.org

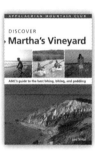